Akrotiri Thera

An Architecture of Affluence
3,500 Years Old

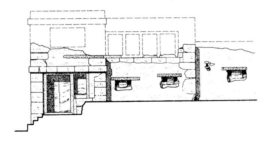

PREHISTORY MONOGRAPHS 15

Akrotiri Thera

An Architecture of Affluence 3,500 Years Old

by

Clairy Palyvou

Published by
INSTAP Academic Press
Philadelphia, Pennsylvania
2016

Design and Production
INSTAP Academic Press, Philadelphia, PA

ISBN 978-1-931534-14-7 (hardcover)
ISBN 978-1-931534-87-1 (paperback)
ISBN 978-1-623030-66-7 (ebook)

Library of Congress Cataloging-in-Publication Data

Palyvou, Klaire.
  Akrotiri Thera: an architecture of affluence 3,500 years old / by Clairy
Palyvou.
      p. cm. — (Prehistory monographs ; 15)
  Includes bibliographical references and index.
  ISBN 1-931534-14-4 (hardcover : alk. paper)
 1. Architecture, Minoan—Greece—Akroterion. 2. Architecture,
Domestic—Greece—Akroterion. 3. Akroterion (Greece)—Antiquities. I.
Title. II. Series.
  NA267.P37 2005
  722'.61—dc22

                                                                    2005014177

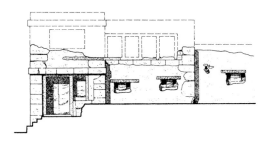

Table of Contents

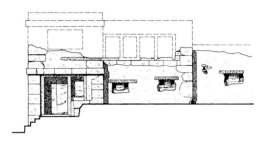

List of Tables in the Text

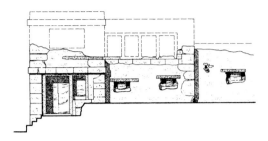

List of Figures in the Text

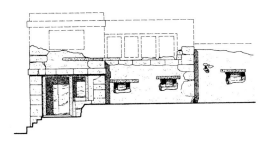

List of Color Plates

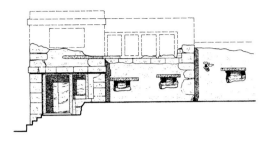

Preface

My first year at Akrotiri was 1977, when I was invited by Professor Christos Doumas who had recently taken over the direction of the excavation after the fatal accident on the site of the first excavator, Spyridon Marinatos. My duties as an architect were multifold from the beginning, but they basically revolved around two tasks: documentation drawings and restoration work.[1] Both of these tasks demand a thorough knowledge of the history of the specific site and its broader region. I soon found myself racing with time in an effort to learn as much as possible—in as short a time as possible—about the Aegean Bronze Age civilization. The first years were a period of informal, albeit thorough, studies in Aegean archaeology. In the field of Aegean architecture, the required knowledge had to be built piece by piece, because there was hardly any comprehensive work on the subject—and one is still lacking. Invaluable companions during this period were the pioneer works of J.W. Graham and J.W. Shaw.[2]

The site itself—a book in vivo—was a true revelation, and by being constantly present during the dig, I learned what no book can teach: the agonies of the archaeologists, the goals and methods of their work, and the fascinating process of interpretation that starts from the moment the spade hits the earth. I also realized the enormous responsibility of all those who work on the site. Doumas used to say "a dig is by definition an act of destruction," and I, too, became anxious to record through my drawings as accurately as possible the "crime" I was witnessing, just as the archaeologists by my side were eager to record their point of view in the daybook.[3] These first drawings, like the daybooks and the photographs, will be the "eyes" to the past for future generations.

The excitement of my first visit to Xeste 4, once I realized that I was actually walking on the third floor of a building erected 3,500 years ago, has remained almost intact to this day. It only grew stronger as my eyes began to "see"—that is, to understand—the astonishing amount of architectural design involved in this building operation and the fine technical specifications guiding this work. Furthermore, the modernity of this 3,500 year-old architecture has never ceased to fascinate me. The use of timber impressed me more than anything else: the "unknown hero" as I dubbed it—unknown because so little has survived of its substance, and a hero because it carries, indeed, a large part of the loads of the edifice.

The small group of scholars that worked under the direction of Christos Doumas rapidly grew. Each new member brought his (mostly her, actually) own "dowry" to the site: yet another point of view, another expertise according to the field of specialization, and a new methodology. The time we spent together each summer was a most fruitful, albeit tantalizing period. Our varying interests, our different goals, and different tools of thought were favorite topics of discussion during the evening hours of relaxation on the veranda of the guesthouse or on the long walks to the nearby village of Akrotiri.

A collective vision of prehistoric Akrotiri was being gradually pieced together. As I was formulating my thoughts about the bustling city and its exquisite houses, other colleagues would add to the picture: Iris Tzachili would provide the looms to manufacture the magnificent dresses described by Christina Televantou; Tania Devetzi and Antikleia Agrafiotou offered the tools, the stone vessels, and the implements to prepare the meals, for which Anayia Sarpaki, Katerina Trantalidou, and Lilian Karali could provide fascinating details; Marisa Marthari, Angelia Papagiannopoulou, and Litsa Katsa would tell us about the ceramic products of their households, and Anna Michailidou would weigh and measure their contents; Christos Boulotis would unfold the hidden messages of the magnificent wall paintings; and Peggy Sotirakopoulou would give us a glimpse of the remote past of this amazing place.[4] And others who later joined the group, too many to mention, would each add yet another stitch to this fascinating, colorful canvas of history. Very seldom, indeed, does an archaeological site present its story in such a vivid manner.

The laboratory for the restoration of the wall paintings was a great school. We all have immense admiration and gratitude for the restorers. Personally, I not only learned much from them, but I am deeply indebted for the undreamed gifts they offer me. Thanks to their work, I can complete many missing parts of the buildings on my drawings. The restored wall paintings of the upper floors of Xeste 3, for example, provide the "skin" of walls that have entirely collapsed. On this skin, I can read the height of the upper floor, the positions and dimensions of doors and windows, even the exact place and outline of each beam of the ceiling.

Akrotiri is a book of pictures with no captions. These captions we all strive to add, each from our own point of view, so as to arrive at a better understanding of the otherwise silent remains of a magnificent civilization. The excavation at Akrotiri—one of the most important worldwide—is a collective work led by Greek colleagues, and it will surely breed many generations of scholars to come. The work is time consuming and tantalizing but, as with every primary research, it is very rewarding. The first generation of scholars—to which I belong—has to a large degree fulfilled its mission of presenting the results of a long-term study. Many doctoral theses have been completed during the past years—though very few have been published—and numerous papers have been contributed to international conferences.

Marinatos' annual reports, *The Excavation at Thera*, vols. I–VII, remain an important source of information regarding the individual finds and the development of the dig for the period of 1967–1974, followed by the yearly reports by Doumas in the journal *Πρακτικά της εν Αθήναις Αρχαιολογικής Εταιρείας*. Doumas' book, *Thera, Pompeii of the Ancient World: Excavations at Akrotiri 1967–1979*, London 1983, is the only comprehensive work on Akrotiri. It is a synopsis of some of the main conclusions by the multi-disciplinary research group working under his direction. The architecture of Akrotiri is, naturally, only briefly discussed. My own doctoral dissertation, *Ακρωτήρι Θήρας: Η οικοδομική τέχνη*, Athens 1999, was published by the Archaeological Society at Athens. The book, in Greek, is a detailed account of the materials and building techniques applied at Akrotiri, but it does not include other aspects of architecture.

It was long felt that an English edition on the architecture of Akrotiri, dealing not only with the building technology, but also with issues of typology, form, and function, would be welcomed. The present book is, thus, an attempt to provide the reader with an overall picture of the architecture of Akrotiri, including an outline of its town plan, a description of the individual houses, and a discussion of its relationship with Crete and its neighbors in the Eastern Mediterranean.

The book is based on personal observations and experience obtained over a fifteen year period (1977–1992) of work at the site as the architect of the Akrotiri dig. The comparative work referring to Crete and the other Cycladic islands, on the other hand, owes much to the work of eminent scholars and excavators of Aegean Bronze Age sites. To these colleagues and friends, I am deeply indebted.

Since 1992 much has been done, especially in regard with the management of the unearthed material. Excavation, on the other hand, was rather restricted, basically in the area of Xeste 4.[5] Since March of 1999, the site of Akrotiri has been going through an overwhelming transformation. A new shelter is being built that will transform the excavation into an in situ museum. The one hundred or more trenches dug for the pillars of the new shelter, in the form of "rescue excavation,"[6] have yielded valuable information, especially regarding the earlier phases of the site. The nature of these finds, however, especially in regard to the architecture, is highly fragmentary and dispersed. Pending the study of this material, which has been undertaken by a younger generation of scholars, this book is confined to the last phase of habitation and the uniquely preserved houses that we see today.

Preface Notes

1. Palyvou 1977; 1978; 1988.

2. Especially their fundamental works: *The Palaces of Crete* (1972) and "Minoan Architecture: Materials and Techniques," *ASAtene* 49 (1971).

3. On the architect's contribution to archaeology, see Palyvou 2003.

4. The reader is referred to the works of these scholars for a comprehensive view of the Theran world. A place to start would be the Theran Conferences (Doumas, ed., 1978; Hardy et al., eds., 1990) as well as Doumas, ed., 1992c and Danezis, ed., 2001.

5. Doumas 1993: 172–176; 1994: 163; 1995: 130–132; 1996: 250.

6. Doumas 2000: 34–35.

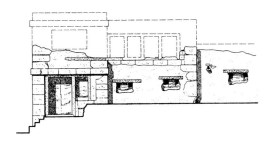

Acknowledgments

The scientific work carried out at Akrotiri is a large scale and long-term interdisciplinary enterprise. Those who work with the material from the site, therefore, are well aware that their work is closely interrelated to the work of many others, and that in this relay-race many more will join forces. In this context I am indebted to all the colleagues working at Akrotiri, to the director and coordinator of the excavation, Prof. Christos Doumas, and to the Archaeological Society at Athens. For the past several years much copious work has been carried out in order to record and organize the diverse material from the dig. Thanks to this—and to the new technology that has invaded our archives—I acquired digital copies of almost all the photographs included in this book, with amazing speed and efficiency. For her support during this procedure, I am obliged to Tania Devetzi, heart and soul of the excavation office for many years now, and to Dimitris Sakatzis and Lucy Valassi, who helped with the preparation of the photographs.

The drawings are almost all my own, and many of them are published in my book *Ακρωτήρι Θήρας: Η οικοδομική τέχνη*, Athens 1999. There are several new drawings as well, prepared specifically for this book, such as the general plans of the site and the ground floor and first floor plans of the best-known houses. These were redrawn (and corrected many times) by architecture students, Maria Karamanou and Penelope Titoni, whom I thank for their patience. The superb three dimensional computer restorations of the West House included in the color plates were made by the architect Apostolos Kassios. They are part of his post graduate dissertation, which I supervised at the Aristotle University of Thesssaloniki (2004).

Last but certainly not least, I am indebted to INSTAP for its generous support and especially to Prof. Philip Betancourt for his support, his wise advice during the preparation of the material, and his generosity in spending so much of his time to check the original manuscript and improve my English.

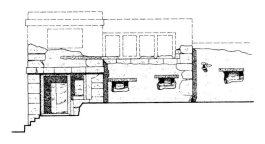

1

The Volcanic Fate of Thera

A Cluster of Volcanos Gives Birth to an Archipelago

Thera is the largest of a group of five islands—Thera, Therasia, Aspronissi, Palaia Kameni, and Nea Kameni—all of which owe their existence to volcanic activity. The islands belong to the so-called "Aegean arc system of volcanos" at the junction of the two tectonic plates, the African and the Eurasian (Fig. 1). This means that volcanism is continuous in the area and has never ceased shaping and reshaping the archipelago. The modern name Santorini was given to this archipelago at the time of the Venetian occupation after the name of the patron saint of sailors, Santa Eirene.

Not one, but several volcanos are responsible for the birth of the archipelago (Fig. 2). The process started under water 2.5 million years ago, first in the region of the nearby Christiana islands, and 1.5 million years later in the area of Thera.[1] The lava coming out of the mouths of these volcanos gradually built up the island of Thera. At least five volcanic centers, five different nuances of the colors of

fire, are all clearly discernible on the colorful landscape of Thera: black and red around the volcanos of Oia and Columbo, white at Aspronissi, red and white at Akrotiri, and dark brown at Skaros. The limestone mountains of Profitis Ilias and Gavrilos were the only non-volcanic cores incorporated in this lava festivity. Several major explosive eruptions and lava flows have occurred on Thera since then, scarring the island in a most dramatic manner. According to McCoy, by the time the first inhabitants appeared on the island in the 5th millennium B.C., Thera consisted of two islands corresponding roughly to modern Thera and Therasia, and a third major island—or highland—between them with a volcano at its summit. A large water-filled embayment dominated the south part of the island compound (Figs. 3, 4). The caldera walls we see today in the southern area, in other words, were not very different then.

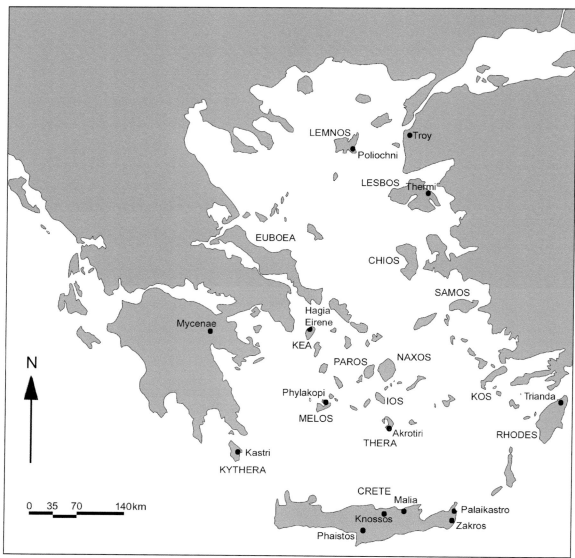

Fig. 1. Map of the Aegean.

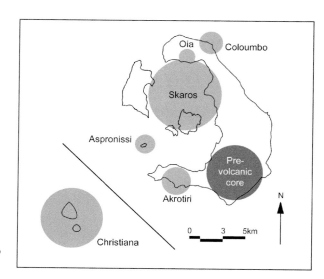

Fig. 2. The genesis of the Theran archipelago (Vougioukalakis 2001: fig. 2).

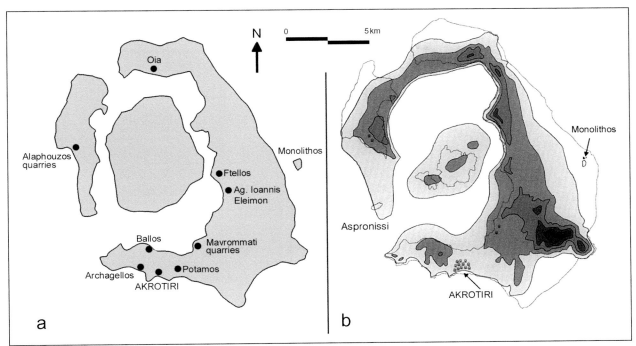

Fig. 3. The shape of Thera before and after the "Minoan" eruption: a) after *Athens News* 2000; b) after Vougioukalakis (2001: fig. 2).

Fig. 4. View of the caldera from Akrotiri.

The Late Bronze Age Eruption

Sometime during the Late Bronze Age, at the hey-day of the south Aegean civilization, a major eruption took place on Thera, causing a "volcanic disaster of epic proportions" as McCoy and Heiken describe it.[2] The remains of Akrotiri, a major harbor town of the time, are a vivid memory of the appalling events. Scientists have long been trying to put together the evidence for the sequence of events that took place during this fatal eruption, and various theories have come forth[3] (Figs. 3, 5). The description presented here is one of the latest and is based on McCoy's and Heiken's studies on the islands of the Santorini archipelago and specifically at the site of Akrotiri.[4] This work, though from the standpoint of a volcanologist, takes good account of the architectural peculiarities at the site of Akrotiri and answers some of the questions arising from the state of preservation of the buildings.

The eruption, according to the two scientists, was of a very high magnitude—only seven eruptions have had equivalent or larger values in the past four millennia! It occurred in four major phases and a fifth minor one, all recognized by distinct tephra layers. It all happened within a few months at most, because the time interval between eruptive phases did not span a rainy winter season.

PHASE I

The "precursor tephra fall" has a varying thickness indicating southeast and south-southeast

Deepening of separate basins within the caldera. Ejection of ash and older debris.

Sea water invades the caldera and produces phreatic eruptions.

Opening of a vent on the Pre-Kameni island and eruption of pumice.

Fig. 5. The eruption sequence depicted on the caldera walls (Friedrich 2000: fig. 6.8).

winds and points to a vent near the modern islands of Kameni. This activity most probably provided warning to the inhabitants.

PHASE II

The "first major eruption phase" deposited about 7 m of pumice and ash all over the island, and the provenance is again near the Kameni islands or farther to the north. Seismic activity related to the eruption caused the collapse of walls during this phase. A short time of 1–8 hours has been estimated for this event, which means that the site of Akrotiri was rapidly covered over with ash. The accumulated pumice is thicker on the north side of the buildings, indicating the direction of the winds, and pumice penetrated through all the northern openings—doors, windows, and gaps in the walls—partially filling the rooms. Roofs were over loaded and collapsed, and walls did as well. Among the debris were various cavities that were later filled with black sand. The tephra that buried the buildings protected them from further damage during the eruptive phases that followed.

PHASE III

The "second major eruption phase" had a different vent placement and a different situation altogether. Water had now accessed into the vent. The coast at the periphery of the island was greatly affected and extended by the deposition of this thick layer (Fig. 6). This phase was also very brief. Pyroclastic surges and flows, typical of this phase, were initially diverted by the buildings and followed the streets, but they consequently became more powerful, destroying all structures that had not been buried under the ash. This explains why some buildings were found with no sign of their roofs.

PHASE IV

The "third major eruption phase" was a massive deposit up to 55 m on central-southeastern Thera. "Ballistic emplacement" occurred during this phase, and boulders up to 3 m in diameter with north-south trajectories hit the buildings causing further damage. The vent was the same, but it was probably extended to the northeast. During this phase, the caldera collapsed to the north of the Kameni islands.

Fig. 6. The flat eastern part of Thera (modern Kamari) was formed after the Bronze Age eruption by the accumulation of enormous quantities of ash (courtesy of the archive of the Deutschen Archäologischen Institut in Athens).

PHASE V

The "fourth major eruption phase" immediately followed, causing further caldera collapse. The lithic-rich deposits came from the same vent as before and were thin along the caldera margin, but they were quite thick along the coast (up to 40 m), forming the prominent sea cliffs we see today in the vicinity of Akrotiri (Fig. 7). Highly erosive torrential rains later were typical of this phase and left behind a rugged formation that was further sculpted by the wind (Fig. 8).

Fig. 7. A "wall" of ash more than 10 m high borders the south coast of Thera.

Fig. 8. Volcanic ash sculptured by the wind.

Thera after the Late Bronze Age

The Late Bronze Age eruption was fatal for the island and affected the broader region as well. It took over 700 years for nature to establish a new equilibrium that was viable enough to attract new settlers. Only a short visit by some rather bewildered Mycenaeans is attested in the meantime: they grounded at the beach of Monolithos for a brief picnic and left without even thinking of exploring further inland. The new settlers arrived around 800 B.C. under the guidance of King Thera. They were Dorians and founded their city on the precarious heights of Mesa Vouno, an extension of Mount Profitis Ilias. They were completely ignorant of the presence of earlier habitation on the island because it was a well kept secret hidden under its thick volcanic mantle. From then onward, Thera reappears on the scene and follows the history of the south Aegean region.[5]

The volcanic heart of Thera never ceased to beat, and many generations of Therans witnessed severe, as much as spectacular, volcanic eruptions that gave birth to islets, some of which appeared only to disappear shortly thereafter (Fig. 9). In 197 B.C., Palaia Kameni was born by an eruption described by Strabo; the most recent eruption was in 1950 on the island of Nea Kameni. Twelve major eruptions took place between these two dates, one of the most severe being that of the submarine volcano of Columbo to the northeast of Thera in 1649–1650 A.D., an event dramatically described in contemporary literature as "the time of the evil." None, however, was even remotely as destructive as that of the 16th century B.C.

Fig. 9. Eruption of the volcano in 1866 (*The Illustrated London News*, 31 March 1866; E. Lignos Collection).

Chapter 1 Notes

1. McCoy and Heiken 2000; Vougioukalakis 2001.

2. McCoy and Heiken 2000: 57.

3. Friedrich 2000; see also Doumas, ed., 1978–1980 and Hardy et al., eds., 1990.

4. McCoy and Heiken 2000.

5. For a general account of the history of Thera, see Doumas 1983 and Danezis 2001.

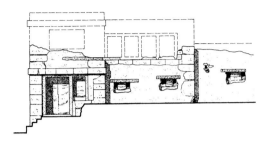

2

The Archaeologist: An Unexpected Visitor 3,500 Years Later

The sealed doors of the prehistoric settlement of Akrotiri were to be trespassed by an unexpected visitor 3,500 years later: the archaeologist. The first to visit the site were the French around the end of the 19th century. The story of these pioneers and the adventures of their first finds is a fascinating one, and it is brilliantly unfolded in Tzachili's recent work.[1] In summary, it starts during the last years of the 19th century, when the French company that was then building the Suez Canal installed a quarry somewhere along the southwest coast of Therasia. Huge quantities of volcanic ash were removed and sent to Egypt for the construction of the canal. This ash, known as *Theran earth*, is an excellent material for hydraulic concretes (i.e., concretes that can harden under water). Once the thick mantle of ash was removed, the remains of "a very old" civilization appeared in the quarry area. We should be reminded that Aegean prehistory was lingering in the sphere of myth at that time, for neither Troy, Mycenae, nor Knossos had yet been discovered. Thanks to the prudence of certain Theran intellectuals and the brilliant work of the French volcanologist Fouqué, these first finds were recorded with an exceptional scientific precision for their time. Two

French archaeologists, Mamet and Gorceix, arrived some years later and briefly investigated parts of the island, including the region of Akrotiri and the nearby area of Ballos. Additionally, soon after the Germans began their campaign on ancient Thera, Zahn undertook a brief investigation in the area of Potamos near Akrotiri.

It was years later, however, that systematic research began. Spyridon Marinatos came to the island in 1967 with a vision in his mind and a specific question to answer: "was the eruption of the Theran volcano responsible for the abrupt end of the Minoan world on Crete?" as he had argued in an ambitious article in 1939.[2] With the information from the earlier surveys at hand, and a wise evaluation of the topography of that part of the island (best anchorage for boats, ample arable land), Marinatos decided to plant his spade in the vicinity of the modern village of Akrotiri,[3] and in so doing he inaugurated a new era in the field of Bronze Age archaeology (Figs. 10, 11). Perplexed by his first discoveries, he could hardly believe that the rooms he brought to light from the very first days of his expedition, during the summer of 1967, belonged to the upper story of a building. Following one of the

Fig. 10. View of the excavation (under the shelter) and its broader region, from Mesovouna.

streets of the town, he attempted to excavate by digging tunnels, hoping to enter the buildings through their doors and windows and leave the fields above intact (Fig. 12). When he realized that he was dealing with the ruins of two and three story buildings (Figs. 13, 14), he gave up the idea and decided to unearth the ruins of the town following the bed of a ravine, in a north-south direction, where the stormy waters had washed away the volcanic deposits.

In ten years time the excavation covered an area of approximately 10,000 square meters. The picture was soon relatively clear: due to an extraordinary whim of fate, Marinatos was bringing to light a uniquely preserved town, destroyed around the middle of the second millennium B.C. by a fatal eruption. It was a flourishing harbor town thriving on trade and seafaring, contemporary with the cities of the legendary King Minos on nearby Crete.

It took years of hard work by many scholars to arrive at the conclusion—long after Marinatos' death—that the Theran volcano was most probably not the main or the only reason for the fatal events on Crete. Yet, the issue is far from being resolved; what's more, to the various theories expressed regarding the two places and their relationship, a new doubt has raised its shadow, that of the date of the eruption. The conventional archaeological chronology of the southern Aegean, in direct relation to the Egyptian chronology, has set the date of the eruption at approximately 1525 B.C., but the calibrated radiocarbon dates give a different estimate

(1645–1615 B.C.). Dendrochronology, ice-cap dating, and climatic perturbations also offer new data on the issue.[4]

It is no wonder that Thera attracts the interest of so many scholars of such varying disciplines. The happy marriage between archaeology and the exact sciences has helped enormously in the common effort to understand the phenomena, both natural and manmade. Dating is a major issue of common interest and strong debate as one can see in the proceedings of the conferences on *Thera and the Aegean World* and the literature thereafter. The date of the eruption has, indeed, become a tug of war, and scholars are constantly pulling the two ends, ranging from the "low" date around 1525 B.C. to the "high" date of 1646 B.C.[5]

The debate has naturally spread beyond the limits of the Aegean world, for each time a date is changed a whole sequence of interrelated events is carried along, greatly affecting the fragile timetables set for each region. Egypt, in particular, is the least flexible in terms of date fluctuations, for by having the early privilege of script, it has a more or less fixed chronological account of events, and hence, more difficulties in coping with such divergences.

Despite the overwhelming preservation of the material culture at Akrotiri, the questions that remain unanswered are many. This is a civilization that reached an incredibly high level of culture in all aspects but one: that of writing. Scant fragments of the undeciphered Linear A script are all that exist. This is a serious handicap for the modern

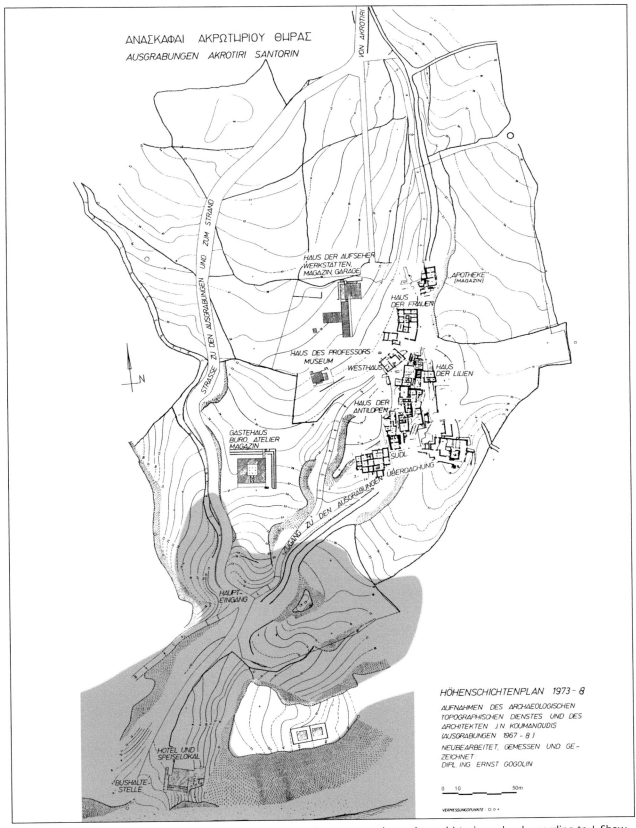

Fig. 11. Map of the Akrotiri region (Marinatos 1976: Plan A). The gray area shows the prehistoric sea level according to J. Shaw.

Fig. 12. Marinatos in the first years of the dig, guiding excavation under the "Tunnel".

Fig. 13. Marinatos standing bewildered in front of the three-story facade of Xeste 2.

Fig. 14. Delta-West at the beginning of the dig. The thick volcanic ash that is being removed is seen to the left.

scholar who seeks to understand a lifestyle through the material remains alone. Understanding the spiritual sphere of this remote past will always remain a nebulous prospect. The amount of information, on the other hand, is so overwhelming that one may easily fall into the trap of thinking one has understood it all. With this circumspection in mind, let us now attempt a description of this magnificent city, carefully avoiding the slippery paths of over-interpretation.

Chapter 2 Notes

1. I. Tzachili, *19th Century Excavations in Thera and Therasia* (in press). According to Tzachili, it was Fouqué who first came to Akrotiri, followed by the archaeologists Mamet and Gorceix.

2. Marinatos 1939b.

3. Marinatos 1968–1976, I: 8–16.

4. Hardy et al., eds., 1990, III: Chronology.

5. Wiener has most recently suggested the date of 1525 B.C. for the Bronze Age eurption of Thera (forthcoming a and b). See also Hardy et al., eds., 1990, III: Chronology; Manning 1999; Bietak 1995: 19–28; Doumas 2001: 95; Warren and Hankey 1989; Wiener 2003.

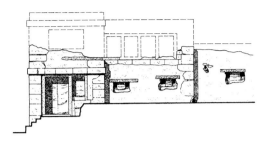

3

The Settlement Pattern of Thera during the 2nd Millennium B.C.

Despite the difficulties in surveying the islands of Thera and Therasia due to the thick mantle of volcanic deposits, the prehistoric find spots are already numerous, pointing to a variety of installations all over the islands (Fig. 3). The earliest human presence goes back to Neolithic times, in the 5th millennium B.C., as P. Sotirakopoulou has shown.[1] Though there is no architecture related to these early finds, they indicate a permanent coastal installation on the flat southwest grounds of Akrotiri. This coastal site was obviously privileged, for habitation was thereafter continuous in the area and of great importance for the southern Aegean. As Doumas often points out, Akrotiri can hardly owe its flourishing rise to agricultural surplus; it was on seafaring and trade that the people prospered.[2]

The Early Cycladic period that followed is rich in archaeological information. There is evidence of settlement in at least six different places during this period, though mostly in the form of cemeteries: near Phira (Phira Quarries, Phtellos, and Hagios Ioannis Eleimon), to the west of Akrotiri (Archangellos and Kalamia), and at Akrotiri itself.[3]

Akrotiri stands out among all Early Cycladic sites in the Aegean for the impressive number and variety of finds it has yielded. The corresponding architectural remains are of two types: rectangular structures built on the bedrock and underground chambers cut in the rock. The picture, though fragmentary (the finds derive mostly from the "rescue excavations" for the foundation of the shelters over the excavations, old and new), speaks of a large and important settlement. Indeed, the early town was so important that its memory survived in the minds of the people for centuries after. This is testified by the Early Cycladic figurines found within a conspicuous stone structure occupying the middle of a public space of the Late Bronze Age town of Akrotiri: a cenotaph, according to Doumas.[4]

As the Early Cycladic period was coming to its end (EC III, in archaeological terms), the settlement pattern of Thera changed:[5] some sites were abandoned (Phira, Archangellos) while new settlements flourished (Phtellos, Hagios Ioannis Eleimon). The latter were situated along the edge of the caldera, perhaps because of the natural protection the high cliffs offered. Akrotiri continued steadily, growing constantly in size and importance.

The tendency now in most Cycladic islands is for the population to gather in large centers, and habitation is limited to one settlement per island. Yet, Akrotiri is not alone on its island during this troubled period, as we have seen—a picture, as Marthari points out, comparable only to that of Melos.

In the Middle Cycladic period the settlement pattern remains more or less the same: life continues at the two sites overlooking the caldera while Akrotiri is now a major site. Of the first part of the MC period, we know very little. During the last phase, however, things change once again: the old caldera sites are abandoned and a new one appears to the south overlooking the caldera cliffs.[6] This is the time of the first palaces on Crete, and the finds show close connections with Crete, especially Knossos. Of the architecture we still have very little to work with, but the pottery finds, according to Marthari, show a

strong influence from Crete, beginning in the early Middle Cycladic, alongside a continuing production of local inspiration. Thera's contacts with the other Cycladic islands as well as the Greek mainland are also attested in this period.

As Thera enters the Late Bronze Age, a major catastrophic event, conventionally called the *seismic destruction* (see Chap. 11), dramatically affects the flourishing town of Akrotiri. The town is destroyed, but it is quickly rebuilt. The remains of the earlier houses are incorporated into rebuilding the new town, and it has more Minoan elements.

The Late Bronze Age is a time of opulence for Thera, and the island seems to have been densely inhabited: Ballos, Therasia, Archangellos, Katsades,

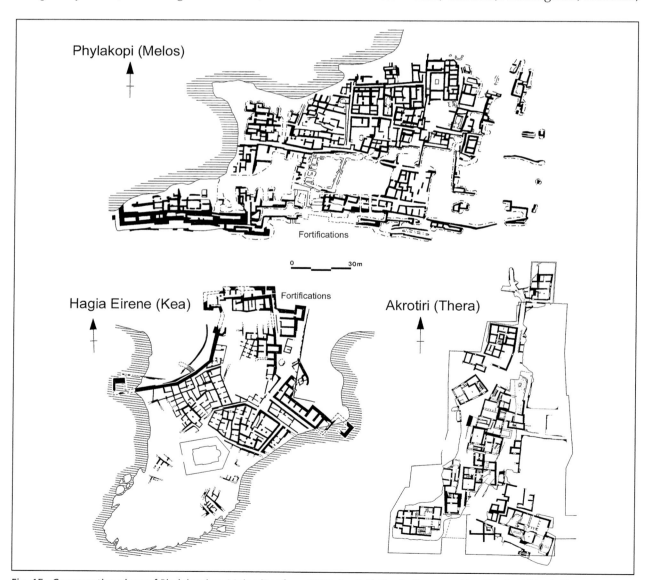

Fig. 15. Comparative plans of Phylakopi on Melos (Renfrew 1985: fig. 2.1), Hagia Eirene on Kea (Davis 1986: pl. 2), and Akrotiri on Thera.

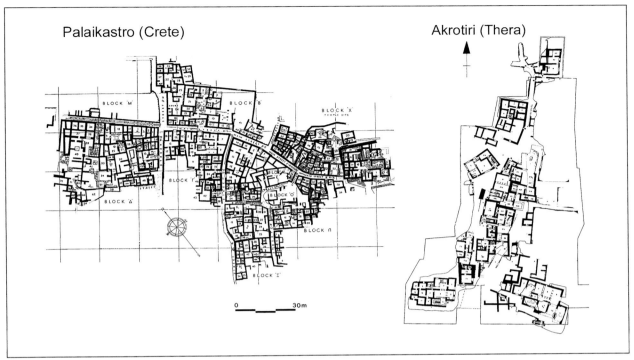

Fig. 16. Comparative plans of Palaikastro, Crete (Bosanquet and Dawkins 1923: pl. 1) and Akrotiri, Thera.

Kokkino Vouno, and Potamos are some of the best known habitation sites of that period.[7] Hamlets, villages, and minor farmsteads or "villas"[8] all attest to the dispersal of the population throughout the Theran landscape.[9] Moreover, the finds and the architecture of these sites speak of a lifestyle comparable to that of Akrotiri.

Davis and Cherry have pointed out that this settlement pattern is wholly unparalleled on Kea or Melos, where the urban centers of Hagia Eirene and Phylakopi are the only significant centers of habitation during much of the second millennium[10] (Fig. 15). It is typical, however, of Crete. It should also be noted that the two Cycladic coastal towns mentioned above are fortified, which implies that the absence of other habitations in the hinterland was due to safety reasons. Cretan settlements, on the other hand, have no fortifications, and neither does Akrotiri so far. Both the settlement pattern of Thera and the absence of fortifications at Akrotiri are features common in Crete but foreign to the Cyclades.[11]

Hagia Eirene and Phylakopi were both built on promontories. The fortification walls protect the settlements only from the hinterland, and they did not extend along the coast.[12] Obviously, the threat was felt only from the land. These walls were built in the Middle Cycladic period, and they remained in use throughout the Late Cycladic period, until LC III.[13] Akrotiri, as far as we can judge today, is not built on a promontory, and it is difficult to envisage a line of fortifications protecting the settlement from the hinterland from all around the site (Fig. 11).

An argument sometimes summoned in favor of the existence of fortifications is the density of the site. Yet, in the case of Akrotiri, it is the style of architecture that is dense (large multi-story buildings, with no open air spaces in their fabric, abutting each other) and not so much the town plan. The latter includes extensive open public spaces and a relatively well organized street network (see Chap. 5). This is not the picture of a building operation restrained within the narrow space limits defined by a fortification wall as is the case with Kea and Melos. On the other hand, unfortified Minoan towns, such as Gournia and Palaikastro, are denser than Akrotiri (Fig. 16).

Fortification is a crucial issue for understanding the identity of Thera in the southern Aegean and in its relations to Crete. If Akrotiri does, indeed, prove to be unfortified, then the socio-political implications are strongly in favor of a direct relationship between Crete and Thera, for in this case, Thera does not share the fears and the precarious fate of the other Cycladic islands.

Chapter 3 Notes

1. Sotirakopoulou 1990; 2001.

2. Doumas 2001: 89.

3. Marthari 2001; Sotirakopoulou 2001.

4. Doumas 1993: 181; 1994: 164.

5. Marthari 2001.

6. Mavrommatis quarries, near Megalochori (Televantou 1982: 358–359; Papagiannopoulou 1991: 358).

7. For references on these sites see Doumas 1983 and Marthari 2001.

8. Barber 1987: 65–66. See also Hägg, ed., 1997, for further discussion.

9. Doumas 1983: 45, Ballos and Mavrommatis are mentioned as suburbs, whereas Potamos was mentioned as part of the city.

10. Davis and Cherry 1990: 191–192.

11. Barber 1987: 167 (on fortifications).

12. J. Davis, *Fortifications at Ayia Irini, Keos*, Ph.D dissertation, University of Cincinnati, 1977, 3, writes: "it is more likely that the fortifications did not enclose the city on all sides. [...] A fortification wall would have been necessary only on the land side." In Bronze Age art there are several depictions of building compounds (towns?) showing large scale, compact walls on their fronts that have been interpreted by some scholars as fortifications. These, however, are commonly along a water line, and their identification as "fortifications" is rather ambiguous. See Boulotis 1990: 436–437, n. 61–64 for references on fortification walls and enclosures both real and in art. See also Marinatos 1968–1976, VI: 52–53; M. Shaw 1986: 112–114; Morgan 1988: 86; Televantou 1990; J. Shaw 1990; J. Shaw and Luton 2000.

13. Barber 1987: 66-69.

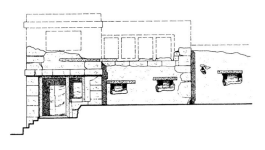

4

The Akrotiri Region:
Landscape, Past and Present

The excavation is situated at a short distance from the south coast, in the vicinity of the modern village of Akrotiri—hence its name (Figs. 11, 17). The southernmost buildings of the dig are about 230 m from the shore, while the village is approximately 800 m to the northwest. Modern Akrotiri dates from Medieval times and was one of the five fortified settlements of Thera; today its *kasteli* (meaning fortified center) stands in ruins on a hilltop (Fig. 18). It was destroyed in the 1956 severe earthquake, and since then the village has been expanding over the east slope of the hill named Loumarades, controlling the southwest tip of the crescent shaped island of Thera.

The village and the hilly land surrounding it form a natural border between two large farmlands called Messa Chorio and Exo Chorio, to the west and east respectively (Fig. 19). The latter is a relatively flat area covered with a thick layer of volcanic ash that was washed down from the surrounding hills. The prehistoric surface several meters below was probably just as flat, providing a broad patch of arable land. Today, the land is covered with rich vineyards. Life on the island has always revolved around wine production, and there is evidence that viticulture was popular in the Bronze Age also (Fig. 20).[1]

Farther east, the fields are bordered by the two non-volcanic mountains of the island, Profitis Ilias and Gavrilos. These limestone outcrops, not far from the site, provided the prehistoric masons with the island's only non-volcanic building material. The thick volcanic layer of the Minoan eruption covering the valley of Exo Chorio is deeply cut by numerous ravines guiding torrential rainwater to the southern coast. These ravines were formed by storms and torrential water following the eruption (Phase V), and when dry, their beds are used as paths. The peculiar ragged formation of these ash banks, sculpted by rainwater and wind, is one of the most spectacular present day features of the island of Thera (Fig. 8). The dig at Akrotiri extends along the bed of one such ravine. Moreover, these ravines are valuable for the archaeological information they offer, because along their banks one can sometimes get a glimpse of the pre-eruption surface.[2] What lies under the volcanic deposits is otherwise a well-kept secret.

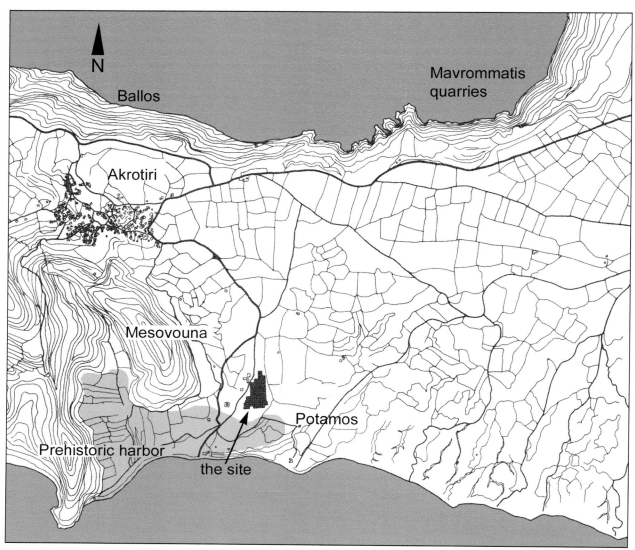

Fig. 17. Map of the Akrotiri region based on aerial photos (C. Palyvou).

Fig. 18. The village of Akrotiri in the early years of the 20th c. The *kasteli* (fortress) dominates at the center (photo courtesy of the archive of the Deutchen Archäologischen Institut in Athens). To the left is the hill of Mesovouna and farther back is Loumaradhes hill. The volcanic ash has been washed away from the slopes of the hills.

Fig. 19. View of the valley and the vineyards (Exo Chorio) to the east of modern Akrotiri. To the left the caldera cliffs are visible, while Mount Profitis Ilias and Gavrilos hill form a natural border at the far end.

To the west the landscape is more diverse: rocky hills and bare low mountains of colorful volcanic rocks alternate with large patches of vineyards and arable land extending in a stepped formation toward the south. These rocky hills present the original "Minoan" landscape, because the volcanic ash has been washed away from their sides and carried down to the flat land below. We can easily imagine that the bright colors of these rocks—a delight to our eyes today—had very much the same appeal to the prehistoric people (Pl. 1A). This impressive colorful landscape could well have been an artistic stimulus for the vivid depictions of nature on the wall paintings, as well as a rich source of building material for Theran houses. It is no coincidence that the colors of these stones, when used as a building material, were carefully matched in orderly compositions, as we shall see below (Pls. 1B, 1C).

One of these hills, Archangellos, to the east of Akrotiri, is famous for its crocuses. During the first weeks of November the flowers blossom and the women of Akrotiri arrange communal expeditions to gather the precious flowers that only last a few days. The "ritual" starts from the chapel of Archangellos where the men are left behind. Having participated in such an excursion, I can hardly emphasize enough the difficulties both in distinguishing the tiny flowers among the thick bushes and in reaching them along the most precarious cliffs. The sight

Fig. 20. Viticulture was always important for the island: grapes painted on a vase from Akrotiri.

of the women with their baskets picking crocus flowers, chatting, and teasing each other had indeed a timeless feeling that unavoidably alludes to the Bronze Age wall paintings of the Crocus Gatherers (Fig. 21).[3] Archangellos, after all, is exactly as it was then, because the volcanic ash has long been washed off its steep slopes. Doumas surveyed the site some years ago and found traces of occupation during most parts of the Bronze Age.[4]

To the north of the excavation, at a distance of approximately 1 km, the land falls sharply into a steep cliff. From an altitude of about 120 m, an impressive view of the caldera opens below (Fig. 4). This view was long thought of as a post-Minoan experience. Thera in the Bronze Age was once believed to be a more or less circular island with a large depression at its summit, corresponding to the volcano. The prehistoric settlement of Akrotiri, consequently, would have been a coastal site lying at the foot of a mountainous mass with the dreadful volcano overhanging to the north. As discussed above, this has been corrected,[5] and the current theory is that the southern part of the caldera already existed and formed part of the Bronze Age landscape.

This new picture radically changes our understanding of the immediate natural surroundings of the prehistoric settlement. The northern limit of the Akrotiri region, in this case, was very much like the caldera cliffs we see today, and prehistoric sites in the region, such as Ballos and Mavrommatis quarry, were situated more or less at the sides of a cliff (Fig. 17). The site on Therasia, on the other hand, was inland, because the land continued all the way to the islet of Aspronissi before the eruption. The settlement of Therasia would have been difficult to reach from Akrotiri.

According to the new theory, the cliffs around the Athenios area—the modern port of the island—were exposed and accessible in prehistoric times. This answers the question of the provenance of the schist-like slabs commonly used for floor pavements at Akrotiri, because such rocks are only found at the Athenios area, which would have been inaccessible according to the earlier view regarding the shape of Thera in the Bronze Age.

Fig. 21. Women from Akrotiri gather crocuses at Archangellos hill (1991, courtesy I. Tzachili) like the "Crocus Gatherers" did 3,500 years earlier.

Fig. 22. The valley of Hagios Nikolaos seen from the north. The west harbor of the town was most probably in this area.

The existence of a deep bay in the middle of the island opening to the west may raise the question of a possible harbor in this area. This, however, seems rather improbable, as J.W. Shaw points out,[6] because of the deep waters and the high cliffs surrounding the bay.

Turning finally to the south of the excavation, the question to be answered is the position of the prehistoric shoreline. Marinatos suggested that it was farther toward the south, in the shallow waters we see today, but most scholars now accept that it was probably more inland instead, and that the new coastline resulted from the accumulation of large quantities of volcanic ash spreading in a southern direction. The ash, weathered by the winds, forms a "wall" about 10 m high along the beach (Fig. 7).[7]

Doumas places the prehistoric harbor to the southwest of the town in the area of the narrow valley of Hagios Nikolaos (Figs. 17, 22).[8] The deep bay is filled with pumice approximately 23 m above sea level. The valley lies between Mesovouna and a rocky promontory of black and red lava farther west, called Mavro Rachidi. The promontory would have sheltered the western side of the deep bay, serving as an excellent natural mole. Even now, boats find refuge from the prevailing north winds in

this part of the island. Doumas has identified this bay with the harbor next to the town depicted on the Miniature Fresco of the West House; the town is seen as Akrotiri itself. The building depicted on the hill to the left of the harbor is identified with Marinatos' finds on Mavro Rachidi,[9] while the peculiar structure by the coast is seen as ship-sheds.[10]

J. Shaw, interpreting the same picture as well as the actual landscape, suggested a different arrangement.[11] The bay at Hagios Nikolaos he claims to be too far from the town because the tendency in most harbor towns of that era was to bring the ships as close as possible to the town. He, therefore, proposes anchorages to the immediate south and to the east of the town where a large depression in the volcanic ash is visible today. This he interprets as a possible bay or a shoreline with an islet at a small distance (Fig. 11). A harbor in this area may also explain the presence of large mansions at the southeast area of the excavation and the impressive Koureton Street leading east. He concludes that a coastal zone, some 700 m long, from Mavro Rachidi to Potamos could have served for anchorage. The idea of a double harbor at Akrotiri is consistent with the picture of most Aegean coastal towns.

Chapter 4 Notes

1. See Giousouroum et al. 1992.
2. Aston-Hardy 1990: 348–360.
3. Tzachili 1994; Sarpaki 2001.
4. Doumas 1983: 27.
5. See Doumas et al., eds., 1978; Hardy et al., eds., 1990, especially Heiken et al. 1990; McCoy and Heiken 2000.
6. J. Shaw 1990: 434.
7. Marinatos 1968–1976, II: 8.
8. Doumas 1983: 55–56. Wells dug in the valley provided evidence for the presence of sea-water before the eruption.
9. Marinatos 1968–1976, II: 35–36.
10. M. Shaw, 1985: 23; Televantou 1994: 327.
11. J. Shaw 1990. The suggestion that the modern 20 m contour line may indicate the ancient shoreline poses a problem because the southernmost buildings of the dig—Xeste 3 area—are at a lower level (+19 m).

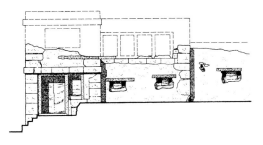

5

The Town

Layout and Public Open Spaces

The excavated part of the town extends over a low hillock sloping south toward the coast at an altitude of 19 to 26 m above sea level, from south to north. To the west, 200 m away, the hill of Meso-vouna seems to have formed a natural border for the expansion of the town in this direction (Fig. 17). The hill has almost no volcanic deposits today and no trace of habitation.

The settlement slopes abruptly to the east in the direction of Potamos, a ravine about 300 m from the excavation created by the torrential waters right after the eruption. Scant finds in this area—including the buildings excavated in 1899 by the German archaeologist Zahn—indicate that habitation here is probably not as dense as within Akrotiri itself.[1]

To the north, there are no natural boundaries or other indications of where the town may end. Perhaps it extended quite far in that direction. The houses excavated by the French at the end of the 19th century in the area of Ballos are too far to the northwest (about 1 km) to be part of the town proper. The same is true for the ruins unearthed in 1982 in the area of the Mavrommatis quarries, about the

same distance to the northeast.[2] Both sites are probably regional installations at the periphery of the town (see Chap. 3). The ancient shoreline to the south and the probable existence of more than one harbor were discussed in the previous chapter. It is quite safe to assume that the town extended all the way down to the coast, which was probably not very far from Xeste 3.

The undulation of the land provided an ideal orientation for the houses, because they face mostly toward the east and the south, with the north to their back. The general impression of the town from far away—for those arriving from the sea—was probably not unlike that of a traditional Aegean coastal settlement today (Fig. 23). One can easily envisage a dense cluster of cube-like buildings with stepped flat roofs, sprawling down the hillside. The color effect may have differed, because the prehistoric houses are covered with a yellowish clay plaster and not whitish lime. Upon closer inspection, however, the differences would have been overwhelming: the sophisticated ashlar facades of the imposing mansions near the coast,

Fig. 23. View from the sea of a typical Aegean town on Karpathos (*Ελληνική Παραδοσιακή Αρχιτεκτονική* 1983–1984, 3: 77, fig. 9). The overlapping effect of the houses, due to the strong inclination of the land, produces an effect similar to that probably rendered by the Town Mosaic from the Temple Repositories at Knossos (Evans 1921–1935, I: fig. 223).

with their orderly indentations and the numerous openings—windows, verandas, and balconies—would have emitted a distinct "urban" look (Pls. 2A, 2B), not to mention the Horns of Consecration that projected above the roofs of some houses. If any comparison with the Aegean vernacular architecture may still stand, it is more toward the direction of the semi-urban architecture developed in many island towns, such as Syros and Oia on Thera (Fig. 24), during the opulent period of the 18th and 19th centuries A.D., when rich merchants and captains brought home architectural ideas and techniques—probably masons and architects as well—from the Neoclassical style prevailing in the west.

Although the total size of the town remains unknown, all indications point to a large town in comparison to the other Cycladic settlements, but also many Cretan sites as well. We know for sure that the excavated area under the shelter—roughly 10,000 square meters—is only part of the town (there are buildings exposed at the periphery of the excavation, in all directions). This part alone exceeds the size of the contemporary settlement of Hagia Eirene, Kea (7,500 square meters), while Phylakopi, Melos is not much bigger (18,000 square meters) (Fig. 15). It also corresponds to the size of the medieval fortified core (*kasteli*) of Akrotiri. In Crete, where no fortifications exist, it is more difficult to estimate the size of the settlements. The absence of a fixed periphery implies that the town could sprawl in various directions as linear extensions following the timeless tendency to build along a road. Finds dispersed in a broader area, therefore, do not necessarily imply that they form a cohesive urban fabric.

Akrotiri was surely a major town, though the size of 200,000 to 300,000 square meters envisaged by Doumas[3] may be rather on the generous side (Fig. 25). My own guess would be more in the area of 100,000 square meters (the size of the modern settlement of Akrotiri). These largely diverging numbers are quite interesting when compared to Crete. According to Branigan,[4] the estimated sizes of Minoan towns fall into two clear groups: those above 200,000 square meters (Knossos, Malia, Phaistos, Palaikastro and perhaps two or three more) and those below 100,000 square meters (Zakros, Gournia, Kommos, Mochlos, Pseira, and others). The small towns outnumber by far the large ones (Branigan anticipates a ratio of 5:1). The size of Akrotiri, therefore, is a strong factor (though not the only one) in understanding its position in the urban hierarchy of the Minoan world.[5] Unfortunately, however, both estimates—Doumas' and my own—remain largely conjectural.

Population numbers are even more difficult to assess, due to the many unknown factors of the habitation pattern (density of houses, number of inhabitants per unit, number and use of upper stories,

Fig. 24. 19th c. mansions in a semi-urban style in the island community of Karterado on Thera (Ελληνική Παραδοσιακή Αρχιτεκτονική 1983–1984, 4: 173, fig. 49).

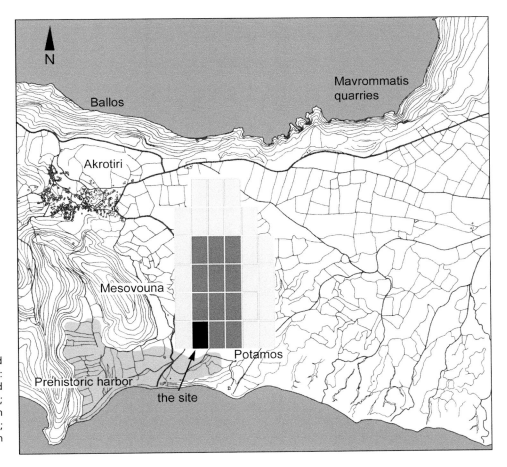

Fig. 25. The conjectured size of the town of Akrotiri: black shows the excavated area (approximately 10 ha); the dark gray grid shows an estimated size of 100 ha; the light gray grid shows an estimated size of 300 ha.

space per person, etc.).[6] Estimates have ranged from 150 to 400 or more persons per hectare. Renfrew[7] suggested 300 for the Aegean: for the large size of Akrotiri proposed by Doumas (30 ha), the population would number 9,000 people (the whole population of Thera and Therasia today, occupying ten different settlements, is hardly over 10,000 persons[8]). Later studies have revised these numbers downward, arriving at an estimate of 150–200 persons per hectare.[9] Accordingly, a moderate estimate of population for Akrotiri on the basis of the smaller size (10 ha), and a low density of habitation within the urban fabric, would produce a figure of 1,500–2,000 people.

The layout of the settlement, on the whole, has been largely affected by the long history of habitation and the natural disasters with which the people had to cope (Figs. 26, 27). The street level was raised more than once, and retaining walls were built in various places in order to hold the accumulated debris. This situation, along with the natural inclination of the land, resulted in the formation of many terraces, both outside and inside the houses. Most houses, indeed, have their ground floors arranged in a highly stepped manner—the seven rooms on the ground floor of the West House are laid on six different levels. Only to the southwest— the area of Xeste 3—does the land seem to be flat.

Some buildings are detached and autonomous, but the majority are arranged in blocks—Sector Delta is such a block, and it includes four different houses. In the latter case, double walls are between adjoining houses. There does not seem to be any special significance in the differentiation between detached buildings and blocks of houses. It may only reflect the time of construction and the restrictions imposed by the local conditions (the detachment of the West House is due basically to the fact that a narrow space to the west was imperative for the sewage system).

The buildings at Akrotiri are relatively standard in form and structure. They do vary, however, in size and probably in function (Fig. 28). Those that can be studied today may be grouped in two general categories: the typical Theran house and the atypical house, discussed below. The typical house ranges in size from 96 square meters to 187 square meters, whereas the atypical houses are large mansions approximately 300–370 square meters (the numbers refer to the area covered by each building

and not the total surface of all the floors). The latter may be considered as buildings of a specialized function, most probably of a communal nature. The distribution of these buildings is noteworthy: there is clearly a zone of public buildings along the south and southeast area, toward the coastline and the harbor area.

The layout of the town—the part that is visible today—shows a latent tendency toward a grid-like order (Fig. 29). Streets and open public spaces follow, more or less, a north-south and east-west direction. Houses tend to follow this orientation as well[10] with some exceptions that are probably due to local restrictions (see the West House, for example, discussed below).

A network of streets and open public spaces runs through the settlement. Depending on their size and function, these spaces can be grouped into six categories, discussed separately below. Open public spaces cover a large portion of the town. The overall picture, therefore, is not that of a densely occupied town, as it is often presented. The high density is actually an architectural feature, because it is attested only within the houses (here the built space is 100% in almost all cases) and consequently in blocks of houses such as Sector Delta, but there is ample unoccupied space between the houses. This is better understood if Akrotiri is compared to Minoan towns, such as Gournia and Palaikastro (Fig. 16).

MAIN STREETS

The main streets constitute the circulatory arteries of the town, accommodating traffic through the settlement as well as within it (Fig. 29, 30). All entrances revealed so far open either on such main streets or public squares. They are 2.00–2.20 m wide and are well defined. The north-south streets can be traced an especially long distance (the excavated segment of Telchines-Daktylon street is over 120 m long). Main streets were usually paved with large flat stones (not slabs) including broken stone implements and discarded millstones. This cobbled pavement is visible in only a few places today (Fig. 31), either because excavation is not complete or because the streets have been covered over with a layer of sand for protection.[11] A well-built drainage system runs under the pavement in several instances (see below).

Streets often have a long history of their own, fading back in time: they may have started as routes established through time as the most efficient and safe way of moving from one point of interest to another. Main streets follow the contours of the land, bypass difficult or dangerous points,

Fig. 26 (opposite). General plan of the excavated area (Akrotiri archive, 1995).

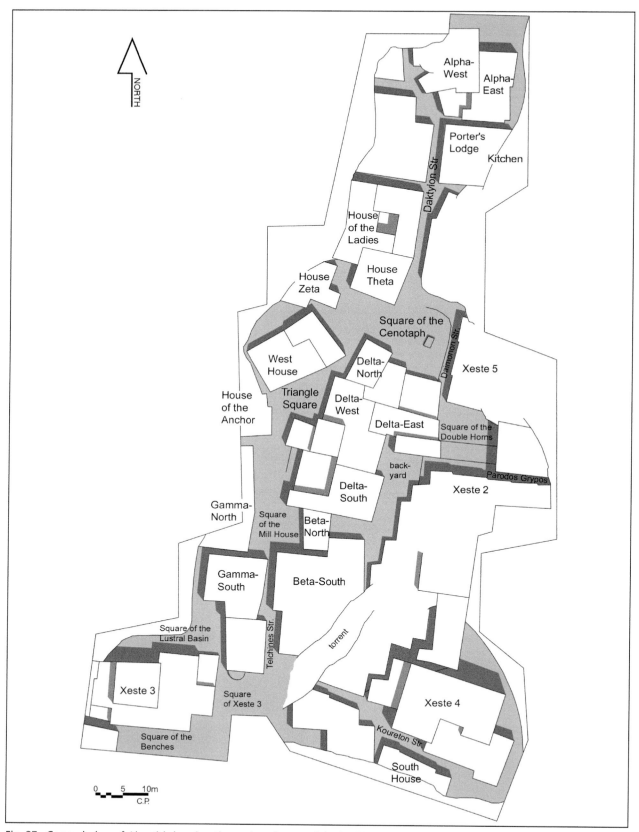

Fig. 27. General plan of Akrotiri showing the main volumes of the buildings and the open public spaces.

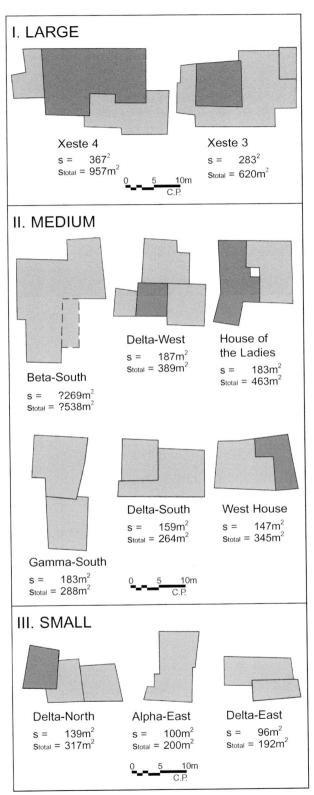

I. LARGE

Xeste 4
s =	367^2
S$_{total}$ = 957m^2

Xeste 3
s =	283^2
S$_{total}$ = 620m^2

0	5	10m
C.P.

II. MEDIUM

Delta-West
s =	187m^2
S$_{total}$ = 389m^2

House of
the Ladies
s =	183m^2
S$_{total}$ = 463m^2

Beta-South
s =	?269m^2
S$_{total}$ = ?538m^2

Delta-South
s =	159m^2
S$_{total}$ = 264m^2

West House
s =	147m^2
S$_{total}$ = 345m^2

Gamma-South
s =	183m^2
S$_{total}$ = 288m^2

0	5	10m
C.P.

III. SMALL

Delta-North
s =	139m^2
S$_{total}$ = 317m^2

Alpha-East
s =	100m^2
S$_{total}$ = 200m^2

Delta-East
s =	96m^2
S$_{total}$ = 192m^2

0	5	10m
C.P.

Fig. 28. Theran houses according to size. S is the surface area of the ground floor, and S$_{total}$ is the estimated total surface area of all the floors (approximately). The darker shade indicates the probable third floor.

and exploit natural passages (in recent times the beds of the ravines are used as paths during the long dry seasons). A route is gradually transformed into a street by the buildings that border its sides (Fig. 32).[12] At Akrotiri, there are almost no front courtyards or other intermediate open spaces that can act as buffer zones between the private domain of the house and the public domain of the street (Xeste 3 is the only exception to date). Their facades, therefore, define the third dimension and delineate the streets. These tall facades (two-story almost everywhere) offered shade and protection from the winds, but also an impressive screen along the narrow streets. Because of the narrowness of most streets, the lower parts of several corners of the buildings were rounded to avoid damage.

The role of these facades in enhancing the urban notion of the street is further emphasized by the indentation of the walls (Fig. 32). This is a well-known trait of the Bronze Age world—popular, in fact, throughout the eastern Mediterranean—and has been interpreted in various ways.[13] It seems, however, that they are largely the outcome of the transformation of a route into a street, discussed above. A sequence of indentations allows a block of buildings to adjust to the fortuitous crooked path following the undulation of the land, while keeping the orientation of the walls toward the cardinal points. Furthermore, it seems that indentations became characteristic of facades facing main streets or major public spaces, such as the north facade of Xeste 2.

The depth of an indentation varies from 0.20 m to a few meters (Xeste 2 and Xeste 4 respectively), the most common dimension being approximately 0.60 m (Sector Delta). It is consistent, however, in a sequence of several recesses, even when different houses—and therefore different owners—are involved, as in the case of both the west and east facade of Sector Delta. This shows that the indentation was a kind of "town-plan regulation" respected by all the members of the community.

Telchines-Daktylon Street is a major traffic axis in the town (Fig. 30). It runs through the settlement in a north-south direction, following more or less the ridge of the hillock, and slopes gently (approximately 5%) toward the sea. It has a minimum width of 2 m, and it is paved.

Koureton Street runs east-west, leading downhill in a southeast direction (Fig. 29). It passes south of Xeste 4 and is quite broad at points, though due to the indentations of the facades, there are some narrow points as well, 1.60–2.00 m wide. It is relatively

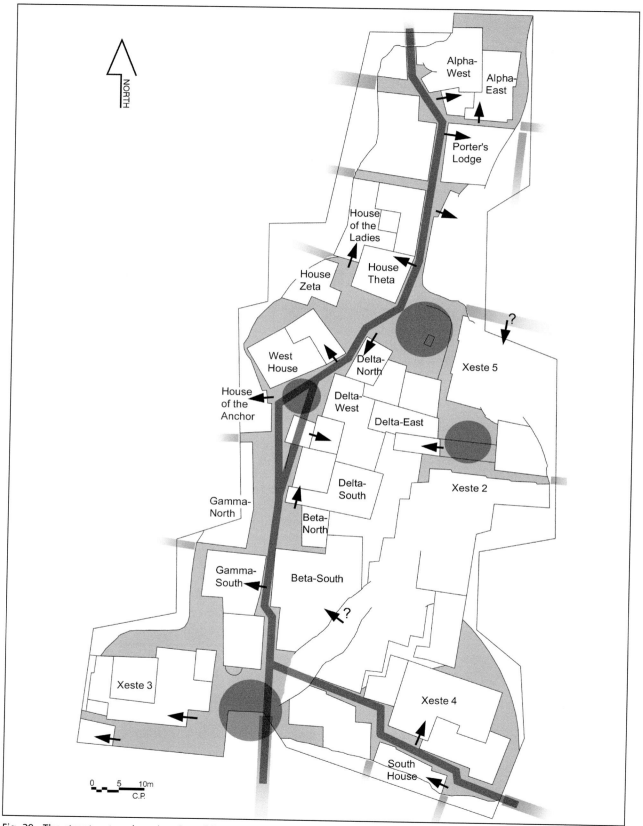

Fig. 29. The street network and main public squares.

Fig. 30. Telchines Street looking north.

Fig. 31. Street south of Alpha-East with visible cobbled surface.

flat to the west, but to the east it has a strong inclination, and it may even prove to have steps.[14] Koureton seems to join Telchines Street near the southeast corner of Sector Gamma (the torrent caused much damage in this area). It continues farther west, bordering Xeste 3 from the north.

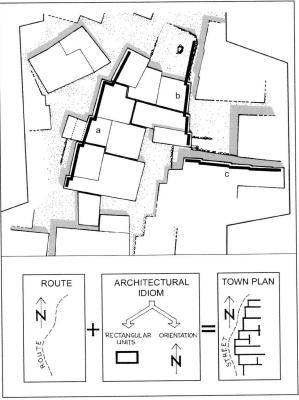

Fig. 32. The indentation of the facades as a means to define the transition from a "route" to a "street".

SECONDARY STREETS

Side streets are part of the street network, but they have a secondary function to accommodate local needs. These streets branch off the main ones and are narrower, 1.00–1.20 m, and of a shorter length. Daimonon Street is a north-south street, 1.20–1.70 m wide. It runs between Sector Delta and Xeste 5 and is most probably connected to the street bordering Sector Alpha to the east. The continuation of this street to the south was blocked by the retaining wall between Xeste 2 and Delta 19.

Other secondary streets are partially showing in several parts of the excavation, such as between the Porter's Lodge and Sector Alpha (1 m wide) (Fig. 31), north of the House of the Ladies, and between Xeste 2 and House ID (1.20 m wide). Several other north-south streets also exist. They are deduced by the outlines of the buildings because they are still unexcavated.

NARROW ALLEYS

Akrotiri was always going through a process of transformation, and it was gradually enlarged through a typical infill development. When a new house was built among an existing group of buildings, the architect had to make sure not to cause any inconvenience to the neighbors—not to obstruct, in other words, access, lighting, ventilation, and drainage of their houses. Ample evidence for such "rules of good neighborliness" exists in the form of narrow alleys and cul-de-sacs.

Narrow alleys are usually restricted to a short length and are not intended for traffic—at least not primarily. They are far too narrow for that (0.60–1.10 m), and no doors open on such alleys. They are more like simple gaps between the buildings for the accommodation of drainage, light, and air. Their presence is due, to a large extent, to the absence of open-air spaces within the fabric of the buildings. The fact that almost all buildings have at least two stories excludes also the possibility for clerestory lighting from above. The "detached" type of house is often the byproduct of such narrow alleys. In other words, the dense, compact architecture of Akrotiri has dictated to some extent its town plan. The narrow alley to the west of the West House is a good example (Fig. 33). It is 0.60–1.10 m wide and 9 m long (the length of the west facade of the building). There are many windows opening toward the alley but no doors. The public drain runs under its pavement. The southern end of the alley was actually

Fig. 33. Narrow alley by the West House serving the public sewage system, blocked by a large slab covering the sewage pit.

blocked by a large slab leaning obliquely on the wall. It covered a large pit, through which the drainage system of the West House is connected to the public drain.

Narrow alleys border the west and north sides of Xeste 4. The situation is not clear here because they are still filled with unexcavated debris up to the height of the second floor of Xeste 4. It is very doubtful, however, that this narrow space, approximately 1 m wide, with the tall facades overhanging, is anything more than a service gap between the buildings. The fact that the north facade of Xeste 4 has no indentations may be a further indication of the minor significance of this alley. On the other hand, the luxurious ashlar facades facing these narrow alleys are a puzzle. This privileged building may have a history of its own.

BLIND ALLEYS

Blind alleys or cul-de-sacs are a further indication of the infill development of the settlement (Fig. 34). They are basically meant to provide light and air—there is no indication so far of providing access as well, as is the case in other dense settlements, such as Gournia, for example. Two cases of blind alleys seem to have resulted from the addition of new structures next to existing buildings, in a way as to avoid obstructing the doors or windows of their neighbors. The group of rooms Beta 5–8b was added between Sectors Beta and Delta. The interesting point here is that the west wall of the new structure is obliquely aligned so as to exploit the maximum space, as defined by the windows of Room Beta 1 to the south and Room Delta 15 to the north. Such deeds speak vividly of a community adhering to rules of common welfare, even when under pressure. They also show that architectural deviations—such as the oblique wall—are never arbitrary.

Another instance is the blind alley in the area between Sector Delta and Xeste 2. The entrance Delta 19 is most probably either an addition or the result of major reformations. Its position, however, was dictated by the need to leave an open space in front of the window of Room Delta 21, because this room both at ground floor level and in the upper story had no other means of acquiring light and air. This is also true for Room Delta 9, of House Delta-West. So, a blind alley was created here in order to accommodate both houses. There is another blind alley nearby, probably meant to give light and air to certain rooms of Xeste 2. The retaining wall that blocked the passage between Sector Delta and Xeste 2 was built 2 m farther west precisely for this reason.

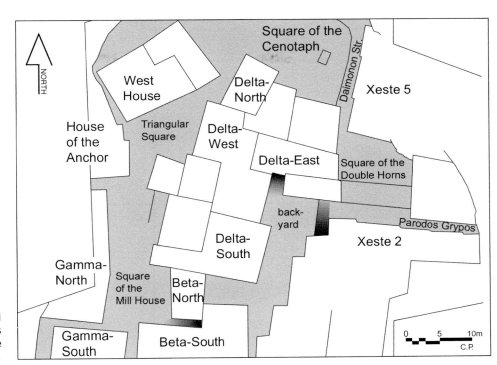

Fig. 34. The darkest shaded areas indicate blind alleys that serve to illuminate the surrounding buildings.

SQUARES

A square is a broad open public space that often plays an important role in the life of the town. Whether irregular, triangular, or actually square, such public spaces are fairly common at Akrotiri. It is not so clear, however, to what extent they were laid out as part of a preconceived town plan, because some of them look more like a casual local broadening of the street. Moreover, they all seem to relate to building entrances. In some cases one may detect the same infill development described above: building operations have reached their maximum, and with further construction, daylight and access rights would have been violated. The largest open public spaces or piazzas are discussed below.

The Triangle Square—to the south of the West House (Fig. 35, 36)—provides access to three buildings: the West House, the House of the Anchor, and Sector Delta-West (through the Gate). Its shape has resulted from the oblique position of the West House. An unexcavated structure farther west, probably belonging to the House of the Anchor, follows the same oblique alignment. The reason for this deviation from the cardinal orientation, typical of the Late Bronze Age, is not so evident for the time being, but it is important to note that remnants of earlier walls under the West House follow the same orientation. It could well be that the formation of the land beyond this point to the west (not visible

today) has dictated the oblique orientation, not only of the West House, but of a larger district to the west. Many examples of this sort exist in other Aegean Bronze Age settlements, such as Hagia Eirene on Kea and Palaikastro.

Daktylon Street leads south through a rather narrow passage between the West House and Sector Delta, cutting through the square, and it continues in two directions: underneath the Gate and bypassing it to the west. The latter is at a higher level, and the two routes meet again farther south, near the Mill House Square. A retaining wall about 1 m high supports the western route. This arrangement resulted most probably from the need to accommodate the accumulated debris (see Sector Delta, Chap. 7). The open public space is paved (visible today only under the Gate), and it has public drainage underneath, discussed below.

The Square of the Cenotaph—to the north of Sector Delta—must have been an important public space.[15] It seems to have acquired its form during the rebuilding that took place after the *seismic destruction*. A long retaining dry-wall was then built at a distance of 1.20–1.70 m from Xeste 5, curving to the northwest so as to hold a broad terrace that was created by the accumulated debris (Fig. 37). A north-south street was left to the west of Xeste 5, running at a much lower level than that of the square. The retaining wall is at least 3.5 m

Fig. 35. The Triangle Square looking north to the West House and east to Sector Delta.

Fig. 36. The Triangle Square looking south to the Gate of Delta-West.

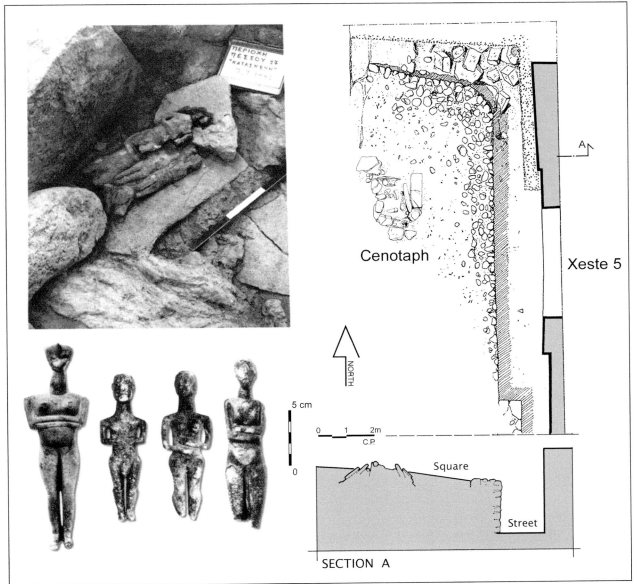

Fig. 37. The Square of the Cenotaph. Left: Early Cycladic figurines as found in the "cenotaph". Right: plan and section of the square.

high here. Bordering the north side of the square, another street branches off Telchines at right angles, leading east with a deep fall (steps should be expected here).

It seems that the upper surface of the terrace was not leveled with a layer of clay, as in other similar cases, because sherds from the artificial fill are protruding. At a central point of the terrace a most peculiar structure was found: it is a rectangle, roughly 1 by 1.50 m, made of slabs half embedded obliquely in the terrace fill (Fig. 37). When the structure was dismantled the excavators came upon the most unexpected finds. A set of seven Early Cycladic marble figurines (3 male and 4 female) were found placed one next to the other, together with other artifacts of that era.[16] Farther down, the remains of a Middle Cycladic building were revealed, and within the rock below were several semicircular rock-cut chambers. This unique correlation of finds of successive eras suggests a monument built in reverence to a remote past, a kind of cenotaph, as Christos Doumas has suggested.[17] The large public space surrounding this structure may have hosted communal rituals. This artificial terrace was accessed only from the northwest, from Telchines Street. The open space continues west beyond Telchines Street, resulting in a very big open public area approximately 8 by 23 m. It should be noted that no evidence indicates any of the surrounding buildings had any special importance.

The Square of the Double Horns—to the East of Sector Delta, between Xeste 2 and Xeste 5—is the most regular square, measuring approximately 10 by 13 m (Fig. 38). It is arranged in at least three terraces stepping southward, and it has a thick artificial layer from the *seismic destruction* underneath.[18] Each terrace probably corresponds to the entrance of a building (the middle level is related to the entrance to Delta-East). Two and three story houses bordered the square with large openings and pier-and-window partitions overlooking the open area. Xeste 2 blocks the south side of the square, to a certain degree. The only way to continue south is by turning east and bypassing Xeste 2 (access to the west is restricted by a tall retaining wall).[19] The north side of the square is bordered by an east-west street running between Xeste 5 and Building ID. This area of the town has the most regular town plan arrangement, with streets crossing at right angles and neatly indented facades bordering a perfectly rectangular public space. This situation, however, need not be overly evaluated: it only shows the underlying ideal model, which is not as clear in other instances when local restrictions dictate strong deviations.

The Square of the Mill House between Sectors Delta and Beta is a small scale public space, mainly intended as an access to Delta-South. It, too, has a thick artificial layer underneath, and it seems that some rooms standing here were demolished and covered over during the remodeling of the area.[20]

The Square of the Benches (South), the Square of Xeste 3 (East), and the Square of the Lustral Basin (North) are large open spaces bordering Xeste 3 on three sides. Only the one to the south, however, is sufficiently excavated: it is a broad area partly paved with large stones forming a beautiful cobbled surface. The House of the Stone Benches,[21] bordering its west side, opens to this Square. The other two sides of the Square are not visible—to the south at least 8 m of free space lies between Xeste 3 and the southernmost limit of the dig. This large open space was heavily used by the rescue parties that came back shortly after the first volcanic events. Ample evidence survives that they were working here shortly before hurrying away. Due to the incomplete picture, it is difficult to say more about this square's function, but it is a large open space, not far from the coast.

The Square of Xeste 3, to the east, is still covered with a heap of ashlar blocks fallen from the building, and it is difficult to judge its size and its relationship to the buildings farther east. The entrance of Xeste 3 has a small forecourt with benches right outside: it opens on this public space. The Square of the Lustral Basin to the north is unexcavated, but there are some buildings showing farther north.

The Square of the Ship Procession, northwest of the West House, is an open space of a very vague

Fig. 38. The Square of the Double Horns. Delta-East to the left and Xeste 2 at the far back.

form and function (Pl. 2B). It has not been cleared of the debris yet. The building to the north of the West House had collapsed during the first phase of the volcanic activity, and the debris spread all over the area was later covered by the volcanic deposits. Other open spaces, only partly identified, exist in various parts of the excavation, such as to the north of Alpha-East.

BACK YARDS AND SERVICE AREAS

The Square of the Monkeys is probably a back yard. It lies between Sectors Beta, Delta, and Xeste 2, and the archaeological finds indicate a place where rubbish had accumulated.[22] Due to the damage caused by the torrential waters, and the incomplete excavation, it is not clear to what degree—and by whom—this open space was accessible. Probably it was once connected to the Square of the Mill House and also to a north-south street running between Xeste 2 and Sectors Beta and Gamma at the other side. This street was blocked toward the north after the *seismic destruction*. The open space, therefore, may have been a service area used only by the surrounding houses.[23]

Managing Water and Waste: The Public Sewage System

The source of clean water in prehistoric Akrotiri escapes us. There are no clear indications of collecting or storing clean water, though the large vessels typically found at the entrances of the buildings are believed to be water reservoirs. Was there a spring nearby, or wells, like the one depicted in the wall painting of the West House, with women carrying jugs on their heads (Fig. 39)? Was there a well within the limits of the town like those at Poliochni and Phylakopi? Or were the residents depending on rainwater as they do today?[24] The latter seems rather improbable, at least on a large scale, because the evidence points to the opposite. The clay or stone spouts found either in situ or in the debris indicate that rainwater was flowing freely off the roofs onto the streets, and no evidence exists so far for gutters of any kind that would collect rainwater from the streets into subterranean cisterns. Such cisterns have not been found. This further implies that the built drain running under the town was meant—at least mostly—for sewage and not rainwater.

Terracotta spouts projecting from the facade of the building at roof level are fairly common and are of two types (Fig. 40, 41). The simplest one is 0.65–0.70 m long and has the shape of a reversed Π in cross section. Two thirds of the spout are embedded in the wall. The other type is shorter: half of it is similar, but the part that is embedded in the wall is flat and rounded at the end. Few terracotta spouts are visible in situ today. A provisional waterspout from a broken amphora is reported from the area of the Tunnels.[25]

In Sector Alpha, Room A1, a clay spout is next to the entrance, 2.30 m above street level. It was built in the wall almost all the way through its thickness, while the projecting part is missing. In Sector Delta, Room Delta 16, two similar spouts border the large window of the western wall. The wall continues above the spouts, forming the parapet of the roof. A spout of the type with the flat rounded end is still in situ at a building to the south of Xeste 4. Though the building remains buried under the pumice, the small part showing today offers valuable information regarding the construction and form of the roof (see Chap. 9).

Fig. 39. Women carrying water jugs near a well. Detail from the Miniature Frieze of the West House.

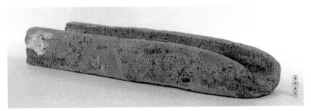

Fig. 40. Terracotta spout.

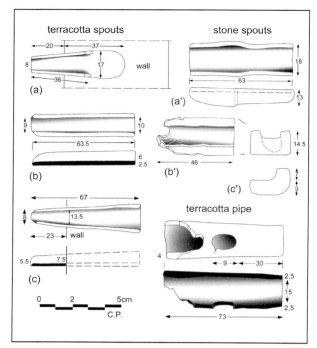

Fig. 41. Terracotta and stone spouts and a terracotta pipe.

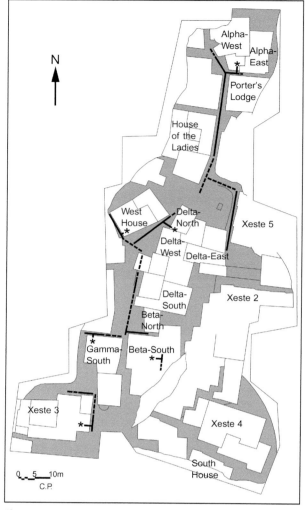

Fig. 42. General plan showing known parts of the public sewage system and connections to the buildings (*). Assumed parts are indicated with a dashed line.

Stone spouts of a crude U-shape in section are also used. Three examples are still in situ, one on the eastern facade of Sector Delta, Room Delta 17, one on the southern facade of Xeste 4, and another on a building to the south of Xeste 4. A neatly dressed stone spout was found in a cavity in the rock on the floor of Room Beta 6. It was broken and presumably discarded there. Spouts are embedded in the wall, and they are carefully sealed with a thick layer of lime plaster.

Many of the activities within the houses were probably of an industrial nature—such as dyeing textiles—thus making the discharge of liquid waste a necessity. But interior lavatories also existed and, judging from the well-preserved example of the West House, they were ingeniously connected to the public sewage system.

An extensive network of underground built channels that lead south toward the sea has been attested in many parts of the site (Fig. 42). The information derives mainly from the daybooks, because many segments of this network were exposed during the excavation of the trenches when building the old shelter over the site and were backfilled afterward. Similarly, many segments of the public sewer have been detected during the excavation of the trenches for the new shelter. Few parts, however, are exposed today and available for a detailed study (Fig. 43).

Piecing together what information is available, we may reconstruct to some extent the picture of the overall system. The main body consists of a network of underground conduits following more or less the streets and open public areas. The largest visible part is along the northern extension of Telchines Street, to the east of the House of the Ladies (Fig. 43). The torrential waters at this point destroyed the surface of the road, thus revealing the sewer that was built on the bedrock. It is rectangular in section, 0.30 by 0.25 m, and runs along the east side of the street, close to the stone foundations of the buildings. The two sides are built with large stones and clay mortar, while the floor is paved with slabs. It was covered with medium sized flat stones with a layer of soil above, followed by the cobblestones of the street pavement. The sewer, in other

Fig. 43. Exposed segment of the sewage channel running under Daktylon Street.

the installations of each house (Figs. 44, 45). The sewer has the same typical construction and the same dimensions described above. At a short distance from the corner of the house, it falls into a large pit, 1.50 by 1 m and 0.80 m deep, occupying the whole width of the narrow alley (see Chap. 6: the West House). This is a remarkable multi-functional pit, on the same logic as those constructed today:

1. It connects the sanitary installation (lavatory) on the upper floor of the West House (described below) to the public sewage system.

2. It accommodates a change of the level of the public sewage: the mouth to the south side of the pit is 0.80 m lower than the mouth to the north. This way a standard inclination of not more than 2% is ensured for each segment of the sewer.

3. It accommodates a direction change: beyond this point the sewer bends to the southeast (keeping the individual parts straight is also essential for its good performance).

4. It most probably included a catch basin at the bottom to retain heavy sediment.

5. It allows for cleaning and maintenance of the whole system, both private and public, hence the large cover slab that could be removed when deemed necessary (a typical manhole).

Farther to the south, near the middle of Triangle Square, another branch—reported in the daybook—seems to join coming from the northeast (presumably the continuation of the main stem revealed outside the House of the Ladies). Not far to the east is yet another connection of the public sewer with the installation of a house: Delta-North, Room Delta 7. This is assumed by the presence of vertical clay pipes embedded in the exterior wall of Room Delta 7 and the pile of stones outside the building pointing to a pit underneath, similar to the one described above. The upper end of the terracotta conduit is not preserved, and it is not clear where it led and what sort of installation it accommodated. The pipes seem to continue above the second floor of the building, presumably to the roof. What is confusing is the fact that the "room" behind the wall with the clay pipes is a staircase. Possibly this conduit is a remnant of an earlier structure, because it is quite clear that the area of the staircase has been remodeled. Similarly, a vertical terracotta conduit was found embedded in the north wall of Room

words, runs deep below street level. There are no signs of lime mortar or any other waterproof treatment—not really needed in this case. The water waste was channeled south toward the sea, with an inclination of approximately 2%, very much like modern standards, so as to ensure a controlled flow. The downward slope of the excavated part of the town along Telchines-Daktylon street is approximately 5%. In order to keep the sewer always at a standard inclination of 2%, deep pits were constructed joining segments of the sewer at different levels.

This underground conduit continues farther north, running along the eastern side of Telchines Street, close to Sector Alpha. It is only a few centimeters below street level here, and small gaps between the covering slabs allowed rainwater to enter as well. At the southwest corner of Sector Alpha, another conduit of the same construction branched off the main stem. It leads east, but its inclination is not clear. It is probably only a small branch, 3 m long, connected to an outlet at the southern wall of Alpha-West. It corresponds to Room A1, and it accommodates a shallow built basin with a clay tub and a mill installation.

Moving south, beyond the area of the House of the Ladies, the next visible patch of the underground channel is to the west of the West House. This is the best preserved part of the sewage system, giving a complete picture of the way it links to

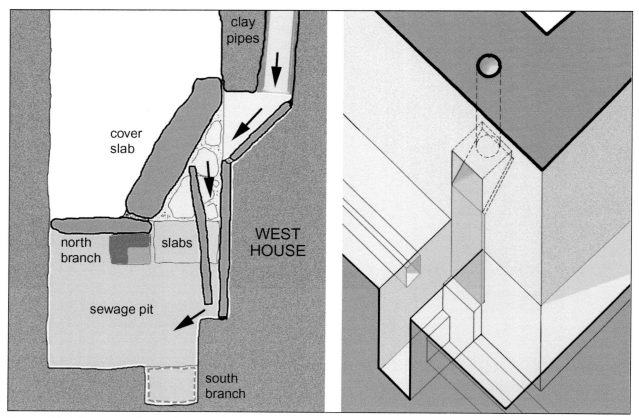

Fig. 44. West House, section and isometric drawings showing the sewage pit and the junction between the lavatory installation and the public sewer.

Gamma 7. It leads waste outside the building to the narrow alley Gamma 8.

Another patch of the sewage system is reported from the area outside Delta 16.[26] It consists of two branches, one running north-south and the other obliquely coming from the northwest, presumably from the area of the pit outside the West House mentioned above. It is roughly 0.30 by 0.30 m in section and 0.80 m below street level. What is of

Fig. 45. The slabs inside the sewage pit of the West House.

special interest here is that the sewer was found halfway within the thick artificial layer (1.70 m) corresponding to the earlier *seismic destruction* of the settlement. This dates its construction after the *seismic destruction*, during the rebuilding activities that took place. What is not clear, however, is whether this applies to the whole sewage system or only to that particular segment, in which case we should be speaking of a remodeling.

To the west of Xeste 5, a built drain leading south runs underneath the street.[27] It is 0.22–0.30 by 0.25–0.37 m high, paved with slabs and pebbles and covered by almost rectangular stones of ignimbrite. Its continuation was brought to light during the rescue excavations for the new shelter in the area of the Square of the Double Horns. It runs directly under the foundations of Rooms Delta 18a and seems to have a vaulted cover (a rather unexpected feature). It is 0.30 m wide and 0.50 m high and is arranged in a stepped formation due to the strong inclinations in this area. The three 'steps' reported are also in varying directions.[28]

The last and southernmost part of the sewage system mentioned in the daybooks is from the area northeast of Xeste 3.[29] This is again a built gutter with a rectangular cross-section running north-south, close to the eastern facade of the building. Its large width, 0.50–0.60 m, was carefully calculated because it corresponds to the lowest segment of the public sewer. A smaller branch most probably extends along the north facade of Xeste 3 leading to the main stem mentioned above: it was found under artificial debris 0.80 m below the street level.

It should be noted that Akrotiri is not unique in its well-designed public sewage system. In densely built settlements, water waste—either rainwater or waste from house activities—can create major problems if not dealt with properly. Communal drains, therefore, are an early technology attested in almost every systematic Aegaean habitation site. Suffice it to look at Poliochni and its superb public drain dating to the 3rd millennium B.C.[30] What is new and extraordinary at Akrotiri, however, is the lavatory inside the house and its sophisticated connection with the public sewage system.

Chapter 5 Notes

1. Zahn's report implies that the building he excavated was alone (I. Tzachili, *19th Century Excavations in Thera and Therasia*, in press). Doumas, however, believes that the town extends to the Potamos Valley (Doumas 1983: 45). During the works for the new shelter the imprint of a tall tree was found near the northeast area of the dig. This is a very interesting find, because it either suggests that trees were included in the urban fabric of the town or that this is, indeed, the fringe of the city.

2. Doumas 1983: 45.

3. Doumas estimates the total size of Akrotiri at 30 times the size of the excavation, i.e., 300,000 square meters (Doumas 2001: 91). His earlier estimate was 200,000 square meters (Doumas 1983: 45).

4. Branigan 2001: 38–41; see also Driessen 2001.

5. See Rackham and Moody 1996: 89 for the four levels in the Minoan settlement hierarchy—hamlets, villages, small towns, and large towns.

6. For a comprehensive account of the proposed sizes of Aegean towns and the various modes of calculating population numbers, see Wiener 1990: 128–133. See also papers in Branigan, ed., 2001.

7. Renfrew 1972.

8. In the first census in 1854, Thera had 18,000 people on the island, while in 1994/5 the population was 9,360. With a total area of 76.2 square kilometers, the density of habitation is 122.8 inhabitants per square kilometer (National Statistic Service of Greece).

9. Branigan 2001: 48.

10. In the Early Bronze Age, the tendency was to have the corners of the buildings facing the cardinal points. See Palyvou 1986: note 30 for further references.

11. Cobbled streets visible today: Telchines Street, in front of the Porter's Lodge, under the Gate, in front of Delta-North, south of Alpha-East, and south of Xeste 3.

12. Palyvou 1986.

13. Palyvou 1986.

14. Some fallen stones from the debris of the building have been wrongly interpreted, I believe, as blocking the road toward the east, thus incorrectly making this major street an "unimportant dead-end" (Doumas 1995: 132). See Fig. 26.

15. Doumas 1994: 164; 1996: 251–252 (on rituals related to the Cenotaph).

16. Doumas 1992b: 181.

17. Doumas 1993: 181; 1994: 164.

18. For a detailed account of the stratigraphical sequence under the Square, see Kariotis 2003.

19. The street leading east has been called Parodos Grypos wrongly implying a side street.

20. Palyvou 1984.

21. Doumas 1994: 157.

22. Tzachili 1990.

23. See Palyvou 2004.

24. Such is the value of rainwater, indeed, that it has dictated to a large degree the form and structure of the vernacular architecture of the island: though stone vaults were used, due to the lack of timber on the island, roofs above are flat so as to collect the rainwater to the cistern below.

25. Marinatos 1968–1976, III: 16.

26. Bernabò-Brea 1976: 23, 30–32, 36.

27. Doumas 1993: 177.

28. Kariotis 2003: 437.

29. Marinatos 1968–1976, V: 27.

30. Bernabò-Brea 1964.

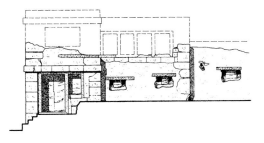

6

The Buildings

Thirty-five different houses can be identified under the sheltered area of the excavation (16 entrances are visible), most of them preserved to the second or even the third floor. Only 10 can be studied to a satisfactory degree, however, because most houses are only partially excavated, and some are identified only from a small part of a facade. The general plan of the site is therefore very complex (Fig. 26). It is also very confusing because ground floor rooms are shown side by side with upper floor rooms depending on the process of the excavation.

An attempt to clarify the picture to some extent presupposes a differentiation of levels: Akrotiri offers the unique possibility of providing plans not only for the ground level, as is commonly the case with other sites, but also for the upper stories. For this reason, at least two plans are presented here for each building, and one general plan shows the volumes of all the buildings (Fig. 27). Needless to say, there are many vague and incomprehensible parts. Moreover, the buildings have a long history of modifications, extensions, and all kinds of interventions, only a few of which are readily recognized at this point. The history of each building is, therefore, only explained when the evidence is strong and of

special interest, as in Beta-South. The description that follows is otherwise confined to the situation shortly before the time of the volcanic destruction. Despite the above hindrances, it was thought worthwhile to attempt a graphic disentanglement of the ruins of Akrotiri, even if it includes several conjectural interpretations, all of which are distinctly marked on the drawings and discussed in the text. Future excavation—an operation that may last several generations—will prove or disprove these hypotheses.

Although the result is an incomplete picture, it is evident that the buildings exhibit striking similarities in structure, form, and interior arrangement. This relative uniformity is of special interest in regard to the social implications, as discussed below. It also helps to deduce "the model of the typical Theran house," in other words, the generic forms of the components and their interrelations, as attested through their variant applications. The "model" does not refer to a prototype or an ideal house but a general concept of what a typical Bronze Age Theran house would have been like.

The West House is a good example of a typical Theran house, and to a large degree, of a typical urban house of the Minoan era in general. Because it is also one of the few buildings where the excavation has been completed,[1] it may well serve as a case study for the description of the "Theran house model." This will facilitate the discussion of the other buildings, whose fragmentary picture does not always offer an overall account of the model.

Among the buildings that do not conform to this model, at least not entirely, are the Xeste buildings that seem to have housed some specialized functions. By outlining the "house model," it will be easier to point out the peculiarities of these large and elaborate edifices. Xeste 3 will serve as an example for this category, for the same reasons as the West House.

Having presented both a typical and an atypical house, we will then proceed to an overview of the other buildings, in the form of a guided tour around the site. These houses will be discussed briefly, focusing on whatever parts and details are best understood. Plans as well as elevations and sections are included only for the houses that present a more or less readable picture. These drawings are simplified and, with the exception of the West House, are based on the existing general plans because detailed documentation of each building is still in progress, following the excavation procedure. Issues of structure (building materials and techniques), design, and morphology are discussed separately because they apply to all the buildings alike.

The West House: A Typical Theran House

The West House is situated at the center of the west part of the excavation—hence its name—and its uppermost walls came to light during the very first years of the excavation (Figs. 46–48).[2] It is a free-standing building, bordering the north side of an irregular open public space (Triangle Square). A broad open space must have extended to the north of the house as well (today covered with the debris of other buildings). To the east runs Telchines Street, one of the major north-south arteries, while to the west a very narrow alley separates the house from other buildings. The West House is visible from quite some distance as one walks up Telchines Street coming from the sea (Fig. 49). It dominates the area today, but this is a deceptive picture because it is due to its large height of preservation in comparison with the adjacent buildings. One should not be carried away, therefore, in overly evaluating its significance. If one restores the second story of Delta-West, with its impressive multiple pier-and-window arrangement facing Triangle Square (see below), the West House will be seen in its proper perspective.

The building is large and compact, with no courts or light wells. It is trapezoidal in plan, and its four facades have no projections or indentations, as is often the case at Akrotiri. The overall dimensions are: north 13.90 m; east 10.75 m; south 15.75 m; west 9.20 m. It covers an area of 147 square meters and has two stories, while a third story occupies a small part of the building (Room 6), thus resulting in a total space of 345 square meters. It has 8 ground floor rooms, with 7 on the upper floor and 1 room

on the highest floor, for a total of 16 rooms. Two staircases are inside the house. These numbers alone point to a large and complex building.

The 8 rooms on the ground floor correspond to 6 different levels (Fig. 50). This is due partly to the inclination of the ground, sloping down from east to west, and partly to the debris of the *seismic destruction* that raised the ground level around the house (approximately 1.50 m). Most ground floor rooms, therefore, look more like semi-basements. The entrance was built on this layer of debris and is, therefore, on the highest level. From the entrance (Rooms 1 and 2) one descends gradually, from room to room, down to Room 4 (this corresponds to a total height difference of 1.80 m) (Fig. 51). From there one ascends up again to Rooms 5, 7, and finally 6. Two or three steps cover the height difference between the adjacent rooms.

The upper floor does not follow the same stepped formation—this would have been too demanding from a technical point of view. Only two changes of levels are attested here. This results in a large variety of heights for the ground floor rooms: the entrance has the lowest, 2.30 m, and Room 4 has the highest, 3.30 m.

The interior arrangement of the house is quite clear, and it will be presented both from the point of view of the resident and the visitor. The only entrance to the building opens on to Triangle Square (Fig. 52, Pl. 2C); it is clearly marked and has all the typical features of the remarkably standardized "entrance model" of the Akrotiri houses: it is situated at the southeast corner of the building and

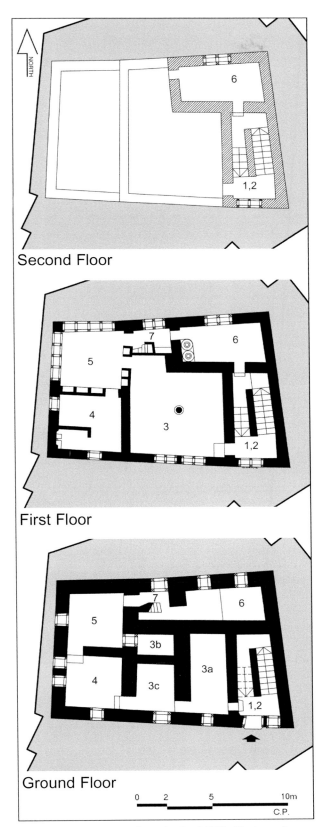

Second Floor

First Floor

Ground Floor

Fig. 46. West House, plans (scale 1:250) Black walls are existing and hatched walls are indicated.

Fig. 47. West House, view from southwest.

Fig. 48. West House model, south facade.

Fig. 49. The entrance of the West House seen under the Gate, as one approaches the Triangle Square from the sea.

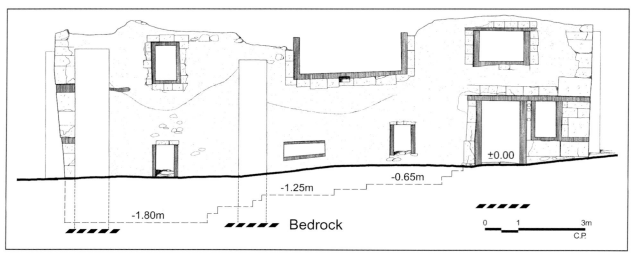

Fig. 50. West House: the south facade and the varying levels of the ground floor rooms in relation to the rock surface.

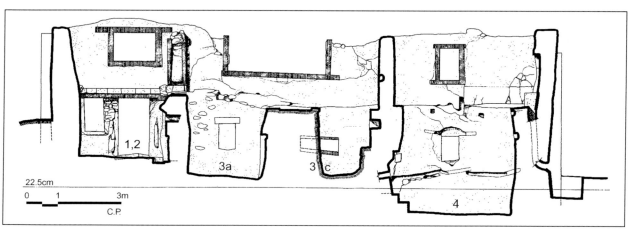

Fig. 51. West House, section through Rooms 1, 2, 3, and 4, looking south.

Fig. 52. West House, isometric drawing of the entrance area.

consists of a large door (approximately 0.90 by 2 m) with a window next to it. Ashlar masonry frames the two openings. A huge monolithic threshold projects slightly from the street level, as well as from the facade of the building. The imprint of the wooden door leaf was visible at the time of the excavation, which means that the door was shut. The door gave access to a small lobby, which is the first landing of the main staircase leading to the upper floors.

Once inside the building, one could follow two routes, both controlled by doors: one, to the left, leads to the ground floor rooms, and the other leads to the upper floor. The latter is a double-leaf door on the first step of the staircase. The space under the second flight of steps was probably used for storage. A large broken stone vessel was found here, set upside down, as a kind of stool. Ground floor rooms

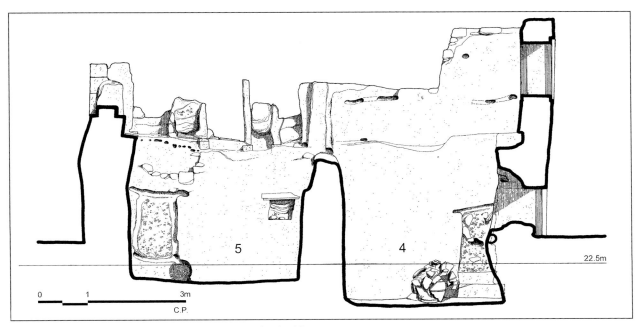

Fig. 53. West House, section through Rooms 4 and 5, looking east.

are arranged in plain juxtaposition, so circulation is controlled by the doors in each room and is planned as one-way traffic from Rooms 1 to 6. All rooms have floors of beaten earth and mud plastered walls, because ground floor rooms were meant for heavy-duty work and storage.

The first room (3a) to be entered from the small entrance lobby (1 and 2) is a long rectangular space: a built bench with three mill stones embedded in its upper surface and accompanying finds clearly show its main function as a mill installation (the preparation of flour was the main activity here). A large stone vessel lies by the door next to the entrance. Such large vessels are commonly found within entrance lobbies or nearby: they may have been reservoirs for clean water brought from outside.

The next room to the west (3b) is half the size of the previous, but initially a room of the same dimensions as room 3a existed here; at some point it was divided in two by a transverse wall blocking off a small part (3c) to the north. The latter has a small window borrowing light and air from Room 5, but it shows no trace of a door, nor was it reached from above through a trap door, as is often assumed in such cases (the upper floor is preserved here). It is possible that the transverse wall was added out of necessity, as a buttress to the main dividing wall, assuming that the latter may have shown signs of too much strain and dangerous deformations. This wall, thick though it may be (actually one of the thickest at Akrotiri, 1.10 m), bears extreme loads

from the upper story due to the central column it supports, and it did, indeed, collapse quite early (the stone base of the column was found almost on the ground floor).

From Room 3b a door opens to the spacious Room 4 occupying the southwest corner of the building. It has two windows and a third that was found blocked. Following a clockwise movement, the next room is Room 5 (Fig. 53). This room was found packed with pottery. It has one window on the western wall. A door to the east leads to a small lobby or corridor (Room 7) with a narrow and steep auxiliary staircase leading to the upper floor. The lobby was well lit with a window looking north. The lower part of the window was blocked to make a stepped cupboard.[3] A door to the east gave access to the most remote room on the ground floor, Room 6, that was found literally packed with vases and other objects.

Turning back to the entrance lobby and the main staircase, we move now to the upper floor. The staircase is well designed for comfortable use: it has low and wide steps and is well lit by a large window at each level. The stairway continues farther up to the third floor and the roof. Due to the many changes of levels mentioned above, the staircase has to accommodate various different levels. This is achieved by using the middle landing for access to an intermediate level—a practice quite common at Akrotiri. In this case the middle landing gives access to Room 6.

The first flight has 8 steps, while the second has only 4 or 5 steps and leads to a landing made entirely of wood. The room entered on the upper floor, Room 3, is extraordinarily large (33.90 square meters), with a column at its center. This is the second largest room at Akrotiri, after Delta 16 (34.80 square meters). It occupies the area of Rooms 3a, 3b, and 3c of the ground floor and has a huge window looking south to Triangle Square. Many loom weights were found here, and taking into account the plain white surfaces of the plastered walls and the ample daylight, it may be assumed that this was the hub of the life of the house, where everyday activities, such as weaving, must have taken place. Its proximity to the entrance—through the main staircase—and its central position in the circulatory pattern of the house are notable.

One has to cross this room diagonally in order to move to the other rooms. A door at the northwest corner leads to Room 5, which along with Rooms 4 and 4a forms a distinct compartment (Figs. 54, 55). These are the most luxurious rooms, decorated with the famous wall paintings of the Fishermen, the Priestess, the Miniature Frieze, and others. Room 5 is paved with slabs stuccoed with red plaster and has an exquisite construction based on a timber framework that was modelled on a grid of 5 by 5 units (its dimensions are approximately 4 by 4 m). The two exterior walls consist of a series of four

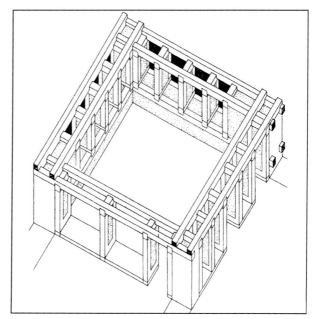

Fig. 54. West House, isometric drawing of Room 5, upper floor.

windows meeting at the corner, while a fifth unit on each end is a rubble wall painted with a Fisherman (Pl. 3A). The other two walls of the room are also divided into 5 parts and consist of cupboards and doors. Numerous planks were detected within the debris of the room, deriving mainly from the doors

Fig. 55. West House, Room 5, upper floor during excavation. The wall painting with the fisherman as found.

Fig. 56. West House model, view from northwest.

of the cupboards. The overall aspect of this room must have had a veranda-like effect and a most delightful interchange of color and light (see Morphology in Chap. 10).

Rooms 4 and 4a form an annex to Room 5 (Pl. 3B). The first room has a floor covered with lime plaster, and the surrounding walls are covered with wall paintings depicting Captain's Cabins. The window on the west wall is decorated with wall paintings showing flower pots and imitations of veined stone. A clay partition wall cuts off the corner of the room, forming a secluded space; this is the amazingly preserved lavatory described in detail below. From Room 5 a door leading east opens to a small lobby, Room 7. Small though this may be, it includes a cupboard, a corridor leading to Room 6a, and a steep auxiliary staircase connecting Rooms 5 and 6 on the upper floor with the storage area below. It was well lit by a large window on the north wall (Fig. 56). Room 6 was a storage or service room. Here, too, numerous vases were found, some deriving from a shelf along the east wall. A built bench with two embedded pithoi occupied the southwest corner of the room.

The main staircase leads up to Room 6 on the third level and continues one more flight to the roof (Fig. 57). This part of the staircase was all made of wood, as one can see from the traces left on the middle wall. The finds that had fallen from the roof show clearly that this was a busy part of the house.[4] The builders would not have gone to the trouble of extending the main staircase all the way up to the roof if it was not an important part of the house.

Comparing the room arrangement of the two levels, one is struck by the flexibility of design—the rooms on the upper floor are much more spacious and better lit than those of the ground floor, and the circulation flow is different. The presence of two staircases plays a very important role in controlling access and also in increasing the possible interconnections.

On the upper floor of the house, Room 4b, a sanitary installation (lavatory) is almost perfectly preserved[5] (Figs. 58–60). The room is 1.30 by 1.95 m, and the west wall has a niche that measures 1.05 m broad, 1.70 m high, and 0.13 m deep. Two stone benches, 0.43 m high, are built within the niche, leaving a gap of 0.08–0.10 m between them. At the far end of the gap, a hole in the floor corresponds to a vertical set of clay pipes embedded in the thickness of the wall. These pipes are cylindrical and specially shaped at their two ends so as to fit one another, while the joints were carefully sealed with hard lime plaster. These details are known thanks to two extra pipes found lying on the floor by the corner of the basement Room 4 (Fig. 61). The vertical conduit of clay pipes ends 0.15 m above the level of the narrow alley outside the building. From an

Fig. 57. West House model, looking east into the main staircase.

Fig. 58. West House, Room 4 with the lavatory at the far corner.

Fig. 59. West House, detail of the lavatory on the upper floor of Room 4a.

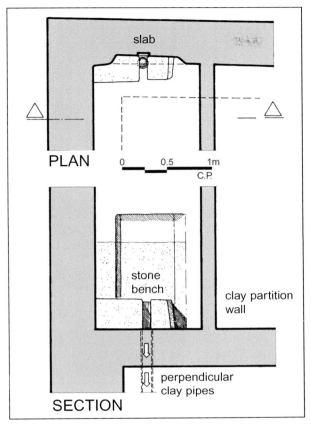

Fig. 60. West House, plan and section of the lavatory.

Fig. 61. West House, terracotta pipe stowed in Room 4, ground floor.

opening in the wall at this point, water-waste could flow into a pit occupying the whole width of the alley. It was found blocked by a large stone in an inclined position. The pit is 1 by 1.50 m wide and 0.80 m deep. The public sewage system crosses through this pit (Figs. 44, 45).

Just below the clay pipes, within the thickness of the wall, a slab is placed at an inclination of 45 degrees. Directly underneath is another slab, perpendicularly placed. This is a very wise arrangement, because it channels liquid waste toward the pit, and it also helps accelerate its flow, thus keeping the system clean.

The pit is unfortunately much disturbed today because of the concrete buttress added at this point. The excavation daybook, however, gives valuable information regarding the finds in this area, and the drawings included in the daybooks, albeit very sketchy, allow for a tentative reconstruction. A number of slabs found within the pit are of special interest. They were fixed in place in such inclinations and combinations that it is quite reasonable to assume that the whole device was meant to function as a siphon, in which case this would be the earliest siphon known in the world! This would prevent smells and gases from coming up to the lavishly decorated upper floor of the West House; a nuisance that added unwillingness among scholars to accept it as a lavatory.[6] Disinfection could also have been practiced—jars containing lime found outside the door of the lavatory could have been for this purpose. The function of this structure as a lavatory was proved beyond doubt by the study of the material contained in the clay pipes and the pit.[7]

Xeste 3: An Atypical Theran House

Marinatos was impressed by the elegant ashlar facades he was bringing to light from the very beginning of his expedition, and he decided to call these houses Xestes, from the Homeric word *xeste* meaning dressed stone. Thus, he labelled the first building with an ashlar facade Xeste 1, and that was the north facade of Sector Delta. He later realized that this ashlar facade was restricted around the entrance, as in many other houses, and downgraded the name of the building to a mere letter of the alphabet. The Xeste denomination was thereafter used for a limited number of buildings that had other characteristics as well. Xeste 2, for example, has only a small part of its northern facade made of ashlar, but it is a distinctively large and imposing building.

Marinatos, in fact, had foreseen the special significance of certain buildings within the settlement. The largest and most elaborate to date is Xeste 4. Its excavation is still in progress and will therefore be described only briefly. The next largest building is Xeste 3 (closely followed by Xeste 2?) and has the advantage of being almost fully excavated. It will serve, therefore, as an example to show the differences and similarities with the "typical Theran house" described above in the example of the West House. It should be mentioned, however, that it is not yet clear which buildings may be assigned to this category: Xestes 3 and 4 are for the time being the best examples; Xeste 2 is practically unexcavated; Xeste 5, despite its name, is most probably an ordinary building, that is, a typical house; and finally, the House of the Ladies is a possible candidate.

Xeste 3[8] lies at the southwest corner of the excavation, on flat land (approximately 19.50 m above sea level) not far from the prehistoric coastline (Fig. 62). Three of its facades are fully exposed, two of which (north and east) are made of ashlar (Figs. 63–65). The south wall is made of roughly hammered blocks laid in rows and covered with a very hard lime plaster that was painted pink/orange (a color resembling the natural red-brown color of the ignimbrite blocks used for the other facades). The house seems to have been surrounded by large open spaces on all three sides, especially on the south, thus adding to its conspicuous position within the settlement. To the west, the house abuts the scarp of the dig. It seems that this side joins another building.

Xeste 3 has a compact interior arrangement, very much like the West House, with no open spaces within its fabric, despite its very large size. It covers an area of approximately 283 square meters (Rooms 1 to 14; the small Room 15 may not actually belong to Xeste 3) and had three floors: the first floor entirely covered the ground floor (except for Room 1 that was probably a veranda), whereas the highest floor covered only the west part of the building. The total surface area of all three floors was approximately 620 square meters and consisted of more than 35 rooms. Because thick stone walls occupy a large portion of this surface, in order to calculate the actual area used for living activities, one should subtract 25 to 30% depending on the thickness of the wall, which differs from ground floor to upper floors. Thus, one would arrive at an estimate of 535 square meters of true useful space. This was a very large building, indeed, comparable only to the Knossian mansions and large villas. Moreover, it is immediately distinguished for its high quality of construction, the elaborate room arrangement at all three levels (Fig. 66), and the superb wall paintings covering almost every single wall of the main rooms.

The building is entered from the east, with a typical entrance system (door, window, and main staircase) occupying the southeast corner (Figs. 67–68).[9] A small forecourt with a built bench is just outside the entrance. A bench is a scarce feature at Akrotiri because Theran houses, as a rule, have no courtyards or intermediate zones between private and public domains. The main staircase inside the entrance is of the typical Π form. The entrance lobby (i.e., the first landing of the staircase) is larger and certainly much more elaborate than usual. It is paved with large slabs and has two built benches, a simple one to the right and an L-shaped one to the left (Fig. 69). The latter is treated with a panel decoration of the kind seen in the palace of Knossos and at Pyrgos. All the walls are painted with scenes from nature, including male figures and animals, extending along the walls of the staircase as well. Even the stone steps, made of ignimbrite, were stuccoed and painted red. The overall effect of this colorful access must have been very impressive. Moreover, the thematic connotations of the depictions on the walls must have had a powerful impact on the visitors and a specific meaning most probably related to the function of the building.[10]

The desire to create an impressive entrance is further attested by a most unexpected and extreme structure: it seems that the builders spared no effort in order to obtain a large entrance lobby and to

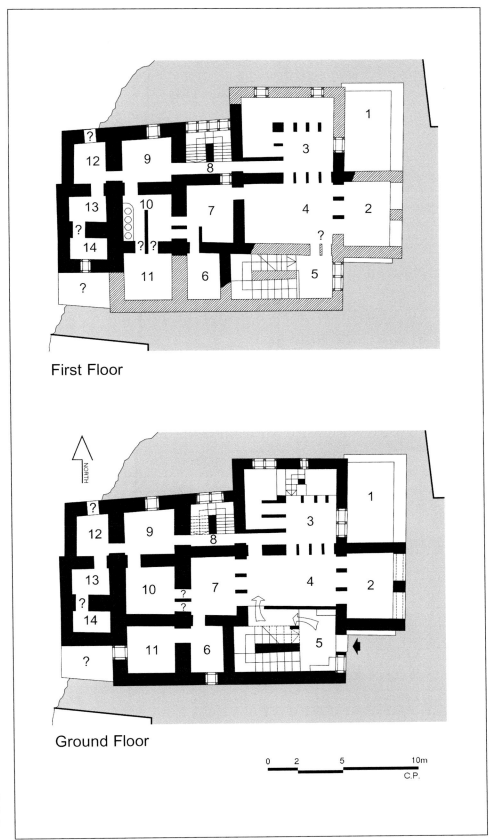

First Floor

Ground Floor

Fig. 62. Xeste 3, plans (scale 1:250). Black walls are existing and hatched walls are indicated.

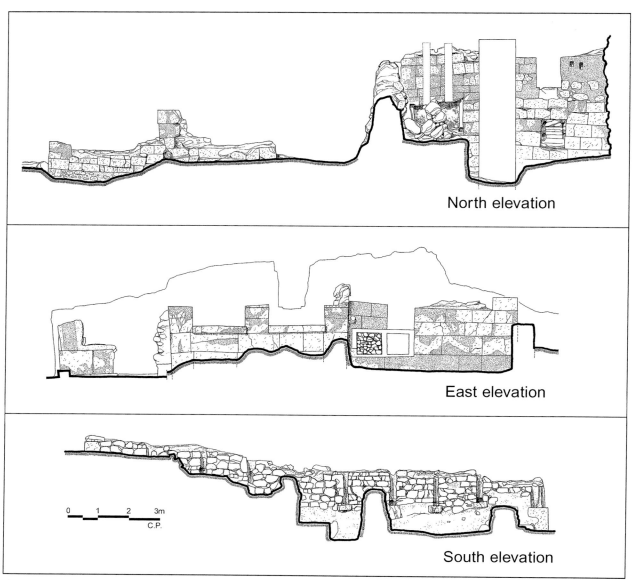

Fig. 63. Xeste 3: north, east, and south facades.

Fig. 64. Xeste 3, east facade.

ensure a specific round-about access to the interior of the building. So, instead of letting the visitors move inside the building by turning to the right, they made them move straight ahead, through a double door and under the second flight of the main staircase, and then enter Room 4. In order to achieve this, they actually eliminated the north wall of the staircase! In its place is a row of sturdy wooden posts placed closely one next to the other (Fig. 70). These posts are embedded in the floor approximately 0.70 m to the north of where the proper wall of the staircase would have been. Thus, the lobby is enlarged, and the area under the second flight of steps is used as access to the ground floor rooms.

Fig. 65. Xeste 3, south facade.

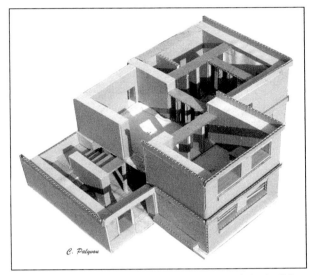

Fig. 66. Xeste 3, model of the eastern part of the building (Rooms 1–5).

Fig. 67. Xeste 3, the ashlar wall and the bench outside the entrance.

On the upper floor, the stone wall of the staircase is in its proper place, which means that it actually rests on the wooden frame below. This arrangement is quite unique, and it shows beyond any doubt the astonishingly high standards of the building technology, especially in relation to timber construction, as well as the design abilities in conceiving such an intricate system.

The first room to enter at ground floor level is Room 4. This spacious room does not abut any exterior walls, and therefore has no windows. It is more like a circulatory nexus surrounded by pier-and-door partitions that provides access to various parts of the house.

To the east is only Room 2, containing a built low basin with an outlet toward the street and a clay tub fixed by its side. Two large windows just under the ceiling offer ample light (Fig. 64). Some light would have penetrated Room 4 through small windows above the pier-and-door partition that separates the

two rooms. This room was once entered from outside: clear evidence for a door and a window that were later blocked is in the north wall.

From Room 4, a pier-and-door partition leads north to a set of rooms (3, 3a, 3b), while another door farther to the left leads to a small corridor that gives access both to the compartment of Room 3 and to the auxiliary staircase 8 and the other rooms to the west. Finally, to the west, yet another pier-and-door partition connects Room 4 to Room 7 and thereafter to the west part of the house (Figs. 71, 72). There are 12 doors altogether around Room 4! This is an amazing arrangement that can provide an extraordinary flexibility of circulation and inter-communication.

Room 3 is a compartment of small spaces, and it is certainly the most intriguing and perhaps the most important part of the house. It is divided by pier-and-door partitions and thin clay walls into small areas: the compound has a central room (3) with a beautiful pavement, a lustral basin (3a) to the north (Fig. 73), and to the west a set of small spaces (3b) and a corridor leading to the auxiliary staircase (8). The so-called lustral basin (or *adyton*) is an idiomatic architectural type well known from Crete. It occupies an area 3.30 by 1.80 m, sunk into the ground, about 0.80 m deep, and approached from Room 3 by 6 steps turning around a pier. The floor is paved with huge slabs, and the walls are covered with dadoes of the same stone. All walls were covered with exquisite wall paintings: the Crocus Gatherers and the Shrine in the area of the lustral basin, and the male figures in the area of the west compartments. The refined architectural aspect of this area and the intricate circulation control are surely dictated by a very specific set of activities in this room—rituals of passage are commonly accepted.[11]

Fig. 68. Xeste 3, entrance
to the building.

Fig. 69. Xeste 3, the stone
benches inside the entrance
lobby.

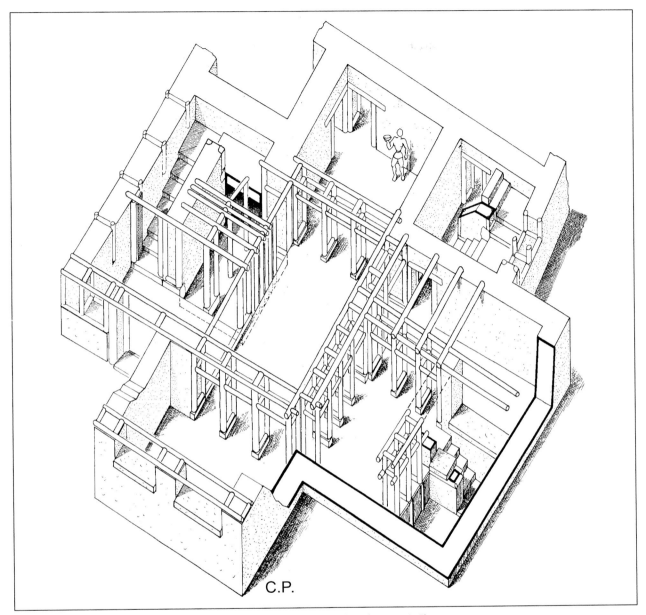

Fig. 70. Xeste 3, isometric drawing of the eastern part of the building (Rooms 1–5).

The other rooms to the west are simple in form and construction and were probably a service area. They are reached either through Room 7 or Room 8. The former is situated in the heart of the building; for this reason, a small opening was left above one of the doors of the pier-and-door partition toward Room 4. The zone above the lintel of the pier-and-door partitions is otherwise built and covered with wall paintings in the form of a frieze.

Returning to the entrance lobby, we may now move to the upper floor. A double door on the first step of the staircase controls the access. The staircase is well designed for easy movement, with broad and low steps. The arrangement on the upper floor is similar to that below: a dense timber framework occupies the eastern part of the building, following the same arrangement of pier-and-door partitions on the ground floor, except for that joining Rooms 4 and 7. Room 4 is again a circulatory nexus. Room 2 had similar twin windows looking east, while the compartment of Room 3 was somewhat simpler: three pier-and-door partitions surrounded the central room giving access to the narrow spaces to the north and west (3a and 3b). All the walls were

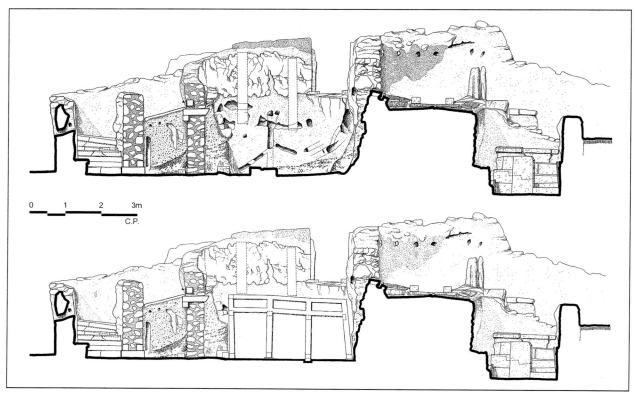

Fig. 71. Xeste 3, the pier-and-door partition between Rooms 4 and 7, before and after restoration. On the upper floor a rubble wall corresponds to two ground floor doors.

Fig. 72. Xeste 3, the pier-and-door partition of room 4.

Fig. 73. Xeste 3, the lustral basin (or adyton).

extensive system of pier-and-door partitions. The staircase in Room 8 is the only access to the third floor, which covered the area of Rooms 7 to 11 and perhaps Rooms 12 to 14 as well. Pier-and-door partitions must have joined several rooms, opening to a broad terrace with a beautiful view to the sea. One may add a light wooden pergola, such as the one in the Archanes Model, and imagine a most pleasant place for relaxation.

The description of Xeste 3, brief though it may be, gives a vivid picture of the grandeur of this building and its main differences from the typical house. From the structural point of view, it differs in the large size and the lavish use of high quality building techniques (i.e., dressed stones and timber frames). From the functional point of view, the difference is even more patent in the importance of the part of the ground floor related to the entrance. The remarkable number of pier-and-door partitions, uniting an area of about 80 square meters, offers the possibility to accommodate a large number of people when all doors are open, while the wall paintings, with all their symbolical connotations, are a dominant feature. This is surely a building that functioned beyond the everyday needs of a family group. Special functions of communal interest were most probably housed in this building, some of which were clearly related to rituals.[12]

beautifully painted with scenes following the Crocus Gathering theme of the ground floor. The auxiliary staircase in Room 8 was reached via a corridor, as in the ground floor level, directly relating the two areas.

A quick glance at the plans of the building shows a distinct difference between the east and the west part. The former is far more complex and elaborate, as described above, while the latter shows a simple juxtaposition of rooms and a plain construction. In Rooms 7 and 10 of the upper floor, clay partition walls divided the rooms into smaller compartments: in Room 10 the partition secludes a narrow area with a built bench incorporating 4 pithoi (Fig. 74). These partitions act more as screens, though they also create rudimentary corridors that channel circulation. Room 7 has a small window borrowing light from the adjoining Room 8 (Fig. 75).

The third floor has not survived, but there is evidence of its form. Dressed stone bases found in the upper level of the destruction layer speak of an

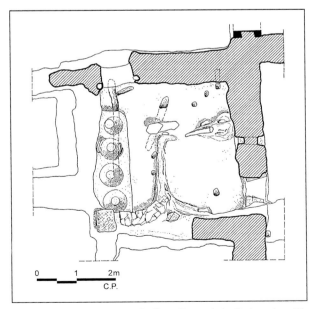

0   1   2m
C.P.

Fig. 74. Xeste 3, Room 10, first floor. A built bench with embedded pithoi.

Fig. 75. Xeste 3, Room 7, first floor, looking toward the door to Room 4 and the small window to Room 8.

Chapter 6 Notes

1. The publications of the West House and Xeste 3 are still pending.

2. For the wall paintings of the West House, see Morgan 1988; Televantou 1990; 1994; see also Michailidou 2001: part I, 41–176.

3. Doumas 1985: 168–169.

4. Michailidou 2001: 133–174.

5. Marinatos 1968–1976, VI: 24–30.

6. See earlier interpretations of this structure as a "kitchen" or a reception for libations (Marinatos 1968–1976, VI: 27–28).

7. Sarpaki 1992.

8. Marinatos 1968–1976, V: 26–28; VI: 15–17 (as Xeste E); VII: 22–28, 32–38; Doumas 1993: 166–170.

9. The southwest corner of the building is not entirely excavated as yet. An entrance may be there, but it is not clear if it relates to Xeste 3. See Doumas 1993: 166–169.

10. N. Marinatos 1984; Doumas 1987.

11. N. Marinatos 1984; Doumas 1987.

12. Doumas 1987: 151–159, refers to Xeste 3 as a public building. See also N. Marinatos 1984.

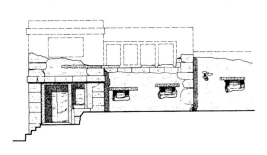

7

A Guided Tour through the Town

Having understood the main characteristics of the Theran houses, typical and atypical, we may now indulge in a more relaxed tour around the site following the imaginary route of a visitor—this is, after all, the identity of the modern scholar. This way we will gradually build an overall picture of the site of Akrotiri. We should be reminded, once more, that the excavation has progressed in varying degrees, differing even from one part of the same building to another. We shall, therefore, discuss only those features that are best understood.[1] These suffice to demonstrate the works of an affluent community living in security and prosperity. We should also be reminded that we see only a part of the town, not far from the harbor, that might well be indicative of the life standards of an upper class. If this is so, then a remarkable number of families enjoyed the privileges of prosperity.

Let us commence our tour through the silent ruins of what was once a bustling town (Fig. 27). We shall start from the south, leaving our boats behind us at the west harbor, and walk up Telchines Street, passing through the dense blocks of Sectors Beta and Gamma. We will stop briefly at Triangle Square to look at the buildings bordering the West House— Sector Delta and the House of the Anchor—and then proceed north, passing by the House of the Ladies. Sector Alpha will be our last stop before we turn back south. We will then follow a different route, to the east. Xeste 5, Xeste 2, Delta-East, and a public square are on our way to the southeast, with Xeste 4 and the South House as our last stop. Here we will take a breath, looking down the Koureton Street trying to imagine what lay beyond this impressive street, perhaps an eastern harbor? If so, we can meet our boats here and depart for the journey back to the future.

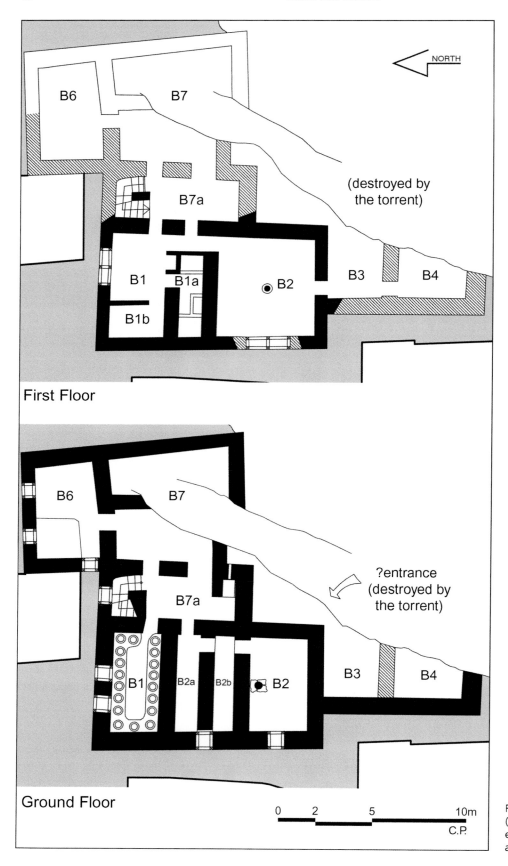

Fig. 76. Beta-South, plans (scale 1:200). Black walls are existing and hatched walls are indicated.

Beta-South

The first building we see today to our left, as we enter the site from the south—from the direction of the sea—is Xeste 3. Opposite this, to the east, stands Xeste 4, an impressive three-story mansion, facing Koureton Street and bordered by various other buildings (e.g., the South House). Between the two Xestes is a set of poorly preserved houses, because this area was damaged by a torrent before excavations began. A clearly defined street leads northward. This is Telchines Street, obviously coming from the sea. The first part of Telchines Street is narrow and crooked, and is bordered by Sector Beta to the east and Sector Gamma to the west (Fig. 30).

Sector Beta[2] is a block consisting of at least two different houses. The eastern part of both houses is badly damaged or completely destroyed by the torrential waters. The house to the south is better preserved and more clear in its interior arrangement (Figs. 76–77). Though there is no entrance visible today, it is safe to assume that it lay in the destroyed southeast part of the house. Thanks to the standardized model of the entrance system at Akrotiri, we can almost detect its exact position: a room with a central column on the upper floor (Beta 2), must have been in direct proximity to the entrance and the main staircase. Beta 2 has two doors: one leads north to rooms with wall paintings while the other

leads south to an unknown space. The latter most probably points to the direction of the entrance (Rooms Beta 4 and Beta 3 may be related to the entrance).

Though the entrance is not there to invite us in, we can still make an intelligible tour around the house. Starting from the upper floor, the room with a central column will guide our way: it has a typical squarish form (4.9 by 5.2–5.4 m) and was paved with beautiful large slabs cut in almost rectangular shapes (Figs. 78, 79). The stone base of the column was still in situ during excavation.[3] There were no frescoes here. No loom weights were present either, which means that the room was not used for weaving as other rooms of this type,[4] at least not at the time it was abandoned. As Michailidou points out, the presence of many vases packed around the column may indicate that they were moved there for safety. Leaving the assumed main staircase behind us, we cross the room toward the north. A door leads, via a small paved corridor, to the elaborate compartment of Rooms Beta 1, 1a, and 1b.

This group of rooms is apparently the formal zone (see Chap. 8). Room Beta 1 is the focal point here. It is slightly trapezoidal in plan (3.4–3.65 by 2.45–2.8 m), and had a floor paved with large slabs, now removed. A large window looks north to the

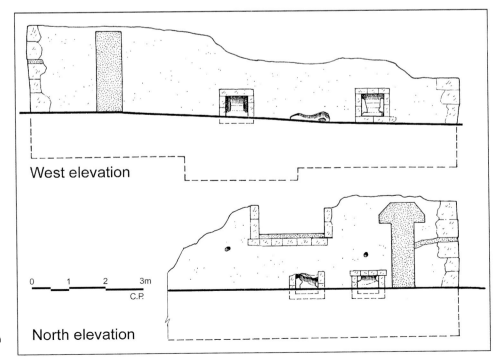

West elevation

0   1   2   3m

C.P.

North elevation

Fig. 77. Beta-South, north and west elevations.

Fig. 78. Beta-South, looking east from Sector Gamma. The west facade of the building facing Telchines Street and the upper floor of room Beta 2 are visible.

Fig. 80. Beta-South, from the Square of the Mill House. The large window to the left belongs to room Beta 1, first floor (the room with the Antilopes and Boxing Children).

Fig. 79. Beta-South, room Beta 2 with the central column and the pavement before the removal of the slabs.

Fig. 81. Beta-South, room Beta 1a from above.

Square of the Mill House (Fig. 80). This room was pierced all around with openings, doors, and cupboards, very much like Room 5 of the West House. Similarly, all the available wall surfaces were decorated with wall paintings depicting antilopes and a pair of young boys boxing (Pl. 4A).

As with the West House, this main room has annexes. To the west, a door leads through a thin clay partition wall to Beta 1b, a small compartment (1.7 by 2.9 m) with a floor of beaten soil and no mural paintings.[5] To the south a door leads to the small compartment Beta 1a, which has four small cases or repositories made of mudbricks set on edge (Fig. 81). This tiny space is covered all over—walls and floor—with white lime plaster. Next to the door is a cupboard made of mudbrick walls resting on T-shaped stone bases with a red painted interior. To the east is another door leading to a lobby (Beta 7a) and an auxiliary staircase.

The corridor joining Rooms Beta 1 and Beta 2 is an important architectural feature: it is paved, just

as the two areas it connects are, and it has two more doors leading east to the lobby Beta 7a. Rooms Beta 1 and Beta 2 communicate with each other, but also independently with the ground floor through the lobby and the auxiliary staircase.

The overall arrangement in distinct zones and the sophisticated circulatory system are all very similar to the West House and conform to the "house model" described above.

We shall now use the auxiliary staircase to move down to the ground floor level. It is built on an artificial fill and has an almost rounded form (Fig. 82). Nine steps lead down to a spacious landing, partly paved with large marble slabs (an uncommon material at Akrotiri). The staircase was lit by a small window looking north onto a blind alley. It is quite probable that the very existence of this dead-end was dictated by the need to provide adequate light to the staircase. An interesting structure is at the south end of the broad landing or lobby Beta 7a: it is a small recess bordered with

Fig. 82. Beta-South, the auxiliary staircase.

Fig. 83. Beta-South, ground floor doors leading to rooms Beta 1 and 2.

Fig. 84. Beta-South, Room Beta 1, ground floor. Pithoi embedded in a built bench.

large slabs standing upright, with an outlet leading waste outside the house. At least three doors open onto this area: one to the east leads to space Beta 7, while those to the west give access to the ground floor rooms Beta 1 and Beta 2 (Fig. 83).

Beta 1 is an oblong storeroom (2.35 by 5.20 m) with rows of large pithoi on all sides, embedded in a built bench, 0.70–0.80 m wide and 1 m high (Fig. 84). Rounded slabs cover the wide mouths of these jars, while numerous vases and rhyta lie around giving a vivid picture of the sort of use this storeroom must have had. It is lit by two small windows, and it had a very low ceiling (approximately 1.90 m). It is interesting to observe that the bench with the pithoi covers the maximum possible area, turning at a right angle and almost blocking the door. This is marginally evaded by the strongly rounded end of the bench, leaving a very narrow space through which to move (the extra pithos was presumably desperately needed).[6]

The next door from Beta 7a leads to a narrow unexcavated space (B2a) through which one enters another narrow space (B2b), similar to the previous.

These two oblong spaces once formed a single room whose window is still visible from the outside, though now blocked by the later wall. This wall was most probably added during the rebuilding that followed the *seismic destruction*. The purpose of this remodelling is clear (Fig. 85): the wall was added for the sake of the upper story, so as to create a large square room with a central support. This was made possible by demolishing the upper part of a wall and erecting a new one at the appropriate distance. Interestingly, the new wall covering two stories is reinforced with vertical posts (a sign of its late date, perhaps, for which see Chap. 9). To the south of these narrow spaces is a door leading to Room Beta 2, found full of cooking pots and vases for everyday use. At a small distance from the north wall of this room, a low stone platform served as the base for a wooden support carrying the load of the central column of the upper floor down to the ground. One small window is on the western wall. Though the entrance is to be expected somewhere in the vicinity of Room B2, the access to the ground floor storage and service area was via the lobby at Beta 7a.

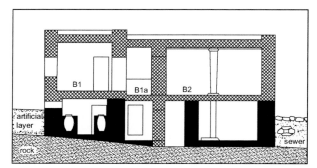

Fig. 85. Beta-South, section through rooms Beta 1 and 2. The hatched walls indicate probable modifications after the *seismic destruction*.

Rooms Beta 3 and 4 to the south are unexcavated, and we have no information about the ground floor arrangement. So let us turn to Rooms Beta 6 and 7 to the east where the picture is slightly better. This area is badly eroded because of the torrent, and as a result the walls have survived to a very low height. Beta 7 actually consists of two rooms, but the north-south wall dividing them is hardly visible. The western part has a door at the north wall leading to Beta 6. This room is better preserved, and its western part forms a separate, very small compartment; the ground floor is unexcavated, and the floor of the story above preserves excellent imprints of the wooden beams supporting it. The ground floor of Room Beta 6 is made of a thin layer of mud plaster laid on the rock. A cavity in the rock is now visible, and a broken stone spout lies in situ within it. Two small windows on the north exterior wall correspond to the two compartments, while a third tiny window looking west onto the dead-end gives extra light to this room. The wall paintings with the Blue Monkeys were found in this area. The plaster pieces were found with slabs obviously belonging to the upper floor.[7] It is not very clear how the two parts of Sector Beta—now divided by the torrent—relate to each other: the presence of rooms with wall paintings on both sides may actually indicate two separate houses.

Beta-North

The area between Sectors Beta and Delta has been rebuilt and rearranged, and Rooms Beta 5, 5a, and 8 were added at some later time to join the two Sectors (Figs. 26, 27). The open space Delta 14 to the east and the Square of the Mill House to the west might well have been united in an earlier phase. This group of rooms was obviously squeezed in this area in such a way as to exploit space to the maximum, without creating any inconvenience to the existing buildings.[8] The three rooms communicate with doors, and a window was probably in the southern wall. The entrance door seems to open from Room Beta 5 to the Square of the Mill House. These very small rooms have no features whatsoever relevant to the "house model" attested in most other buildings; indeed, they make very little sense unless they are interpreted as an auxiliary building for purposes other than those accommodated by the ordinary houses of Akrotiri.

Gamma-North (Building IΓ)

To the west of Sector Beta, across Telchines Street, lies the partly excavated Sector Gamma (Figs. 26, 27). It consists of two different houses separated by a narrow alley, Gamma 8. Gamma-South is the house we can visit today, because only two rooms of the other house, Gamma-North,[9] are visible: Rooms Gamma 9 and 10. The former was destroyed during the earthquakes that preceded the final eruption. The rescue parties that arrived shortly after levelled the debris and put three beds there, two side by side and one on top.[10] There were several vases and other implements by the beds, vividly showing the outdoor activities during the short period before the final eruption.

Gamma-South

This building is a free-standing house covering an area of 183 square meters (Fig. 86). The northern part had two stories (Gamma 4 to 7), resulting in a total surface of 288 square meters. The situation is rather peculiar in this building because the two stories actually correspond to a basement and a ground floor. The entrance door of Gamma-South opens on to the narrow Telchines Street, a feature uncommon at Akrotiri, because entrances usually have a broad public space in front of them (Figs. 87, 88). No window is next to the door—yet another uncommon feature—though it may be explained by the peculiar arrangement of the main staircase that lies beyond. The missing window was probably on the north wall of Gamma 5/6 that collapsed (perhaps precisely because of the window[11]). Ashlar blocks within the debris to the north (area Gamma 9) may derive from the ashlar frame of this window. The whole entrance system is rather exceptional, though this may well be the result of modifications and rebuilding activities in this area. The staircase typically found inside the entrance does exist, but it is restricted to only one flight (Gamma 6). The other flight is actually a paved corridor (Gamma 5) leading from the entrance to a middle landing where one or two steps lead up to Room Gamma 7. This large room belongs to the upper floor, which means that the entrance we see today is more or less at the level of the upper floor! The overall arrangement explains why a window was needed in the north wall and not by the door, where it would be of no use to the stairs of Gamma 6.

The flight of steps of Gamma 6 leads up to the roof. This flight was made of wood, as one can see from the traces on the middle wall. Underneath is another flight of steps (only partly visible today), leading down to the basement rooms. To reach this flight, however, one has to cross through Room Gamma 7. It is possible that an opening was present, and a ladder led to the basement from the entrance as well, as Marinatos suggested. A peculiar gap is in the floor as one enters the building to the left—just behind the entrance door. A direct access between the entrance and the service area is actually a logical necessity and very common at Akrotiri. Of the basement rooms, only Gamma 4a is partly visible today (with many large vases), while the other rooms are not excavated. Rooms Gamma 4 and 4b show only their two tiny windows, obviously placed high up just below the ceiling. Their sills define the street level outside. Because we can

say no more of the ground floor rooms (or basement), let us go to the upper story again.

Room Gamma 7 is partially revealed. Its dimensions (5.10? by 4.90 m) show that it is a typical square room with a column in the center.[12] The north wall of the room is an exterior wall, but with no windows (it faces a very narrow alley). Probably the west wall (badly damaged) is also an exterior wall with a large window of the type accompanying such rooms. The other two walls of the room have one door each, both by the southeast corner of the room. One door leads east to Gamma 6, to what must have been a small landing giving access to a flight of steps leading up to the roof. From the same landing, one may access Room Gamma 4.

The other door of Room Gamma 7 leads south to Gamma 4a (a similar door is below). The relationship between Gamma 4, 4a, and 4b is not so clear, because the walls between them are destroyed (Fig. 89). From Room Gamma 4b, a door leads south to a small staircase of five steps going down to the semi-basement Rooms Gamma 1, 2, and 2a. The building was obviously adjusted to the sloppy ground, and a difference of 1.85 m exists between the entrance threshold and the floor of the southernmost Room Gamma 1.

Sector Gamma, and the broader area in general, has suffered greatly from earthquakes. The earlier disaster—50 years prior to the volcanic destruction—produced large quantities of debris that were laid down on the street outside the building. The new street surface was approximately 1.50 m higher, resulting in at least one window being blocked (Gamma 4). It is due to this rearrangement of levels that the new entrance built on top of the accumulated debris resulted at more or less the same level as the upper floor.

Fifty years later, another earthquake hit the house, soon to be followed by the fatal eruption of the volcano. A rescue party came back after the earthquake and started cleaning the narrow street of debris. This is the first priority in such circumstances, in order to re-establish circulation within the settlement. The stones were selected from the debris to be reused, and they were provisionally piled at the spot, along the eastern exterior wall of Sector Gamma, hence the deceptive picture of a "double" wall there. This piling was probably not very high (as high as they could easily reach without scaffoldings). After the residents left, the upper part of the wall that had survived until then fell

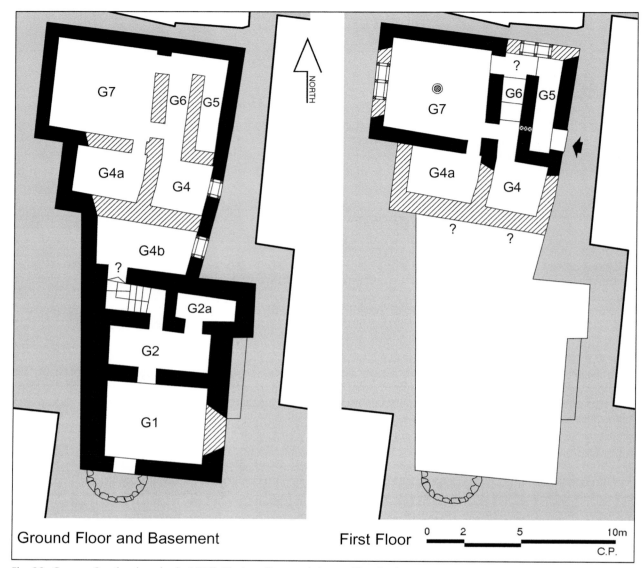

Fig. 86. Gamma-South, plans (scale 1:200). Black walls are existing and hatched walls are indicated.

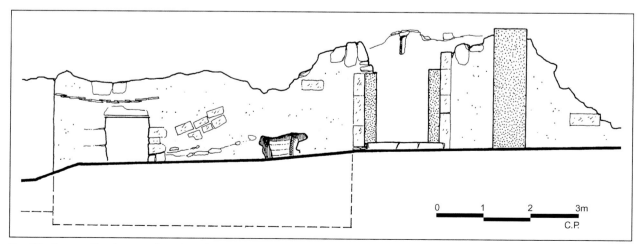

Fig. 87. Gamma-South, east elevation along Telchines Street.

Fig. 88. Gamma-South, the entrance door.

Fig. 89. Gamma-South, Rooms 4 and 4a looking north.

outward, covering the piled stones and Telchines Street.[13] The thick west wall, on the other hand, may have resulted from an intentional reinforcement some time after its construction (maybe after the earlier earthquake destruction). Next, the residents blocked the entrance door (see Chap. 11) and the doors in Gamma 4, cutting off the access to the stairs down to Gamma 2.[14] In doing so, they actually blocked off the entire northern part of the house,

which must have been in a bad state. It seems that only the southern part of the building could be used at that point (perhaps it suffered less damage because there was no upper story here). They had to open a door for that: this is the peculiar, atypical entrance seen in the south wall of Gamma 1. The numerous stone and metal implements found in this room speak vividly of the kind of activities that were taking place up to the last moment of departure. It is this picture of metallurgical activities that inspired Marinatos to name the street outside Telchines after a mythical race of metal workers.

Delta-South

The extensive building compound known as Sector Delta, occupying the central area of the excavation, consists of four distinct albeit adjoining houses. The delineation of each building is quite clear thanks to the double walls separating different buildings, but also because of the "house model" identified in all cases. The four distinct entrances of Sector Delta suffice to point to the four different compartments, and it is through these doors that we shall find our way inside.

Delta-South covers an area of 159 square meters and had two stories except for Room 16, which was single storied—the total surface was 264 square meters (Fig. 90). The entrance to Delta-South, Room Delta 15, faces a small open public space, the so-called Square of the Mill House (Fig. 91).[15] It is a typical entrance system in all respects: it occupies a corner of the building and has a large door-and-window opening, bordered by ashlar stones with a

narrow (0.18–0.20 m) stone cornice projecting above. Crossing the huge monolithic threshold, which is dressed with a pronounced rounded edge, one enters into the typical rectangular room with the main staircase. In the narrow entrance lobby, corresponding to the first landing of the staircase, are two built benches: a taller one, with mill-stones embedded in its top, and a lower one for sitting (Fig. 92). Some vases were found lying on the benches. The entrance door looks very wide today, but this is due to a mistake during the restoration of the east jamb (its correct position is evident by the faint traces of the timber frame on the stone threshold) (Fig. 93).

Of the typical staircase, only the southern flight is now visible, consisting of seven steps leading up to a middle landing (Fig. 94). One or two more steps give access to the second story. The landing is lit by a window looking south. The flight of steps has

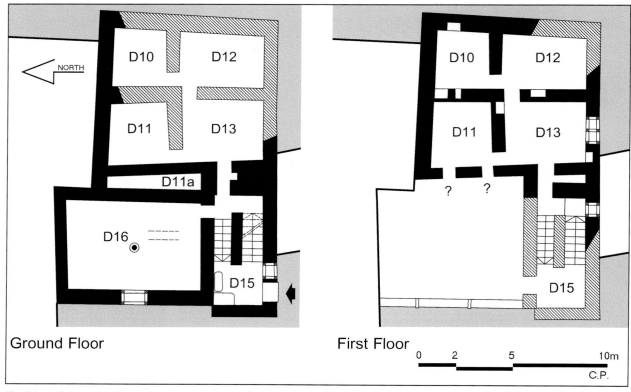

Fig. 90. Delta-South, plans (scale 1:200). Black walls are existing and hatched walls are indicated.

Fig. 91. Delta-South, the entrance.

Fig. 92. Delta-South, entrance lobby. Marinatos displaying the function of the mill installation.

actually be the only access to Room Delta 16 but also to the ground floor (or semi-basement) Rooms Delta 13, 11, 12, and 10. A door is partly visible from within Room Delta 13 leading to the landing at the bottom of the main staircase.

From the main staircase we move down to the large Room Delta 16. This room is the largest covered space known at Akrotiri: it measures 4.90 by 7.00–7.10 m and has a stone base at its center for a wooden column supporting the ceiling. A large window is at the western wall, and the beam holes

subsided in a manner indicating that it rested on wooden beams with sottoscala underneath. The other flight to the north is covered with debris, and the area cannot be examined. It is quite safe to assume, however, that a second flight of steps led down to the semi-basement rooms. This would

Fig. 93. Delta-South, the entrance threshold. The arrow shows the traces of the timber jamb.

Fig. 94. Delta-South, the main staircase.

Fig. 95. Delta-South, west facade along Telchines Street.

above its lintel clearly show the construction of the roof. This is a single story room, as can be attested by the two clay spouts jutting out from the western wall at a level slightly above the lintel of the window (Fig. 95). The span of the room was too large to carry an upper story.

Back to the landing of the staircase, we may now move on to the other rooms of the ground floor, Delta 10 to 13. These rooms are actually semi-basements, a familiar picture throughout the site, due to the modifications that took place after the *seismic*

destruction (Fig. 96). The earlier cobbled pavement of the street was found outside Delta 16[16] at the same level as the floor of the room inside the building (i.e., 1.50 m below the street level we see today). Moreover, the entrance Delta 15 is clearly a new addition, built on top of the accumulated debris. The ashlar corner stones of what was once an exterior wall (Delta 16) are clearly visible (Fig. 95). The addition is also evident by the awkward way the west wall of Delta 15 abuts Room Delta 16, forming an indentation, yet with no bonding whatsoever. It

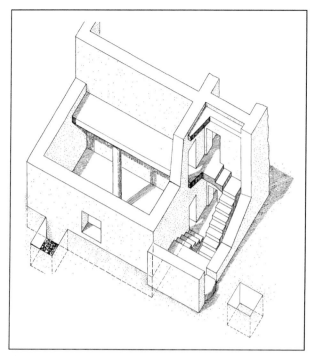

Fig. 96. Delta-South, isometric drawing of Rooms 15 and 16.

Fig. 97. Delta-South, the two parallel walls between Rooms 15–16 and Rooms 10–13.

Fig. 98. Delta-South, Delta 16. The earlier dividing walls cut in the rock are partly visible under the later floor.

seems that the morphological aspect prevailed over the structural in this case.

At the semi-basement level, information is very restricted because the rooms are practically unexcavated. Room Delta 13 is the first room reached from the entrance and the main staircase. This fairly large room (approximately 3.40 by 4.40 m) has at least one small window looking south to an open public area (Delta 14). We can hardly say anything more about the other rooms; they seem to have the same outlines as those on the upper floor, and they communicate with doors perhaps corresponding to those seen on the upper floor. Room Delta 12 is badly damaged by the torrent, while Delta 10 and 11 abut the house to the north, hence the thick double walls. A large fragment of Horns of Consecration as well as large pithoi were found within the debris of Room Delta 11.[17]

Between Delta 16 and 11 is a peculiar narrow space, Delta 11a (0.65–0.80 m wide), which seems to be accessible from Delta 11 (Fig. 97). This strange narrow gap cuts the building in two. It is probably the result of the rebuilding that followed the earlier *seismic destruction*.[18] Earlier walls divided Delta 16 into four smaller spaces (their foundations are still visible under the floor; see Fig. 98). These walls were demolished, and a new eastern wall was added (it has no bonding with the north wall). The new wall

was placed so as to achieve the maximum width that could be spanned, i.e. 4.90 m, to create a large room with a central column. A gap was thus created between the new and the old wall. The narrow area may have been used for storage, but it is also quite probable that it housed an auxiliary staircase, approached by the landing of the main staircase (a common arrangement at Akrotiri). Further excavation will certainly illuminate the situation.

Moving now to the upper floor from the main staircase, we reach a landing crossing the two walls and the above mentioned narrow space and leading east to Delta 13. This room has a large window looking south to the open space Delta 14. Next to the window is a small niche veneered with slabs. The northern wall has a door on one end and a niche plastered white on the other. The latter actually has the dimensions and structural details of a door, and only its back is closed off by upright clay slabs. Such niches, not so common in other buildings, are found in all four rooms, Delta 10 to 13, and together with the smaller ones they form a typical feature of this house. Numerous loom weights found in Delta 13 suggest that this amply lit room was used for weaving.

The door to the north leads to Room Delta 11. This room lies deep within the fabric of Sector Delta, and it most probably had direct access to the roof or terrace above the adjoining Delta 16. Room Delta 11 has no other access to the rooms of the upper floor. Going back to Delta 13, another door leads east to Delta 12 and on to Delta 10. Room Delta 13, in other words, offers access to all other rooms. This is an arrangement common at Akrotiri. The east and south walls of Delta 12 are exterior walls, and though they do not survive to a great height, at least one window was there. A door at the northern wall leads to Delta 10. This room has three niches, one of which is of the type resembling a blocked door, while the other two are small niches

within the thickness of the wall high above the floor level. The walls and the niches were covered with red plaster. Though no traces of a window have survived, probably one was present at the eastern outer wall of the room. The northern limit of this room and Rooms Delta 11 and 16 is a thick double wall separating this house from the adjoining one to the north.

It is not clear if the main staircase continued up to the roof, as is usually the case. One flight of steps starting from the middle landing at the eastern end of the staircase would suffice to climb to the roof of Delta 16. This was more like a veranda accessed from within the house as well. This flight may have been wooden, because no stones corresponding to steps have been reported from the higher levels of the debris of the staircase. It is rather unlikely that the staircase continued up another flight so as to reach the roof above Delta 10 to 13.

Delta-West

This house occupies the central area of Sector Delta, covering an area of 187 square meters (Fig. 99). It had two stories throughout and an estimated total surface of 389 square meters. The entrance of Delta-West lies under the so-called Gate or Pylon (Figs. 100–102). This structure juts out from the western facade of Sector Delta that is otherwise well articulated and has a uniform indentation along Telchines Street. The Gate is a later addition, as it can be clearly seen at the points where it abuts the outer walls of Sector Delta. It consists of a very thick outer wall to the west and two wide openings—not doors—allowing free passage in a north-south direction. Actually, it forms a part of Telchines Street that was roofed over, and its floor is the continuation of the cobble pavement of the street. The purpose of such a structure is not readily understood, and its impressive form gave rise to fanciful speculation— hence the name Gate or Pylon.[19] The technical details in this area, however, show that this was most probably constructed during the rebuilding phase after the *seismic destruction*, with the goal of solving the typical problem of how to deal with the accumulated debris in the streets and open public spaces. The answer was to arrange the material in terraces kept in place with a retaining wall that runs down Telchines Street, opposite the west facade of Delta 16. This wall is 2.20 m from Delta 16 and approximately 0.90 m high near the Gate. The accumulated

debris reached a marginal level coinciding with the level of the entrance to Sector Delta. The Gate was, therefore, built in order to shelter the entrance and protect the house from being flooded by rainwater (it is the only case where the threshold of the entrance door is slightly below street level instead of above it). Because this entrance was in the middle of the building compound, and not at a corner as in almost all other cases, the interventions and height differences that could be achieved here were limited.

In all other respects, the entrance is typical: it has a wide door and a window next to it with ashlar stones bordering the two openings. The door leads to a typical main staircase with two parallel flights and a middle landing. The area occupied by Delta 9g, d, and e is only partially excavated, but enough architectural features are visible to allow for a tentative reconstruction of the entrance system. The entrance door opens to a small lobby corresponding to the landing of the main staircase. The two narrow, corridor-like spaces, Delta 9d and g, are the first and second flight of the staircase. Only the last two stair steps are visible today, at the upper floor of Delta 9g, but they suffice to reconstruct the remaining staircase according to the "Theran house model."

Within the entrance lobby two doors lead to the ground floor rooms, instead of one as with the West House. The door to the south, however, gives access

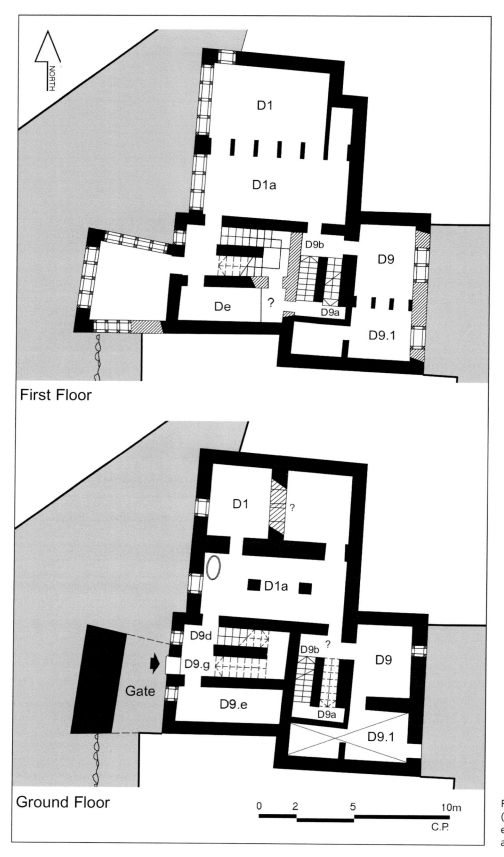

First Floor

Ground Floor

0   2   5   10m
                            C.P.

Fig. 99. Delta-West, plans (scale 1:200). Black walls are existing and hatched walls are indicated.

Fig. 100. Delta-West, the entrance under the Gate.

Fig. 101. Delta-West, along Telchines Street, looking north toward the Gate.

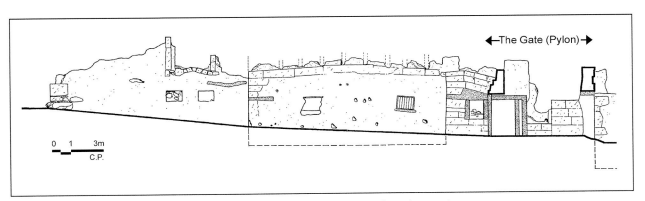

Fig. 102. Delta-West, west facade and section through the Gate. To the left, Delta-North.

only to the small Room Delta 9e that serves like an annex to the entrance (see also Alpha-West, and perhaps Beta-South). The other door, to the north, is the one that leads to the ground floor rooms.

The first room to enter is Delta 1a. It is a large, rectangular room (3.30–3.50 by 7.30 m) with one or two piers in the center (Fig. 103). This room contains a large number of vessels and most notably a large bathtub like those regularly found near the entrance. The room is lit by a relatively small window looking west to Triangle Square, and four doors are symmetrically positioned at the two ends of the long walls. The southwest door is the one we just entered coming from the entrance.

The two doors of the northern wall lead to two rooms not visible today because of the unexcavated mass of the upper floor of Delta 1. It should be noted, however, that the floor has collapsed in such

a way that it implies a void underneath. Indeed, when Marinatos opened a small trench through the upper floor of Delta 1a, he found very little evidence of the dividing wall. It is possible that a kind of pier-and-door partition here collapsed soon after the destruction. This idea is further corroborated by the fact that the eastern room has no direct source of light and air, so the dividing wall might have had some extra openings for this purpose.

Though excavation is far from being complete in this building, it is relatively safe to assume that Delta 1 has no further access to the north or to the east, and that the adjoining rooms belong to different houses. So, moving back to Room Delta 1a, we may now explore the fourth door, at the southeast corner. This leads to an area that has not been cleared of the debris at the ground floor level. One may anticipate, however, an auxiliary staircase occupying the two

Fig. 103. Delta-West, the pier at ground floor level in the center of Room 1.

narrow corridor-like spaces, Delta 9a and b. The former is probably the first flight of steps, and the latter is the second flight leading to the second story. It is quite possible that the middle landings of the two staircases—main and auxiliary—communicated at this point (this remains to be proved by excavation). Such an intricate arrangement of staircases, difficult even to describe, provides a remarkably sophisticated circulatory pattern throughout the building. Had there not been many other examples of such complex patterns, it would admittedly look quite likely. Yet, this direct communication between the main and auxiliary staircases is repeated several times at Akrotiri: the House of the Ladies, Delta-North, Xeste 4. At the landing of the auxiliary staircase there is a door leading to Delta 9 and 9.1. The latter has a basement as well, approached presumably by the auxiliary staircase.

Clay partition walls organize the area, screening off the staircase. Room Delta 9.1 was paved with large slabs and has a door at the eastern wall. This

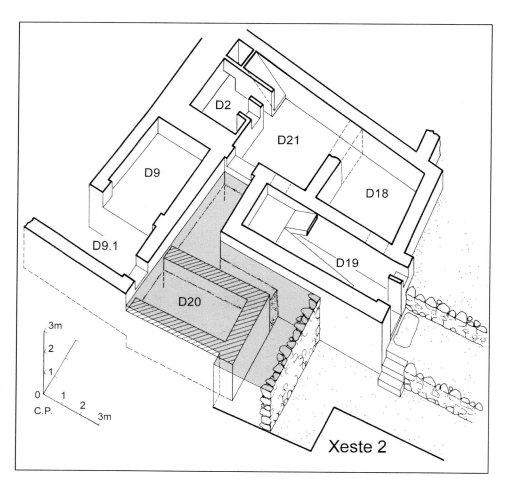

Fig. 104. Delta-West, the terrace outside Room 9.1 was formed when Room 20 was filled with debris after the *seismic destruction* (Rooms 2, 18, 19, and 21 belong to Delta-East).

Bases

Fig. 105. View of the first floor of Delta-West, Rooms 9 and 9.1. The bases of the pier-and-door partition are visible.

door opens on to what may have been a private terrace.

Excavation in this area, to the east of Delta 9.1, was resumed in 1979 and provided some very interesting information. It was expected that a street parallel to Telchines Street, separating Sector Delta from Xeste 2, would be revealed, but instead a tall retaining wall was found blocking the passage and leaving just a small courtyard in front of the northwest corner of Xeste 2, presumably to avoid blocking the windows of this building (Fig. 104). Further investigation showed that about a meter behind this dry retaining wall was a room (Delta 20) that had been filled in during the remodelling that followed the *seismic destruction*. It soon became clear that this was once a ground floor room communicating with Delta 9.1 with a door still visible, though blocked. Most probably an upper room had been demolished, and the ground floor room had been filled in with the debris and covered over with a thick layer of clay. Due to this rearrangement, Room Delta 9.1 became a true basement, and the door on the upper floor became an exterior door. This explains the presence of an exterior door that

has all the typical features of an interior door. The situation to the south of this veranda-like platform is vague because the area lies in the bed of the torrent and has not been fully excavated. We cannot be sure of the degree of privacy of this open space because it is possible that it was accessible from the south. It looks more like a backyard and service area and a continuation of the open space Delta 14, which was found full of litter.[20]

But let us close the door behind us and go back into the house. Going back to the auxiliary staircase and climbing up to the first floor we may enter Rooms Delta 9 and 9.1, united with a pier-and-door partition (Fig. 105), or approach the largest compartment of the upper floor, the largest known from Akrotiri. Two large rooms, Delta 1a and 1, communicate with the longest pier-and-door partition known at Akrotiri (Fig. 106); it has six doors and is 7.30 m long. The easternmost door leads to a small space, cut off from Delta 1 with clay partitions. This double compartment can also be reached directly from the entrance via the main staircase. The floor was of packed soil, and no wall paintings were present. The two rooms were more

Fig. 106. Delta-West. The bases of the pier-and-door partition joining Rooms 1 and 1a on the first floor are visible. A large pithos was found blocking one of the doors.

than amply lit: the western outer wall, looking toward Triangle Square, consists of a long row of windows, four for each room, plus one at the northern corner (Pls. 2A, 2B). The sill of the pier-and-window arrangement is 0.56 m high, and numerous loom weights were found on its threshold. This would have been a most pleasant compartment to live and work in—weaving was obviously a major activity—with a good view toward the public square below. The residents could even chat across the square with the ladies weaving at the West House (Room 3).

Yet another room on the upper floor can be explored: it lies above the Gate and is approached only from the landing of the main staircase. The floor is of packed soil with large sea pebbles bordering the sides. The walls survive to a low height that

probably corresponds to the sill, and windows were placed all around (Pl. 2C). Probably the room had some mural decoration, perhaps above the windows, in the form of a frieze of spirals.[21] This was certainly a beautiful room with a commanding view over Telchines Street and Triangle Square, though its importance need not be overestimated.

On the whole, Delta-West is a relatively large building with many oddities though still adhering to the "Theran house model." Its plan was probably dictated, and restricted, by the fact that it lies in the heart of a block of houses. Of special interest is the fact that the house is practically divided in two parts, with an intervening zone of staircases channeling circulation among various levels in a manner indicative of a sophisticated design procedure.

Delta-North (Xeste 1)

The northern part of Sector Delta is partly damaged by the ravine (Fig. 107). Its size may be estimated at 139 square meters, with a total surface of at least 317 square meters (it had an extensive second story, and Delta 3 had 3 stories). The entrance to this house faces north to a wide public open space. The rooms inside are not all well preserved

or excavated, and circulation within this compound is not so clear. Yet, having defined the limits of the other houses comprising Sector Delta, it will be easier to understand what is left.

The northern facade with the entrance juts out, forming a typical indentation (Fig. 108). It is preserved to a height of 0.77 m from the level of the

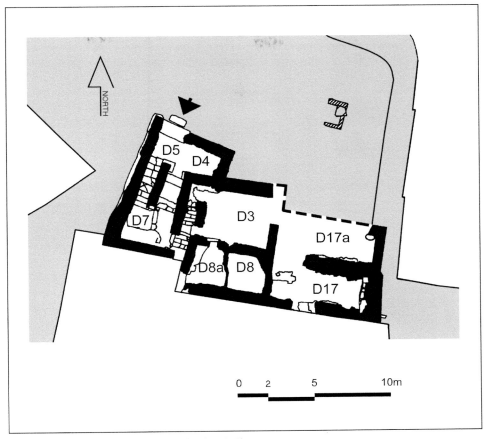

Fig. 107. Delta-North, general plan (scale 1:250).

Fig. 108. Delta-North, the entrance.

Fig. 109. Delta-North, the entrance lobby and the main staircase.

threshold, and though no clear traces of the window next to the door survive, we may well assume that this is the level of a window sill. The wall around the entrance was typically made of ashlar blocks. Numerous dressed stones were in the debris in front of it, and Marinatos named the building Xeste 1 after the Greek word for dressed stones. The huge monolithic threshold bears traces of the rotation of the wooden door, and a pivot hole at one end shows that this door had only one leaf opening to the right (see Chap. 9). This was a heavy door that had worn the wooden pole holding it, so that a lead plate had to be inserted in the cavity of the pivot to raise the door.

Crossing the threshold, one enters a typical lobby paved with large slabs (Rooms Delta 4 and 5).[22] Ahead lies the main staircase (Fig. 109). To the right (west), one can see the stone steps of the first flight leading up. They are cracked and broken, and the whole structure has subsided, showing clearly that a void was underneath. Eight steps lead to a middle landing, and from there the stairs continued, presumably in wood, because only one stone step is in place, and no large stones were found in the debris.

Once inside the entrance, we face two double doors, one on each side of the middle wall of the staircase. Access into the building was obviously controlled not only by the entrance door, but also by the two doors inside the building, as is the case with other houses as well. The double door to the right is fixed on the first step of the stairs (the scratches of the two door leafs are visible).

Taking the door to the left (east), there are two options. The first is to go down the stairs (space Delta 6) to a semi-basement area, which has two small windows on the western facade of the

building, underneath the second flight of steps. The basement of Delta 3 was also reached by the same flight of steps (it was found full of bronze vessels[23]). The other option is to move under the auxiliary staircase into Room Delta 3, on the ground floor. Such a door is actually visible from within Room Delta 3. This, after all, is the only way to enter the eastern rooms at ground floor level.

Back to the entrance lobby and up the first flight of the main staircase, we reach the middle landing (Delta 7). A peculiar shallow basin occupies much of this small space. A wooden staircase must have continued upward to Rooms 4[24] and 3 (Delta 3, in other words, had three stories). From the middle landing, a door leads directly to an auxiliary staircase of the most remarkable design (Fig. 110). It is a combination of four small flights of steps joining three different points in the building. The south end of this staircase protrudes inside Room Delta 1, inside the adjacent house Delta-West. The situation at this point is not very clear and may easily mislead the visitor into thinking that the staircase actually leads to Room Delta 1.

Room Delta 3 communicates with Delta 8a. This is a small dark room containing 3 box-like structures built of upright mudbricks along the west wall.[25] It is separated from Delta 8 by a thin mudbrick wall. Room Delta 8 has a pier-and-door partition facing toward another room to the east, while farther east it opened on a veranda above Room Delta 17.[26] The remaining rooms to the east (Delta 17 and 17a) are badly damaged by the torrent, and the situation is unclear. Delta 17 has a plain facade facing toward the Square of the Double Horns with a spout at roof level. This indicates that no upper floor was present here, as suggested above, though as Michailidou points out, fragments of wall paintings along with fallen slabs are reported from this area.[27] The four rooms from Delta 17a to 19, though they belong to at least two different houses, have a neat eastern

Fig. 110. Delta-North, the auxiliary staircase.

facade with a uniform and continuous indentation (Fig. 32).

Double walls to the south separate Delta-North from Delta-East and Delta-West. These walls, however, are only attested at ground floor level, whereas on the upper floor, those of the north house do not continue. It seems that the upper floors of this specific house were extensively remodelled, presumably after the *seismic destruction*.

House of the Anchor

Triangle Square is bordered to the west by a building showing only part of its eastern facade (Fig. 111).[28] It is preserved to the height of the first floor, and the wall is indented in the familiar way. A large window occupies the southern part of this facade. It has a low sill, as if the intention was to have easy communication between the interior of the house and the public space outside (like the window of Sector Alpha-East, Room Alpha 1). To the north of this facade, in a recess, lies the entrance. It consists of a door with a monolithic threshold made of limestone (unique at Akrotiri). No window is by the door, unless it is the one to the left, corresponding to the protruding facade. A bathtub is inside the entrance to the right, and though the rest of the building disappears under the pumice, we may anticipate the presence of a main staircase in the vicinity of the entrance door and even the presence of a room with a central column next to it. This is indicated by the facade of the room with the large double window to the south of the entrance and the typical dimension of 4.90 m.

Fig. 111. A view of the House of the Anchor (to the right) and the Gate from Triangle Square.

House of the Ladies

The building complex consists of at least two adjoining houses, one to the north and the other to the southeast. The House of the Ladies,[29] where the homonymous frescoes were found, is the northern compartment. The house—assuming that the eastern limit seen today is the limit of the house as well—covers an area of 184 square meters (Fig. 112). It has three stories and an estimated total area of 463 square meters.

Leaving the Square of the Cenotaph behind us, we continue our way to the north. The north extension of Telchines Street—now called Daktylon Street—is a well defined road, 2 m wide. The torrential waters have carved deep below the original paved surface, revealing part of the sewage system running under the street (see Chap. 5). Two other streets branch off Daktylon Street at this point: one goes east toward Xeste 5, and the other leads west.

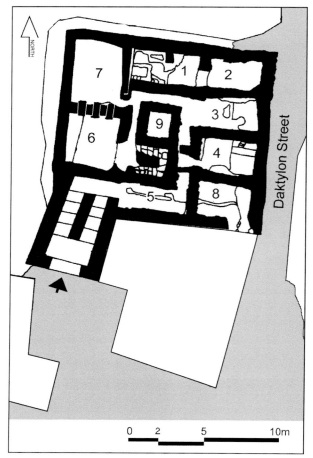

Fig. 112. The House of the Ladies, general plan (scale 1:250).

Fig. 113. The House of the Ladies, the small window in the light well.

Fig. 114. The House of the Ladies, Room 1, clay bins.

If we follow the latter, we bypass House Zeta and arrive at the entrance of the House of the Ladies.

The entrance projects from the otherwise rectangular outline of the building in a manner suggesting that it might be a later addition, as in many other instances. This hypothesis is corroborated by the fact that the entrance is at a higher level than the ground floor rooms of the building (half the height of a story), which is an indication that it had to be adjusted to a new street level, after the accumulation of debris from the earlier *seismic destruction*. It has the typical door and window arrangement at the south wall, and the entrance lobby corresponds to the first landing of the main staircase: the east flight leads down to the semi-basement Room 6, while the west flight leads up to the first floor and continues farther up to the second floor and perhaps to the roof as well. An L-shaped stone bench is reported in the lobby, similar to the one seen at the entrance of Xeste 3.

The House of the Ladies had three stories (or rather, a semi-basement and two stories above). At the lower level access is through Room 6—the door

is visible at the southwest corner of the room—and presumably through Room 5 as well. For the upper two floors, the access to the interior of the house is only though Room 5. The ground floor—or semi-basement—is inadequately known, but the higher floors present a relatively clear picture.

The most conspicuous feature of this edifice is the small rectangular light well, 1.50 by 1.70 m, at the heart of the building compound (Fig. 113). Two small windows framed with ashlar stones occupy the center of the north and the west wall, while the southern wall has a larger opening. The latter corresponds to an auxiliary staircase, which is closely related to the main staircase at the entrance of the house, just like Delta-North, Delta-West, and Xeste 4 (see below).

A corridor giving access to various rooms borders the other three sides of this light well. This arrangement is unique at Akrotiri. It probably derives from the position of the auxiliary staircase in the center of the house: having no exterior walls for windows to give light to the staircase, the builders resorted to the construction of a light well for this purpose—a true light well, in fact. This is by no means similar to what has wrongly been labelled a light well in Crete.[30] It is actually strong proof of the strict "lighting regulations" applied to staircases.

The rooms are arranged around the light well in three zones: the north zone (a compartment of the two adjoining Rooms 1 and 2) is where the Frescoes of the Ladies were found, coming from the second floor. On the first floor, Room 1 has a set of clay bins (Fig. 114). The east zone is a set of rooms of more or less equal size (Rooms 2, 3, and 4) accessed by the corridor but also intercommunicating. The west zone, finally, consists of Rooms 6 and 7 joined with a pier-and-door partition into one compartment on the second floor (Fig. 115).

The House of the Ladies, as far as one can tell for the time being, has little in common with the house model and belongs most probably to the category of the atypical houses.

Fig. 115. The House of the Ladies, Room 7 looking northwest.

House Theta and House Zeta

House Theta abuts the House of the Ladies to the southeast (Figs. 26, 27). A double wall is along the joint of the two buildings, so that each one retains its structural autonomy. An indentation of the east facade appears at the point where they meet. The house is unexcavated and quite damaged from the torrent. Its outline, however, is more or less visible, and it probably covered an area in two stories like all the other houses. Its entrance is showing on the east wall, opening on Daktylon Street, and the presence of a staircase can be assumed by a dressed stone of a typical trapezoidal form with two mortices that shows among the unexcavated debris.

House Zeta stands between the West House and the House of the Ladies. Its south wall must have collapsed at an early stage, because the debris had spread over the open space between the two buildings before it was covered with pumice. The only hypothesis one may attempt at this point is that the rectangular room sticking out toward the Square of the Cenotaph is the entrance and main staircase of the building.

Porter's Lodge and "Kitchen"

At the other side of Daktylon Street, opposite the House of the Ladies, lie more unexcavated buildings (Figs. 26, 27). Their facades along the street are badly damaged by the torrent, so there is very little one can see. Shortly before we reach Sector Alpha, we see a narrow alley leading east. At the junction of the two streets, Marinatos excavated a small space (1.90– 2.10 by 2.70 m) with all the characteristics of an entrance, which he named the Porter's Lodge.[31] It, too, lies in the bed of the ravine and is badly destroyed.

This entrance door—0.82 m wide—gives access to a building extending southeast. It occupies the corner of the building and has a large though atypical threshold (the walls are preserved to a very low height, and there is no way of detecting the window). The entrance lobby inside, paved with large greenish slabs, has a neatly built bench 0.40 by 1.60 m along the southern wall. The room has an elongated form, and the staircase is probably at the eastern end. Marinatos reported fragments of wall paintings from the upper floor,[32] and to the east of this entrance he excavated a room that he called a kitchen.[33] It has a window and a cupboard and most probably belongs to the same building as the entrance.

Farther to the southeast, a wall jutting out from the unexcavated volcanic layer probably defines the eastern limit of the building. It is more or less in line with the eastern facade of Sector Alpha, so a street parallel to Daktylon Street is here. This wall has the typical ashlar cornice of a pier-and-window partition, attested also by the wooden imprints and the lime mortar on the sill (see Chap. 9). It belongs to the upper floor and is most probably part of the building entered through the Porter's Lodge.

Alpha-East

Having reached the northernmost end of the excavated area, we arrive at Sector Alpha. It consists of two separate buildings meeting along a north-south axis. Alpha-East is fully excavated.[34] It includes three main rooms, Alpha 1 to Alpha 3, aligned from south to north (Figs. 116, 117). Its rectangular outline covers an area of 100 square meters and had two stories with a total surface of 200 square meters. The eastern facade faces a north-south street and has a typical shallow indentation (Fig. 118). The indentation does not correspond to a transverse wall and seems to have been produced by some kind of remodelling in this area (the wall to the south is thinner). The indentations of the south facade are of a similar nature.

The entrance, at the SW corner of the building, is poorly preserved because it is situated along the bed of the ravine. The threshold is missing, and it has no other features, such as a window or ashlar stones. Beyond this doorway is a small paved lobby with a large clay vessel still in situ in one of its corners. A crude partition wall at the northern side of the lobby defines a deep narrow space. This is probably a staircase leading to the upper floor. The staircase must have been wooden and rather narrow for a main one, but all this could be due to remodelling. Or perhaps it may be due to the fact that we are now leaving behind the "upper class" harbor district, and the houses are becoming smaller and less elaborate.

From the entrance lobby, a door opens to Room Alpha 1 (Fig. 119). This is a large squarish room, 4.90 m by 5.10 m with a central column. It was full of large pithoi still in place, arranged in rows along the north and south walls. A large window opens to the east. It is divided in three parts by intermediate posts and has a low paved sill facilitating communication with the public space outside. It has been suggested that it functioned as a kind of shop. A low rectangular stone is embedded in the floor, which has some traces of fire on its surface. It has been identified as a hearth.[35] A stone basin, a large tripod cooking pot, and grinding stones add to the picture.

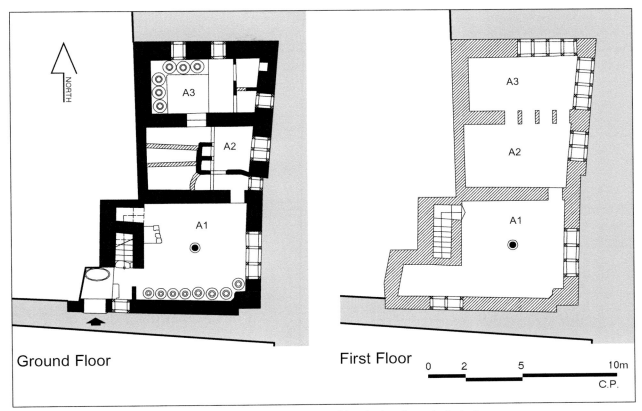

Fig. 116. Alpha-East, plan (scale 1:200). Black walls are existing and hatched walls are indicated.

Fig. 117. View of Alpha-East, ground floor rooms from the north.

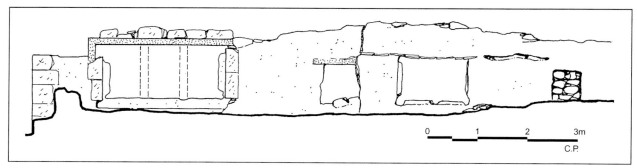

Fig. 118. Alpha-East, east elevation.

Fig. 119. Alpha-East, Room 1.

Fig. 120. Alpha-East, Room 2. The cupboards were made of upright clay slabs fixed in a timber frame.

Fig. 121. Alpha-East, looking south from Room 2.

Crossing this room diagonally—very much like Room 3 of the West House—is a door leading north to Room Alpha 2 (3.20 by 5–5.40 m). This room is 0.20 m lower than Alpha 1, and the door was found blocked with pithoi (Figs. 120, 121). It has an interesting arrangement: it is divided into many smaller compartments by thin clay partition walls forming cupboards or closets. Circulation is channelled through this area in a very intricate manner. A rich variety of finds, most notably a pair of scales and a complete series of lead weights, shows that this compartment served many purposes, and it could have been an annex to Room Alpha 1. Next is Alpha 3 (2.75 by 5.10–5.50 m), reached by a door from Room Alpha 2. It is divided into two parts, the western one being on a lower level. This part is a storeroom with pithoi arranged along its western wall. The north wall looks out onto an open public space.

The upper floor of this building is virtually missing and unknown. What is certain, however, is that the first room entered from the main staircase by the entrance is a large, almost square room with a central column (comparable to Room 3 of the West House). The column base was found in the debris of the ground floor, next to the base of the ground floor column (see Chap. 9). Dozens of loom weights were found fallen into the ground floor, indicating that, as with the West House, weaving took place here.[36] If the typical "house model" applies here, then we should be looking for a compartment equivalent to the decorated Rooms 4 and 5 of the West House as well as an auxiliary staircase. The former might correspond to Rooms Alpha 2 and 3. Frescoes would be expected in this area. An auxiliary staircase, on the other hand, may well correspond to one of the small compartments of Alpha 2, separated by clay partition walls.

Alpha-West and the "Tunnel"

Alpha-West is only partially revealed (Fig. 122).[37] It has a row of rooms abutting house Alpha-East and more rooms to the west. The west facade of the house includes the entrance and a room jutting out farther north.[38]

The entrance is excellently preserved (Fig. 123): it is close to the corner of the building and consists of a large door bordered by a window (this actually belongs to a room next to the entrance, and judging from the awkward wall separating the two, it may be the result of remodelling—or it shows how imperative the presence of a window next to the entrance was). The monolithic threshold preserves the traces of the door pivot hole and bolt (a unique element so far). Inside this entrance is a neatly paved lobby (1.30 by 2.60–2.90 m) with a built bench along the wall at the far end. To the right (south), a door leads to a room that is readily recognized as a mill installation: it has built benches with mill stones embedded upon them, and a clay bathtub connected to a shallow built basin that has an outlet through the southern exterior wall of the building guiding waste into the public sewage system right outside. This room is an annex to the entrance proper.

The northern area is virtually unexcavated, but the walls and room features exposed so far permit a tentative reconstruction. The door opening to the north from the entrance lobby leads to what seems to be a small corridor. The main staircase, though not visible today, is most probably situated nearby.

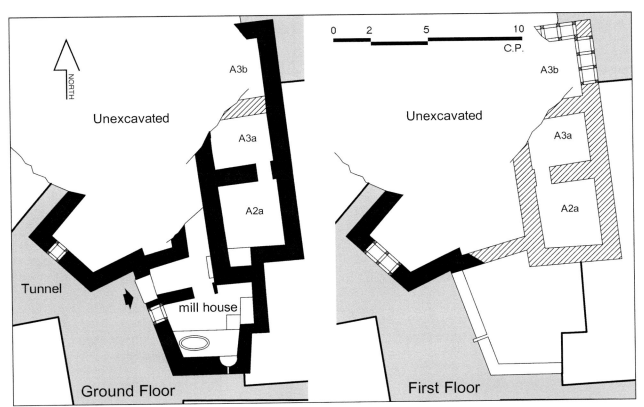

Fig. 122. Alpha-West, plans (scale 1:200). Black walls are existing and hatched walls are indicated.

Fig. 123. Alpha-West, the entrance in the "tunnel" area.

Three or more rooms to the north belong to this building.

At least four rooms are on the upper floor. The mill installation next to the entrance had no upper floor, as is indicated by the presence of a clay spout still in place on the western facade, at a level corresponding to the upper floor (in this case the roof). The rooms to the north are of the type known from the West House and the "house model": the first room entered from the staircase is most probably the large, almost square type with a central column. Evidence for this is found on the outside of the building, on the western facade seen with difficulty when moving deep into the tunnel. Three windows are here: two small ones at the ground floor level and a larger one above. This is a most typical arrangement of openings, seen in many examples, and is a strong indication of the interior of the building because it probably consists of two small rooms on the ground floor united into one large room with a central column on the upper floor.

Farther to the north is yet another recognizable type of room: two of its walls are seen today, the east and the north, and they have clear traces of pier-and-window partitions (see Chap. 9). The eastern wall, specifically, had the typical four windows occupying most of its length (the ashlar cornice can be seen at the level of their sills). The northern wall shows signs of the beginning of a window, and though the existence of more windows cannot be confirmed at present, it is enough to identify this room with Room 5 of the West House (in which case frescoes should be expected here). More buildings are beyond this point, with parts of their facades along the two intersecting streets in the area of the "tunnels."

Xeste 5

The building called Xeste 5[39] lies to the east of the Square of the Cenotaph, at a much lower level (Figs. 37, 124). A tall retaining wall holds this side of the square, and Daimonon Street, 1.20–1.70 m wide, runs below with a north-south direction leading to the Square of the Double Horns. The retaining wall is roughly built and has a pronounced rounded corner at the northeast. A street branches off in an east-west direction at this point. It joins with Daktylon Street with a strong inclination (steps should be expected here), but it also continues east to an unexcavated area.

Xeste 5 shows only part of the west facade and the tops of some of its walls (Fig. 125); in other words, it is practically unknown. It is a challenge, however, to anticipate its interior arrangement by applying the specifications of the "Theran house model."

The west facade has two indentations dividing the wall in three parts. It is all made of ashlar masonry, and numerous dressed blocks were found among the debris in front of the wall. The entrance to the building is not visible, but it most probably corresponds to one of the three indentations of the visible facade at the northwest corner of the building. This is assumed by the large, Type C, window, typically seen above an entrance (see the West House) and from the scanty structural details visible in the area (ashlar wall and timber imprints). The sill of this window is 1.60 m lower than that of the very large window farther south; it is clear that the levels of the corresponding floors do not match.

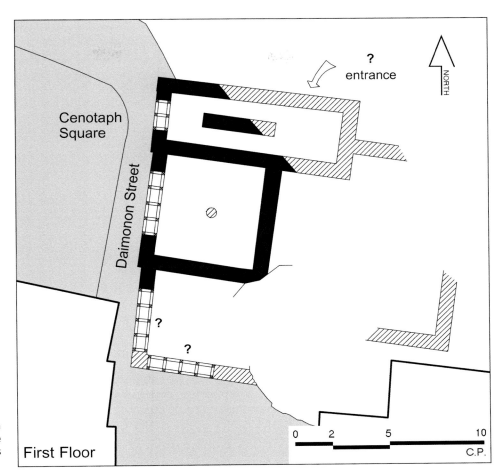

Fig. 124. Xeste 5, plan
(scale 1:200). Black walls are
existing and hatched walls
are indicated.

This is a typical picture of the middle landing of a
main staircase giving access to the adjoining rooms.
A well dug for one of the pillars of the shelter inside
the assumed entrance has given further proof: a
large stone vessel and a paved floor were reported.
This trench was broadened recently for the foundation of the new shelter. The middle wall of the main
staircase was thus revealed. Interestingly enough,
at the other end of the staircase (east) there seems to
be an even larger landing: this suggests that the
entrance door is probably from the north.

To the right, next to the entrance, the picture of
the west facade is quite familiar: there are two (or
three?) small windows below and a large multiple
window above, 3.80 m wide. The situation is similar to that of the West House, Room 3. This kind of
arrangement implies a room with a central column
on the upper floor and two or more small storerooms at ground floor level. Judging from the
length of the wall corresponding to the room with
the central column, it is very possible that the north-
south dimension of this room is the typical 4.90 m.

Fig. 125. Xeste 5, west facade looking from the Square of
the Cenotaph.

The fact that this room is next to the entrance is a
further confirmation of the "house model." What is
even more typical is the relationship between the
different levels: the entrance level is clearly in the
middle between the levels of the ground floor and
the upper floor—one would expect a typical main

staircase inside with two flights each leading to the respective levels. Finally, one more room farther south may conform to the "house model:" it is a corner room, with its south facade facing the large public square. It would not come as a surprise if pier-and-window partitions appear on both sides, and of course wall paintings would be in this part of the house. The overall arrangement, in this case, would be very similar to that of the West House, and the eastern zone of the house would be the storage and service area.

Delta-East

This is the smallest house known from the town: it covers an area of 96 square meters and had two stories, with an estimated total of 192 square meters (Figs. 126–128). The entrance of Delta-East corresponds to Room Delta 19. It has all the typical characteristics of the Theran entrance model: the wide door (1.00 by 1.86 m) and the window next to it, the ashlar wall surrounding the two openings, and the projecting ashlar cornice above them (0.30 m wide). The door has a large monolithic threshold with a shallow hemispherical depression to hold the pivot and a long groove showing clearly that it had a one-leaf wooden door. Indeed, this door left a detailed imprint on the volcanic material that covered the building.

The door opens into a typical entrance lobby: an elongated room holds the main staircase to the upper floor (Fig. 129). This room has three outer walls, and only the northern side abuts to Room Delta 18. As usual, there are two possible accesses: one to the ground floor rooms and one to the upper floor, via the staircase. The former, however, is under the second flight of steps and not directly to the right, to Delta 18a, as one would have expected. This may have been intentional so as to assure a roundabout way to the storerooms.

Moving under the staircase, one arrives at Room Delta 21, at the center of the house. It is approximately 3.50 by 4.30 m with a large window on its southern wall, looking out to a small blind alley, whose very existence was obviously dictated by the need to give light and air to both Delta 21 and also Delta 9 of the neighboring house. In the middle of this room, a low stone platform, 0.60 by 0.70 m, has been interpreted as a hearth, though it may be the base of a wooden support for the ceiling.

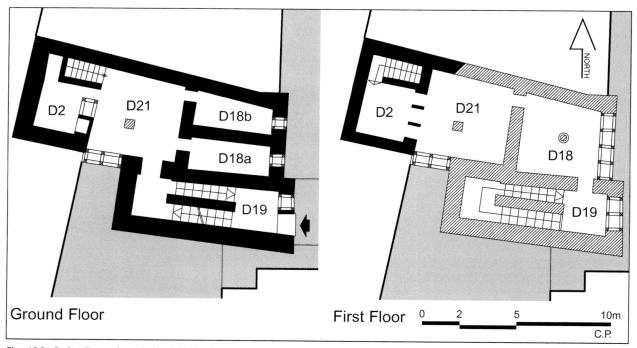

Ground Floor

First Floor

Fig. 126. Delta-East, plans (scale 1:200). Black walls are existing and hatched walls are indicated.

Fig. 127. Delta-East, east facade looking on the Square of the Double Horns.

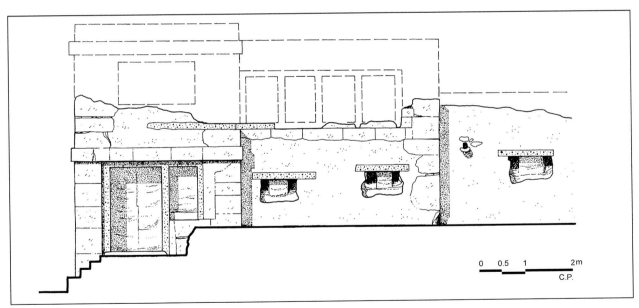

Fig. 128. Delta-East, east facade.

This room has five doors giving access to all the other ground floor rooms. To the west, it has two doors, one of which leads to Delta 2, the room with the famous Spring Fresco (Fig. 130, Pl. 4B). This was a small room 2.10 by 2.50 m, situated deep in the fabric of Sector Delta. It has many interesting and well preserved architectural features, such as a shelf along the west wall at a height of 1.75 m above the floor. Its east wall is actually a series of openings: a door, a window, and a cupboard. This sort of arrangement, based on the concept of the pier-and-door partition, is quite popular at Akrotiri.

Its northern side is a light partition wall made of thin clay slabs set upright within a wooden

Fig. 129. View of Delta-East, Rooms 17–19 looking toward the east. The torrent has destroyed part of the building.

Fig. 130. Delta-East, the room with the Spring Fresco during excavation. The gypsum cast of the bed is still in situ.

frame. Behind this wall lies a narrow blind space, Room Delta 2a. The western end of this wall has an opening forming a low cupboard that was found full of vases and other objects. This arrangement can now be explained: the narrow space is an auxiliary staircase leading up to the first floor, accessible by a door opening to Delta 21 (Fig. 104). The steps were probably made of slabs supported by a wooden framework (the first step was of stone and is still in situ). This interpretation is further reinforced by the recent discoveries at the West House, where such an auxiliary staircase was found quite unexpectedly in a very narrow space separated by clay partition walls. Moreover, it has since become clear that the "house model" at Akrotiri includes at least two staircases: the main one situated at the entrance, and a much smaller auxiliary one, found in various unpredictable places. The double walls on three sides of Delta 2 aid in the interpretation.

Going back to the circulatory nexus of Room Delta 21, we now turn east, toward the two narrow spaces, Delta 18a and 18b, found literally packed with vases, pieces of furniture, and other artifacts—most notably clay sealings of Cretan origin and fragments of Linear A tablets.[40] Room Delta 21 lies right in the bed of the torrent, and the eastern wall dividing it from the two narrow storerooms has almost completely disappeared.

Back to the entrance lobby, we may now move up to the second story via the broad staircase. The landing on the second floor was broad and well lit by a large window similar to the one we see above the entrance of the West House. To the north, a door

opened to Room Delta 18. This was a large, almost square room, with its eastern outer wall occupied by four windows forming a typical pier-and-window partition (Figs. 127, 128). The sills of these windows, at a height of 0.60 m, had the same finishing as the floor of the room: a fine mosaic made of small sea pebbles embedded in clay mortar. A flat rounded slab is still in situ approximately in the center of the room, and it may well be the base of a vertical wooden support. In this case, Room Delta 18 would correspond closely to Room 3 of the West House. The wall to the north is preserved to a low height, but it is high enough to testify that there was a double wall here with no door. The western wall of this room has not survived; the torrential waters have swept it away. Its position can be estimated by the remains of the ground floor wall, but its form remains unknown (was there a pier-and-door partition?). Room Delta 21, completely missing today, had the same almost square shape and dimensions as its companions below it on the ground floor and most probably the same large window to the south.

To the west, however, we know for sure that a pier-and-door partition connected this room to Delta 2; the stone bases, cut in the form of a double T, are still in place (Fig. 131). One of the doors leads to the auxiliary staircase giving access to the ground floor—part of the clay partition wall separating the staircase from Room Delta 2 is still in situ, resting on a thick wooden beam. The walls of Delta 2 are preserved to a low height, but it is clear that the double walls continue on all three sides, though the thickness of the upper wall is diminished.

Fig. 131. Delta-East, view looking west at Room 2. The bases of the pier-and-door partition of the first floor are visible above the door and window. The window to the left in the image corresponds to Room 21 and looks out to a blind alley.

Xeste 2

To the south of Xeste 5, Daimonon Street leads to a large open public area (Figs. 26, 27). This is the Square of the Double Horns bordered on the west by Sector Delta, on the east by an unknown building of which we can only see the topmost part of its western facade, and on the south by Xeste 2. This is a neat orthogonal open public space.

Xeste 2[41] is a three-storied building extending south to an unexcavated area, and it is most probably very large (Figs. 132, 133). Only its north wall that is approximately 23 m long has been revealed, and it shows an intricate arrangement of horizontal and vertical wooden beams that reinforce the rubble walls. The projecting ashlar cornices define the floors between the three stories of the building.

The northwest corner is built with ashlar blocks only at the upper floor. A large window at its center, preserving an imprint of its balustrade, was mistaken for a ruined wall and was cemented over early in the excavation. The northwest corner of the building is actually all made of ashlar blocks. A large opening looks west onto a small blind alley.

Over the years various trenches were dug beyond this facade, to the south, revealing rooms that probably belong to Xeste 2. An earlier find, in a trench dug for the first shelter, may be indicative: a trapezoidal stone baring two mortises was reported, and because such stones are typical of the middle wall of a staircase, one may assume the presence of a staircase nearby or even perhaps the entrance.

Fig. 132. Xeste 2, north facade (computer restoration based on an old photograph by C. Palyvou).

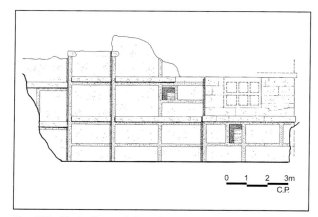

Fig. 133. Xeste 2, north facade.

Xeste 4

Xeste 4 is the largest and most impressive building revealed to date (Fig. 134).[42] It occupies an area of approximately 367 square meters and had at least three floors. The first floor was the same as the ground floor, while the second floor covered part of the building—perhaps Rooms 2 to 11. In this case, the estimate of the total area of the building would be 957 square meters. All the facades of the building are exquisitely constructed with ashlar stones of white/green tuff (Figs. 135, 136). This practice is unique at Akrotiri and distinguishes Xeste 4 from all other buildings. One should not hasten, however, to attach to it a "unique" significance as well, because more elaborate buildings may be revealed in the

future. What it might suggest, on the other hand, is that the southeast district of the town is of special importance—Koureton Street, a well-defined broad street, corroborates this hypothesis. A harbor in that direction would confirm this.

The entrance to the building occupies the southwest corner and opens on Koureton Street. Typically enough, it consists of a staircase with two parallel flights and two landings (Fig. 137). The wall paintings unearthed during the past years from this area are breathtaking in their beauty and magnificence, as much as in the information they deliver: large scale male figures are depicted walking up the stairs, carrying various objects, perhaps as gifts to some important resident of the house or as offerings of some kind. The grandeur of this access speaks vividly of the special importance of the building.

The entrance system is typical in yet another way: the middle landing has two doors, one of which connects the main staircase to an auxiliary staircase, and the other to a room with a central column, both well known features attested in other buildings as well. The window lighting the auxiliary staircase is visible at the south facade of the building. It is positioned higher than the other windows, directly under the projecting cornice, precisely because it corresponds to the middle landing of the staircase.

The square room with a central column is 4.30 by 4.90 m. Only the upper floor was visible until recently, but judging from the large hollow space in the middle, one could anticipate the presence of a similar room with a central column below. Such a room was, indeed, found when excavation progressed. A cast of the wooden column was made possible. The room on the upper floor had its walls painted red, and a large window faced south.

Crossing this room in the familiar diagonal manner, we come to a door opening directly onto a narrow staircase. This is the third staircase of the building, connecting the second floor with the third.

The third floor is only marginally preserved. A set of rooms connected with pier-and-door partitions occupied the north part of the building (Fig. 138). These rooms must have had windows to the north and doors leading out to a veranda, because the third floor occupied only the central part of the building, very much like Xeste 3. A paved corridor borders these pier-and-door partitions to the south, with its two ends leading to the two auxiliary staircases. This ingenious arrangement allows for an amazing flexibility of circulatory patterns within the building, especially because the auxiliary staircase to the west is also connected to the main staircase and hence to the entrance of the house. It is, indeed, a remarkable example of the high level of architectural design attested in the houses of Akrotiri, equal only to the palatial architecture of Crete.

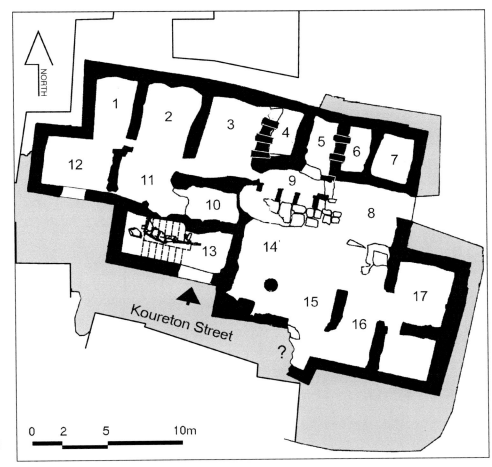

Fig. 134. Xeste 4, general plan (scale 1:250).

Fig. 135. Xeste 4, west facade.

Fig. 136. Xeste 4, north facade.

Fig. 137. Xeste 4, the main staircase.

Fig. 138. Xeste 4, the bases of the pier-and-door partition of the second floor.

South House

Directly across from Xeste 4, on the other side of Koureton Street, are various buildings whose facades face the street. One of them, the South House, can be better understood (Fig. 139). Although it has not been excavated, we may safely anticipate its interior arrangement by applying the "Theran house model," just as we did with Xeste 5.

What we see today is basically the north facade (Fig. 140) and the northeast corner of the building where the typical entrance system has been identified. The entrance door and window face east (they were visible within the well dug for one of the pillars of the first shelter). The main staircase behind the entrance door was partly investigated by Marinatos when he removed the volcanic deposits

and revealed the upper part of the staircase (Fig. 141). The visible part belongs to the upper floor: a flight of 9 stone steps, approximately 1 m wide, leading westward to a middle landing. The eastern landing corresponding to the entrance below is paved and is broader, as expected. There are two windows here ensuring ample lighting of the staircase (Fig. 142). The middle landing, on the other hand, gives access to a room to the west via a door. The door incorporates two steps, because the level of the rooms to the west is approximately 0.50 m higher than the middle landing.

The picture is surprisingly familiar: just like the West House, the main staircase gives access to an intermediate level. The other flight of steps (south)

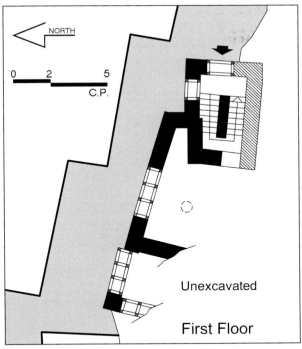

Fig. 139. South House, plan (scale 1:200). Black walls are existing and hatched walls are indicated.

is hardly visible, and it seems that the last flight to the roof was made of wood. The rather awkward shape of the staircase and the small left-over space to the west may also indicate that, as with many other houses, the entrance is a later addition and an adjustment to a new level of the street.

The north facade of the building has a series of shallow indentations of 0.12 m. The facade easily betrays the interior arrangement of the house (Fig. 140). The middle part, next to the entrance/staircase, shows a typical arrangement of windows: two small below, one large above. This means that two storerooms are probably at ground floor level, and a room with a central column is on the upper floor. This room is typically situated next to the entrance. Farther west, the next room has a pier-and-window partition (Fig. 143). It is a corner room, and it is quite possible another pier-and-window partition is on the other side as well. This is again reminiscent of the compartment of Rooms 4 and 5 on the upper floor of the West House. It is in this area, therefore, that one would expect wall paintings to appear.

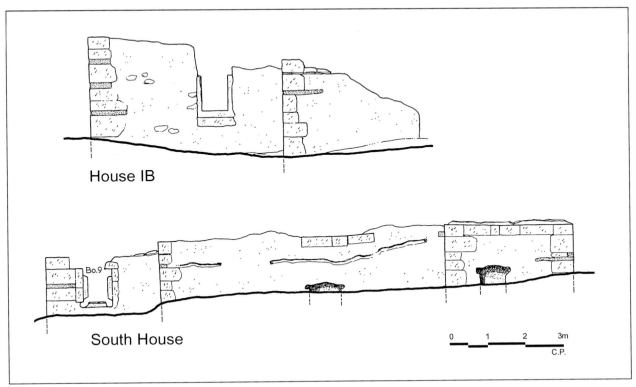

Fig. 140. South House, north facade. The large window of the first floor probably corresponds to a room with a central column, and the two small windows below to two small rooms. House IB lies to the west of the South House.

Fig. 141. South House, the third flight of the main staircase leading from the first floor to the middle landing.

Fig. 142. South House, a window at the first floor of the main staircase.

Fig. 143. South House, the pier-and-window partition of the first floor.

Chapter 7 Notes

1. The references to each individual house are far too many to mention here. The main sources of information are Marinatos 1968–1976; Doumas 1983 and 1976–1996; Palyvou 1999a; Michailidou 2001a.

2. Marinatos 1968–1976, I: 38–47 (the area B1–B2 under the name Bronos 2); II: 10–15 (Bronou 2); III: 32–38; IV: 28–33; VII: 17–21.

3. The floor was found intact by Marinatos who removed it later in order to excavate below (Marinatos 1968–1976, VII: 19).

4. Michailidou 2001a: 294.

5. Michailidou 2001a: 296 suggests that it may have functioned as a bedroom.

6. The arrangement is very similar to a later storeroom in the Mycenaean palace of Pylos, as Marinatos has already observed (1968–1976, VII: 17).

7. Marinatos 1968–1976, III: 35.

8. Palyvou 1986.

9. Marinatos 1968–1976, III: 25, 38–52.

10. Doumas 1993: 180.

11. A window on the north wall of Xeste 3, next to the lustral basin, collapsed in a similar manner. This probably indicates that the earthquake movement was in a north to south direction. See also McCoy and Heiken 2000.

12. The column base must be the one revealed during the excavation of one of the nearby wells for the new shelter (see Fig. 188).

13. Marinatos 1970: 40–41, pls. 33.1 and 33.2.

14. Marinatos 1968–1976, III: 45, pl. 42 shows the blocked doors as found.

15. Marinatos 1968–1976, III: 28 (also called North Court).

16. Palyvou 1984.

17. Marinatos 1968–1976, IV: 27, pl.100b.

18. Palyvou 1984.

19. Marinatos 1968–1976, VII: 16 suggests influence from the East.

20. Marinatos 1968–1976, IV: 28.

21. Marinatos 1968–1976, VII: 16.

22. This area was called Bronos 1a by Marinatos (1968–1976, I: 34).

23. Marinatos 1968–1976, IV: 17.

24. Fresco fragments are reported from the upper story (Michailidou 2001a: 312).

25. Doumas 1993: 181, pl. 108a.

26. This is attested by the spout at roof level still in situ at the eastern facade of Delta 17.

27. Michailidou 2001a: 308; Marinatos 1968–1976, VII: 14, pls. 15, 16a; Michailidou 2001a: 333, suggests that D17a probably had an upper floor.

28. Marinatos 1968–1976, VI: 18–19.

29. Marinatos 1968–1976, V: 11–15, 38–41; VI: 8–11; Doumas 1990: 224–232; 1992b: 176–180.

30. See Palyvou 2004.

31. Marinatos 1968–1976, II: 28–29.

32. Marinatos 1968–1976, II: 28.

33. Marinatos 1968–1976, II: 28–29; V: 15–16.

34. This area was one of the first to be excavated by Marinatos. It was named, initially, Arvanitis Sector Alpha: Arvanitis 1. This is where Marinatos began, in front of the cave (Marinatos 1968–1976, I: 16–34; II: 15, 30–33; III: 8–15).

35. Marinatos 1968–1976, I: 28.

36. Marinatos 1968–1976, I: 21, 28.

37. Marinatos 1968–1976, II: 33; III: 15–16.

38. This room was called the Sunken House (Marinatos 1968–1976, III: 15–16).

39. Marinatos 1968–1976, VII: 12. Doumas 1993: 176–177.

40. Doumas 1995: 129–130.

41. Marinatos 1968–1976, VI: 13–14, Arvanitis 2, Xeste 2, and D18, D19; I: 51–55.

42. Marinatos 1968–1976, VI: 15; VII: 21–22; Doumas 1993: 172–176.

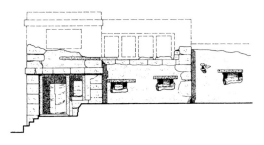

8

A Synopsis of the Theran House Model

Having overviewed the houses visible today, we may now attempt to summarize the main characteristics of what we have termed "the Theran house model," both in its typical and atypical form.

Theran houses are fairly large, with a clear distinction between the typical and the atypical houses—the latter being at least twice as large (Fig. 28). Of the typical houses, there are two sizes, the small (roughly 100 square meters) and the medium (roughly 140–190 square meters). The medium type is the most common. The different sizes of the typical houses do not seem to imply a different social status, because the quality of the architecture, the wall paintings, and the equipment is more or less the same. It probably reflects the adjustments of the house model attested in urban areas where space is often restricted. The overall sample (11 houses) is too small for further observations of a statistical nature.

General Layout

All houses consist of rectangular units in a plain juxtaposition, especially at ground floor level. This is a simple means to ensure static efficiency (see Chap. 10). Houses are either free standing or part of a building block, depending on the local conditions each time. In the latter case, each house has its own walls (in other words, there are double walls where two houses abut). Their practice is dictated by practical needs, but it also shows differentiation of ownership.

Two features prevail in the overall design of the Theran houses, both characteristics of their urban character:

THE PRESENCE OF AT LEAST ONE FLOOR ABOVE GROUND

Many ground floor rooms are actually semi-basements, for reasons discussed elsewhere. All, however, have a second story, and only a very small number of rooms are single storied (e.g., Delta 16).

Third stories are not as common, but they are not an exclusive privilege of the large atypical houses. As Michailidou points out, the presence of a second floor indicates vertical expansion and is not a matter of technology but of socio-political requirements,[1] but the technological implications should not be underestimated. This vertical expansion is typical of urban centers and allows for zoning and distribution of functions.

THE LACK OF PRIVATE OUTDOOR SPACES

The absence of private outdoor space is more strong evidence for the urban character of the settlement—rural tasks and animal keeping need open spaces such as light wells or courtyards, either within the building or at its periphery—but it also shows a clear preference for compact building.

Xeste 3 is an interesting case: the building consists roughly of three rows of rooms, but the middle section (Rooms 2, 4, 7, 10, 13) has no exterior walls and therefore no proper windows. Light and air are accessed and circulated from the adjoining rooms by means of interior windows and skylights over the doors. A light well in the middle of the house would have been a better solution, but this was obviously not included in the architectural vocabulary of Akrotiri. The small light well in the House of the Ladies, on the other hand, is a different case related to the function of the staircase, as argued elsewhere. Suffice it to point out that all the rooms surrounding this light well were built with windows looking to the exterior of the building and do not depend on the light well for illumination. It seems that the flat roofs of the houses at Akrotiri compensate more than adequately for the absence of private outdoor spaces.

Circulation

Circulation within the building is carefully designed and fairly intricate (Fig. 144). Access to the house is well marked, and the entrance system is highly standardized in all the buildings, typical and atypical alike. Once inside the building, the resident or visitor has two choices: either to move to the ground floor rooms (residents only) or to climb up to the living room/reception area on the upper floor, via a spacious staircase that is included in the entrance lobby. Both accesses are controlled by doors. The small lobby at the entrance acts, therefore, as a buffer zone between the public and the private domain and helps determine a hierarchy of circulation within the house. Service areas situated on the ground floor are directly related to the public space outside, via the entrance. Just as direct is the access from the "urban-public" space to the "private-public" area of the upper floor (the room with a central column) thanks to the staircase included in the entrance system; the access system guides the visitor straight to the upper floor.

Circulation within the house is basically organized by the number, position, and distribution of the doors (see, for example, the round-about circulation at the ground floor of the West House). Doors are typically situated at the corner of the room, as in Crete,[2] and not at the center of the wall as is common in Hagia Eirene on Kea, Phylakopi

on Melos, and in Mycenaean architecture later on. This arrangement is significant for the circulation pattern it creates and the use of the space inside the rooms. Sometimes the first room reached from the entrance plays the role of a circulatory nexus, channeling circulation around the house (Room Delta 21 has 5 doors). This is often due to the fact that the entrance is situated at a corner of the building, making it difficult to access all the rooms easily.

Circulation is more complex where pier-and-door partitions are involved, which is usually on the upper floor. These architectural elements are, indeed, one of the most ingenious novelties of Aegean Bronze Age architecture because they offer an exquisite flexibility of space arrangement controlling inter-communication from the total barrier (all doors closed) to the void (all doors open) (Fig. 145); the composite function is not unlike the screen walls of Japanese architecture (Fig. 146).

Mudbrick partition walls often play the role of dividers, especially on upper floors. Due to their light weight and thin dimensions, they can be easily incorporated anywhere. They often function as screens, separating part of a room, and in doing so they form rudimentary corridors. True corridors are otherwise scarce.

Vertical circulation has a distinct hierarchy. This is evidenced by the presence of more than one point

A SYNOPSIS OF THE THERAN HOUSE MODEL

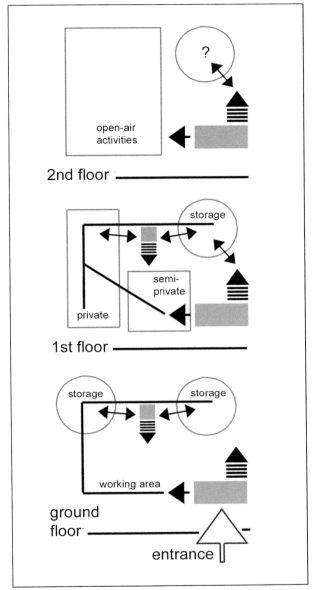

Fig. 144. West House, schematic representation of the functional zones and the circulatory pattern.

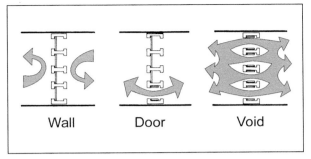

Fig. 145. The pier-and-door partition as a flexible barrier.

Fig. 146. A Japanese screen wall (Grillo 1975: 130).

of vertical communication and by the position of staircases within the fabric of the house. The fact that the builders often go to extremes in order to provide a second staircase shows their concern in differentiating between the two circulatory systems: the more "public" related to the visitor and the "private" used by the resident. The hierarchy is further emphasized by structural differences between the two staircases, in terms of size and quality of construction. The function of the auxiliary

staircase is basically to privately link the service area of the ground floor with a specific part of the domestic area above. In several instances the two staircases, main and auxiliary, relate directly to each other through a middle landing. This is indeed remarkable, because it is no easy thing to design (i.e., anticipate and co-ordinate) a communication system relating many different levels through adjoining staircases that vary in form and size! The result is an impressive multiplicity of interconnections. The fact that the main staircase usually leads to the roof is a further emphasis of its functional importance. The atypical houses seem to differ in this respect: the roof—or veranda—is reached from within the house (from the auxiliary staircases) and not from the main staircase at the entrance.

The intricate 3-dimensional circulatory pattern resulting from the combinations of pier-and-door partitions, corridors, and staircases is far from being arbitrary or chaotic; it was wisely designed to perform in a multi-functional manner. It is a circulatory pattern that offers multiplicity of choice and not complexity.

Functional Zones

Functions are carefully distributed within the house and grouped into zones (Fig. 144). The typical presence of an upper floor corresponds to a basic separation between working and living areas. The ground floor level—or semi-basement in many cases—is given over to storage and home industry, while the upper floor is basically for domestic use and corresponding service areas. The atypical houses differ in this respect: judging basically from Xeste 3, part of the ground floor is an important area of the house, most probably given over to rituals. The flat roof, finally, is the only outdoor space belonging exclusively to the house, hence its great importance, well attested by the finds and the fact that staircases lead all the way up to the roof. It was probably a multi-functional space, related both to working and living activities.

Functional zones and related types of rooms[3] may be grouped as follows:

HEAVY-DUTY WORKING AREA

This area includes various workshops or working areas that are usually on the ground floor level. The mill installation is a distinct part of this zone: situated in close proximity to the entrance of the house, obviously for easy everyday access, it is identified by the built benches with mill stones embedded on their upper surface. Water seems to be important for these activities, as is attested by the large vessels and the built basins found nearby. The size of the installation and the number of mill stones may indicate the size of the "house group" of each building. This zone has a separate, direct access from the entrance lobby.

STORAGE AND SERVICE AREAS

These areas were dispersed throughout the house, at all levels, accommodating different functions. Storage is a major necessity in any house, and it ranges from a shelf and a cupboard to a whole room or a series of rooms. Storage areas were usually annexes to various activities. Heavy-duty service areas at the ground floor, for example, were commonly annexed by a storage space (one or more rooms). Food supplies may have had a storage area of their own. On the upper floor, the formal zone often included small storage areas in the form of cupboards, niches, and clay bins (repositories), but also service rooms (e.g., Room 6, West House). High quality objects were usually kept here. Auxiliary staircases were commonly related to these areas for direct intercommunication.

MULTIFUNCTIONAL ZONE

This area was used for everyday activities and informal receptions. It occupied part of the upper floor and was commonly identified with the large squarish room with a central column, though it could appear in other forms as well (Delta 1 and 1a, for example). It was a plain spacious room,

Fig. 147. The Archanes model of a house (Sakellarakis and Sakellaraki 1991: fig. 36) and a similar roof shelter in Veroia, northern Greece (*Ελληνική Παραδοσιακή Αρχιτεκτονική* 1990, 7: 83, fig. 46).

Fig. 148. Balconies and roofed verandas in Aegean Bronze Age art: left, wall painting, Knossos (Evans 1921–1935, II: 603, fig. 376); middle and right, detail from the Miniature Frieze, Akrotiri (based on Doumas 1992a: 85, fig. 48 and restored by C. Palyvou).

adequately lit, that could accommodate various functions, especially weaving.[4] It had two points of access: one linked the room with the entrance of the building, hence its further function as a reception area, and the other linked it to the innermost private areas of the house. It acted, therefore, also as a kind of buffer zone between the semi-public and the private domain.

FORMAL ZONE

This innermost area was used for rituals and formal receptions. It included the rooms with the frescoes and the elaborate rooms often involving pier-and-opening partitions. They were typically far from the entrance and were reached in an indirect manner. Auxiliary staircases were related to these areas as well.

OUTDOOR ZONE

The roof was the main outdoor area of the house. Because we know practically nothing about the arrangement of space on the roof (the Archanes model is helpful in this respect [Fig. 147]),[5] we can only assume that various activities took place here, especially during the long periods of pleasant weather living. Sheltered verandas and balconies may also have existed in reality as depicted in art (Fig. 148).

Problems in Identifying Function

With all the remarkable information that Akrotiri has to offer, it is very frustrating that we cannot adequately define the areas corresponding to two most essential everyday functions: cooking/eating and sleeping. This situation persists, despite the fact that a considerable number of cooking pots, plates, cups, and even beds have survived.

One of the reasons for our inability to define the sleeping areas is the fact that the furniture of the house has been moved around to a large degree.

This was done during the rescue phase, when people were trying to save some of their belongings or to create provisional living areas outside the houses, for safety reasons. The only bed found within a house is the one in Delta 2, in a rather unexpected context. As for cooking, the only thing we can say at this point is that there is very little evidence for fire within the buildings (Alpha-East, Room Alpha 1, has the only certain hearth) and no clear indication of an installation that would resemble an oven or a cooking place, though Marinatos identified a

Fig. 149. Informal worship within the house may not leave an archaeological trace (Nelly's, Santorini 1925–1930, D. Tsitouras Collection).

few hearths.[6] Cooking, perhaps, took place in areas that have not survived—the roofs, for example—or in movable ovens, as those found in the houses. Two "kitchens" with ovens and chimneys were unearthed recently while expanding the excavation for the needs of the new shelter. They are well preserved and may give us valuable information when studied and published. They were in use during the last phase of repairs and rehabilitation and may prove to be provisional communal ovens.[7]

On the other hand, another everyday activity, and a very demanding one for that matter, has left unexpected evidence: lavatories were included in these houses. The only complete example to date, that of the West House, is not enough to draw general conclusions. For all we know, its place on the upper floor and the specific corner may have been dictated by technical requirements (i.e., the position and level of the public sewer outside the house).

These last notes lead to a series of questions that often recur in archaeology: can we read function from architecture alone? How much can we trust the finds within a room—or their absence—for assuming its function (Fig. 149)? How do we deal with the discrepancies between function as the needs of the client (the user) expressed in the building program prior to construction, and function as the numerous potentials of use that a built space can offer in its lifetime? And this refers not only to the "initial" building program but to all subsequent ones, for every single modification, adjustment, or addition that may occur to a building through time, any act of building, has a design concept (a building program) behind it. In this consumer-producer-consumer cycle, values and significance may diverge largely. Moreover, time is an important variable of function. Within the same room, and by the same people, different activities may take place in different times—times of the day or seasons of the year. The full range of activities of a lifetime may find shelter in one and the same room in certain cases (Fig. 150). A room of this type, if found empty, can tell almost nothing of the life it housed.

The Modern Movement that prevailed throughout most of the 20th century saw function as rational and scientific and assumed that form in architecture is "transparent to function," implying that a direct correspondence can exist between specific forms and specific functions. As Nesbitt points out, however, "this correspondence requires codes to create meaning, since meaning is not inherent in the forms, but is culturally constructed."[8]

Archaeological thought was greatly influenced by the "form follows function"[9] dogma underlying such ideas, especially when dealing with architecture. Form is what we believe we have in our archaeological records, and function is what we think it should be pointing toward. But form is not what we have—that, too, is deduced to a large extent—and form alone does not lead to function. Structure, on the other hand, has been underestimated as a key

Fig. 150. A typical single-space house in Rhodes that accommodates a variety of functions (Ελληνική Παραδοσιακή Αρχιτεκτονική 1984, 3: 197, fig. 62).

to understanding both form and function. In a way, the "form follows function" idea has retained in archaeology the "Romantic and thoroughly American" concept that Sullivan's axiom enclosed: that architectural forms should express human functions and needs, not structural laws.[10]

These last notes should act as a word of caution toward overinterpretation of the archaeological data.[11] Nevertheless, though we may be quite aware of the circumstances of this function-hunting, our need to envisage people using this architecture is imperative, and for the time being we have no alternatives to propose. Problems of this sort, after all, are not generated only by the archaeological motivation to define function—that is human behavior—through architecture. They are inherent in architecture itself, as is evident in the agonizing efforts of the theoreticians to understand how architecture is produced and what its meaning is.[12] They dwell in the divergence between architectural theory and practice. As with the other sciences that archaeology has been flirting with (ethnography, anthropology, etc.) architecture brings to archaeology its own innate problems of interpretation.

Chapter 8 Notes

1. See Michailidou 2001: 27–29, for extensive references to examples of second stories in the Aegean, the Mainland, and elsewhere, as early as the Neolithic (Hacilar, Choirokitia, Sesklo, and maybe Knossos).

2. In Hagia Eirene and Phylakopi interior doors are often placed in the middle of the wall, a trend related to Mycenaean architecture.

3. For a discussion on functions and types of rooms see also Michailidou 2001: 419–440.

4. Tzachili 1989.

5. Lebessi 1976: 12–43.

6. Room A1 (Marinatos 1968–1976, I: 28); Room G1 (III: 42); Room D7 (IV: 15).

7. I am grateful to Kiki Birtacha for this information. See Nikolakopoulou 2003: 564–565.

8. Nesbitt 1996: 45.

9. This powerful dogma of our time has been the fundamental axiom of the modern movement, expressed in the 20's by Sullivan. It was first published in the *Journal of the American Institute of Architects* 10–11, 1922–1923 (Kruft 1994: 355–363). The statement was inspired largely by the study of vernacular architecture and was believed to apply to primitive cultures in general. See also Palyvou 2003.

10. Kruft 1994: 357.

11. Palyvou 2003. See also Michailidou 2001: 419 on a theoretical approach regarding the use of space, and issues such as house vs. family and object vs. activity. She, too, concludes that most functions are not identified through architecture (377).

12. See, for example, Kruft 1994 and Nesbitt 1996.

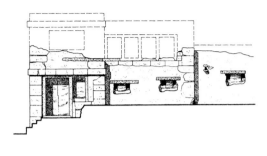

9

The Art of Building:
Materials and Techniques

Building with Stone, Wood, and Clay

The choice of materials and building techniques is determined to a large extent by natural factors, such as local resources and their availability and climatic conditions.[1] These, however, are not the only factors at play: at the other end of the environmental determinism, cultural factors—religious beliefs, exhibition of power or prestige, etc.—can be equally influential, though they are not always easy to detect.[2] The importation of Knossian gypsum at Akrotiri, for the pavement of a specific floor of the House of the Ladies (see below), is an interesting case of this sort.

The basic building materials used in the construction of the houses at Akrotiri, as in most pre-industrial communities for that matter, are those supplied by nature: mainly stone, wood, and clay. Yet, even when the materials are exactly the same, their treatment and the way they are applied (i.e., the building techniques) may vary significantly from place to place. The choice of the load-bearing elements basically defines the building technology in each case: the peculiarity of Minoan architecture is that stone goes hand in hand with wood, to such an effect as

to speak of *a half-timber building technology*. This technology was carried over, and in some cases further advanced, by the Mycenaeans.

Strangely enough, the lavish and elaborate use of wood in Minoan architecture was not properly evaluated in the beginning, although Evans himself emphasized its use as early as 1927 and pointed out in referring to the half timber technique that "the expectation of earthquakes may have influenced the style of building in Crete."[3] This misconception was due largely to the material absence of wood (very little of its substance has survived), but perhaps also because of a biased view of the Prehistoric world. The fact that timber technology is not a prevailing element of Greek and Roman architecture was perhaps subconsciously projected to the Aegean world as well.

Akrotiri provides ample evidence for the use of wood as a basic building material. Despite the fact that the wood itself survived only in very few instances, it has left remarkably clear imprints on the clay mortar or the volcanic ash surrounding it, because the disintegration of the material was slow

Fig. 151. The bed in room Delta 2 was recovered by pouring plaster of paris in the imprints left in the ash. The Spring Fresco is still hanging on the walls.

and gradual. These imprints provide detailed "negatives" that are used as casts: by pouring plaster of paris into these molds, numerous wooden items have been recovered—most remarkable are the highly sculptured pieces of furniture (Figs. 151, 152).

Though the quantity and quality of timber available at that time on Thera cannot be definitely asserted—tamarisk and olive wood have been

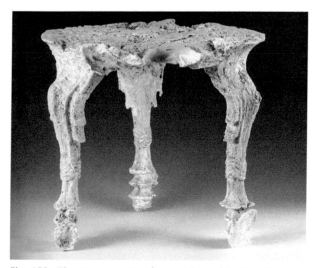

Fig. 152. The gypsum cast of a wooden table in high relief.

identified at the buildings of Thera and Therasia—it is almost certain that large quantities of high quality timber, such as cypress and other conifers, were imported.[4] The Therans could easily have undertaken this operation with their own boats. What is more, they did not have to travel far: nearby Crete, Naxos, Euboea, the Dodecanese, and Anatolia were potential suppliers of timber.[5]

One of the questions arising is why the Therans adopted a style of architecture that was so dependent on a material lacking in their homeland. Several possible answers exist:

a) Timber was a material familiar from ship-building.

b) The Therans knew that the incorporation of timber into a stone wall was an excellent earthquake-resistant measure.

c) The builders could afford to import wood, if necessary.

The experience in shipbuilding and its effect on house building must not be underestimated. P. Touliatos regards a boat, "as a structure containing human activity which is constantly in water (rain) and under dynamic loading (earthquakes)."[6] Homer, he continues, attributes the low level of the civilization of the Cyclops to "the fact that they ignored boat-building techniques, didn't travel and so didn't develop their culture" and concludes that "if they had them [boats] then their house structures would have been built in a more correct way."[7]

Most importantly, however, timber was an integral part of the architecture the Therans imported from Crete. Timber was plentiful there, and the Cretans had been building with it since the beginnings of the Bronze Age (Vasiliki, Malia Hypostyle Crypte), long before Akrotiri. The Therans, in other words, borrowed the technological tradition of a forested land. On Kea and Melos, on the other hand, timber was used much more sparingly—as was the ashlar technique as well. These Cycladic islands not only had less wood but also a lesser interest than Thera in adopting the architecture of Crete.

Stone was the most common building material on Thera, used for the construction of all the main walls, from the foundations to the roof, whether the building involved one, two, or even three stories. This is also the case on Kea and Melos because the rocky Cycladic islands offer ample stone for building purposes. In Crete, on the other hand, mudbrick walls for the upper parts of the buildings are also common, especially in areas were stone is sparse and clay prevails, as in the flat region of Malia.

The prevailing rocks in the vicinity of Akrotiri are ignimbrite, scoria, andesitic lavas, black and red lava, and tuff (Pls. 1B, 1C).[8] Some of the local stones are easy to dress, and this must have played an important role, because Theran architecture involves lavish use of ashlar masonry, not only for the facades of buildings but also for corner stones, window and door frames, and cornices, steps, and door bases.

The main stone used for the ordinary rubble walls is the red-brown to black scoria. Large resources are in the area, and they are easy to extract. Red-brown and black porous lava is also a common material for dressed blocks used as corner stones, frames, and steps. Pebbles of different volcanic rocks are mixed with clay and used for floors (small size) and as fillers in the rubble walls (large size). These pebbles were picked up from the nearby beach or the beds of the torrents.

The virgin rock under the site, extending over a large area, is ignimbrite. The bedrock is visible today along the modern ravine called Potamos to the east of the excavation, where traces of a possible prehistoric quarry have been identified (Fig. 153).[9] Ignimbrite is a pyroclastic material—dark brown with black obsidian-like lenses—that was easy to dress with bronze tools. It is a popular building material at Akrotiri, applied in many cases (walls, frames, and steps), though it is avoided where the requirements of durability are very high, as with the thresholds and the bases that carry heavy loads. Many ashlar walls are made of ignimbrite, and in some cases the stones are badly cracked and deteriorated (Fig. 154). This may be due to an inadequate knowledge of quarrying techniques, because it seems that the workers cut stone from the surface, where the rock is brittle, instead of discarding this layer and moving farther down.

Dacitic tuff has a whitish color, and it is sometimes slightly green. It is abundant near the modern village of Akrotiri, and most of the modern houses are actually founded upon tuff outcrops. The nameplace Petrokopia (meaning "Cutting the Stone") to the south of the village speaks of quarrying tuff. No indications of prehistoric quarrying exist in the area, however. Ashlar stones made of tuff are often incorporated into rubble walls at key positions—cornices, corner stones, and frames—or used as steps and bases of pier-and-door partitions. In only one case, in Xeste 4, tuff was used for the construction of all the ashlar facades of the building. This is surely the most lavish use of tuff known so far.

Dacitic lava was used sparingly. This rock provides the strength and durability necessary for special cases such as entrance thresholds and column

Fig. 153. Traces of quarrying in the Potamos region.

Fig. 154. Xeste 2, the blocks of ignimbrite are badly cracked.

bases, but it is a very hard stone that can only be treated with copious hammering (with stone hammers).

Dense volcanic rocks with a natural slab-like formation were ideal for pavements and, despite their weight, they were used extensively on the upper floors. The provenance of these light to dark gray slabs has been a puzzling question for some time, because they only appear near the modern harbor of Athenios, at the lower part of the cliffs of the caldera. Our new knowledge regarding the shape of the island and the existence of that part of the caldera during the Bronze Age has now answered this question, because it means that the outcrops of these slabs were accessible during Minoan times.

Non-volcanic rocks, such as phyllites and greenish chlorite schists from the region of Profitis Ilias, are occasionally used for sills and pavements. Limestone slabs from Gavrilos or Profitis Ilias were also used occasionally for pavements (in Sector Beta). Smaller pieces of limestone, in the form of gravel, were incorporated in the mosaic-like floors and in the thick lime mortars that derive from the roof of Xeste 3. Finally, the gypsum slabs found in the area of the House of the Ladies should be mentioned separately: they are dressed in a perfectly rectangular shape, and they were imported from Crete, straight from the Knossian quarries.[10]

Local clay has a light yellowish color. It is used as a bonding mortar for all the stone walls. It is also used for the construction of sun-dried mudbricks (and a few baked bricks as well). Mudbricks at Akrotiri were exclusively used for the construction of thin partitions inside the buildings whereas in Crete, mudbricks were also used for load-bearing walls. Various minor materials such as straw, hair, shells, and weeds supplement the list of building materials.

Metal, finally, is practically absent: a plate of lead in the cavity of a threshold and a couple of bronze pins (rather doubtful as to their use) is all that has been found. Bronze hinges of a very small size—obviously for boxes—have been found at the site. They look exactly like the door hinges we know today, but no samples are large enough to assume that they were used for building purposes. Bronze

Fig. 155. Bronze tools and stone hammers.

tools were, of course, quite common, but it seems that they were too precious to leave behind when the residents abandoned the town. Those that have been found among the ruins of the settlement—chisels, saws, knifes, daggers, razors, etc.—are similar to Cretan tools (Fig. 155).[11] They were used both by masons and carpenters, and ample evidence survives indicating that the two worked side by side. Stone tools are abundant at the site, as they were too heavy to carry away.[12]

Walls

Rubble walls are the most common type of wall construction at Akrotiri. The stones collected from the fields are relatively small; larger stones are used for the two faces of the wall and smaller ones for the core—along with pebbles, slabs, fragments of stone vessels, etc. (Fig. 156). Long stones set transverse within the wall are rare. Such stones would have been important in "locking" the two faces of the wall. The coherence of the wall, therefore, depends basically on the thick bonding material (clay mortar) and the timber reinforcement, as in Crete.

Our knowledge of the methods applied for the construction of the foundations derives mainly from the trenches dug for the supports for the protective shelter, as well as a few stratigraphic sections. The

evidence, though fragmentary, shows that a large part of the settlement is built on the rocky substructure of the area. The rock (ignimbrite) has been leveled in several cases in order to obtain an even bedding for the wall and to protect the foundations from sliding, which is especially dangerous in case of an earthquake.[13] Rubble walls, as a rule, are uniform throughout their height, with no distinction for the foundation. Some walls rest on remnants of earlier ones, especially in the central and northern parts of the site. A few rest on protrusions of the rock that have been cut in the shape of the wall (Delta 16).

The thickness of the walls varies considerably, adjusting to the load bearing requirements of each part of the building. Rubble walls at ground floor

Fig. 156. Rubble wall: large stones form the two faces, and smaller ones fill in the gaps.

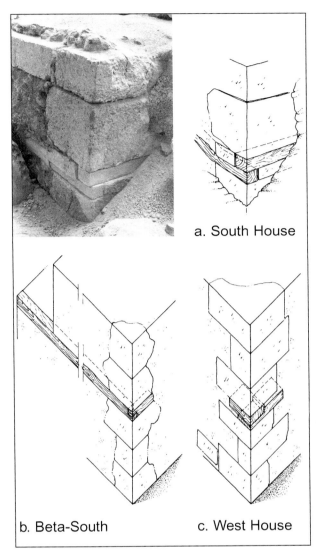

a. South House

b. Beta-South   c. West House

Fig. 157. Ashlar corner stones and timber reinforcement: a) South House, northwest corner; b) Beta-South, northwest corner; c) West House, northwest corner.

level are commonly 0.60 to 0.75 m thick (maximum 1.20 m). Their thickness diminishes on the upper floor, thus forming ledges approximately 0.20 m wide. The most slender walls are found in the area of the main staircase, especially the middle wall, which is hardly over 0.45 m thick. This is mainly due to the fact that the construction of the staircase is based on a timber load-baring frame, as we shall see below.

Dressed stones are incorporated into rubble walls in certain important places. A very common case is the corner stone (Fig. 157) applied in almost all of the buildings at Akrotiri (a rare exception is the northeast corner of the West House). This practice is a means to consolidate the corner of the edifice, and it is further achieved by tie beams set between every second or third stone. These beams are either restricted to the corner, or they constitute part of the timber reinforcement of the wall, running all around the building. The two beams join at the corner either by means of cuttings and mortises or by simply securing one on top of the other.

Corner stones have their edges rounded along the lower part of the building for protection from damage caused by the traffic through the narrow streets. Ashlar corner stones are not as common in Crete and constitute a typical morphological feature of Theran architecture. The aesthetic effect is further enhanced through color, because of a tendency to arrange the stones in alternating colors.

Ashlar frames around entrance doors and many windows are made of rather small dressed stones of varying sizes and colors (Pl. 1C). The construction procedure in the case of windows is as follows: the wall is built up to the height of the sill, where the bottom side of the ashlar frame is inserted. Thus, the position and dimension of the window has been determined. Then, the wooden frame is fixed on the wall, and the building is continued around it, incorporating the dressed stones of the other three sides of the frame. This procedure is evident by the fact that the lintel consists of small stones resting on the wooden frame. In some cases, the horizontal beams of the window frame may extend beyond the opening, interrupting the ashlar frame at the corners.

Elsewhere, a corner stone is cut in an L-shape in order to fit the existing timber frame. These details clearly show that the ashlar stones were placed after the full construction of the timber frame.

The dressed stones are level with the clay coating of the wall. This means that when they were put in place, they projected from the rest of the wall so they could function as a guide during the final plastering of the surface. The timber frame of the window, on the other hand, is recessed a few centimeters. The function of the stone frame is to create a neat border and protect the wood from the humidity of the wall.

Projecting ashlar cornices usually indicate the level of an upper floor but are otherwise independent of the actual structure of the floor (Figs. 118, 158). They appear either locally, in relation to the entrance (e.g., Delta 19), or as a continuous zone embracing the building. The north facade of Xeste 2 is a good example of the latter: cornices appear on both stories. Toward the east end of the facade, they change levels, dropping down approximately 0.30 m and indicating most probably a similar change of level inside the building. A thick layer of lime plaster seals the joint between the projecting stones and the wall. The function of the projecting cornices may be to slow down the rainwater as it runs on the surface of the wall, as well as to protect the timber beams underneath. Their morphological value, however, is also important (see Chap. 10).

Thin slabs are commonly inserted in the rubble walls in the form of rows projecting from the wall surface approximately 0.20 m. Such slabs are applied either to shelter a window opening (Fig. 159) or to form a cornice at the upper end of the building along one or more facades. In the case of the windows (Alpha-East, Room A2; Gamma-South, Room G4; House of the Anchor) the slabs are often simply wedged right above the wooden lintel. Cornices at roof level are not directly related to timber elements, but their function is the same, to protect the building from rain. This simple means of protection is very common in vernacular Aegean architecture.

The lower parts of certain interior walls are covered with slabs standing upright within a timber framework. Examples of such dadoes are in Xeste 3, Room 3 and an unidentified space southeast of the House of the Ladies. The first case is the best known (Fig. 73): slabs of the same volcanic stone as those used for floor pavements cover the three sides of the lustral basin. They are 0.80 m high and of varying widths, and they were held in place by wooden posts between the slabs. Similar slabs cover the east wall of the adjacent Room 3, at a height of

Fig. 158. Xeste 4, north wall.

0.40 m, like the height of the sill of the window. The purpose of the dadoes may have been to protect the lower zone of the wall and/or to create a more elaborate finish. The technique is well known in Crete, but it is common in other Aegean sites as well. In Crete, dadoes are sometimes made of high quality stones, such as alabaster, a technique imitated through wall paintings both in Crete and Akrotiri (West House, Room 5; Pl. 3A).

Ashlar walls are one of the most impressive architectural features at Akrotiri. They are commonly applied around the entrance of a building, but also for the construction of one or two facades. Few ashlar walls exist inside the buildings, all in small surfaces: the lustral basin of Xeste 3 and the House of the Ladies, Room 1, are such instances, both of special functional significance. Xeste 4 is the only known building with all its exterior walls made of ashlar. It is also the only building where greenish tuff has been used instead of the dark colored ignimbrite. In Xeste 4, one has the opportunity to see that the foundations are made of large boulders protruding from the wall.[14]

Aegean Bronze Age ashlar walls (including the Mycenaean world as well) have certain features in common. Most characteristic is the elaboration of

Fig. 159. Slabs inserted in the wall as drip-stones is a popular technique from vernacular architecture as well.

the individual block: the only surface of the stone that is fully dressed is the face (Fig. 160). A fine chisel was used for the final dressing, and judging from the traces on the stone, this proceeded from the mid-top edge downward, in a radiant manner. All the other sides of the block were roughly dressed with a much broader chisel. The final shape of the stone is roughly reminiscent of a pyramid. All sides but the face, in other words, are slanted so as to facilitate the building. The upper and lower surfaces are only slightly slanted, but the other two sides form acute angles. A difference exists between the ignimbrite blocks of most ashlar walls and the tuff blocks of Xeste 4; the former have a more rounded backside, while the latter are clearly angular in shape. This distinction may point to an early and a late dressing technique, as has been suggested for similar instances in Minoan architecture.[15]

The ashlar blocks occupy approximately two thirds of the width of the wall, while the inner side is filled in with rubble. While building the wall, the clay mortar of the bonding material is kept at a distance of at least 0.20 m from the facade, so that the interstices can be sealed at the end with lime plaster

Fig. 160. Xeste 3, showing the chiseling on the faces of the blocks that has left clear marks. The small gap in the wall is unidentified.

Fig. 161. Ashlar block of ignimbrite with a lime plaster border.

Fig. 162. Xeste 4, the interstices of the ashlar wall were sealed with lime plaster, and a line was drawn over with the fingertip.

to protect the wall from humidity. Sometimes the lime plaster overflows in all directions in order to fill the anomalies and chipped edges of the blocks (Figs. 161, 162). In these cases, the interstices are drawn on the plaster with the aid of a sharp tool or the finger. In walls made of tuff, the plaster stays white, while in those made of ignimbrite it is painted dark red to match the color of the stone. It is obvious that the intention is to make the irregular plaster as discrete as possible.

An interesting practice concerning the ashlar walls is the calculation of the height of the rows. In Xeste 4, the well preserved north facade shows clearly that the height diminishes from bottom to top. Actually, it remains the same for two adjacent rows and changes only every third row. It is clear that elaborate calculations were involved in building an ashlar wall (see Chap. 10). This rule is applied, more or less, to all ashlar structures, be it corner stones, or the small-scale ashlar walls inside Xeste 3. Room 1 of the same building has two exterior ashlar walls that seem to deviate from this rule (Fig. 63). On closer inspection, however, it becomes evident that the walls, made of small-size ashlar blocks, are a later addition. The blocks used in this rather provisional structure ("Room 1" may be an open air space) derive most probably from the upper rows of an earlier ashlar wall that was destroyed (this would explain the small size of the stones).

The length of the ashlar blocks varies. No specific rule exists as to this dimension except that

Fig. 163. Ashlar walls in art and Xeste 4. Unidentified gaps are seen in both cases. To the left, an ivory plaque from the Royal Road area at Knossos (Hood 1971: pl. 23) and to the right, a sketch of the northeast corner of Xeste 4 (C. Palyvou).

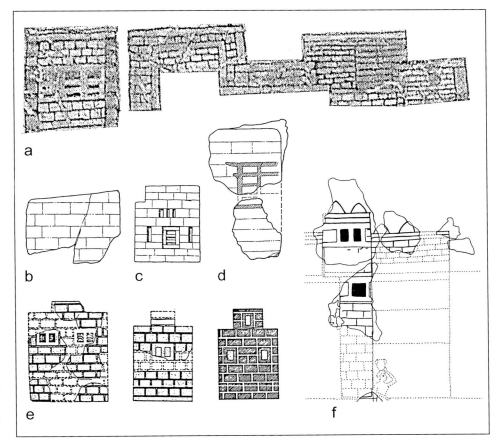

Fig. 164. Ashlar facades in art: a) Miniature Frieze from Akrotiri (Doumas 1992a: 71, fig. 36); b) marble plaque from Pseira (Lebessi 1976: pl. 16); c) plaque from Royal Road, Knossos (Hood 1971: 75, pl. 23); d) Tylissos (Evans 1921–1935, III: fig. 49); e) Town Mosaic from Knossos (Evans 1921–1935, I: fig. 226); f) Miniature Frieze, from Kea (Morgan 1990: 254, fig. 1).

vertical interstices are never aligned. Certain gaps in the walls of Xeste 4 cannot be understood at present (Figs. 160, 163). They do not seem to be loopholes, as Marinatos suggested, because they are most probably blocked halfway. A plaque depicting the ashlar facade of a building from Knossos shows exactly the same gaps, but it is not illuminating as to their function.

A conspicuous feature of all ashlar walls is the absence of timber reinforcement. This is understandable, because it would have interrupted the coherence of the wall.[16] Similar conventions are present in depictions of ashlar walls in Bronze Age art, for example in the Town Mosaic (Fig. 164).

Square mortises cut on the upper surface of dressed stones are attested in several instances, all of which are related to timber elements (a practice that is common in Crete). Their usual dimensions are 0.04 by 0.04 m and 0.07 m deep. They are intended to secure a wooden beam upon the stone with the aid of wooden pegs (never to fasten stone to stone, as in Greek/Roman architecture) (Fig. 165).

Mortises are quite common in the area of the entrance, where ashlar blocks, orthostates, and corner stones relate to timber elements. The entrance is one of the most vulnerable areas of the house because it consists of large openings set right next to a corner. For this reason, the timber frame of the door-and-window opening and the timber reinforcement of the wall in this area are carefully anchored to the wall with the aid of tenons and mortises.

Fig. 165. Xeste 3, Room 2. Wooden beams were fastened on the block with pegs inserted in the mortises.

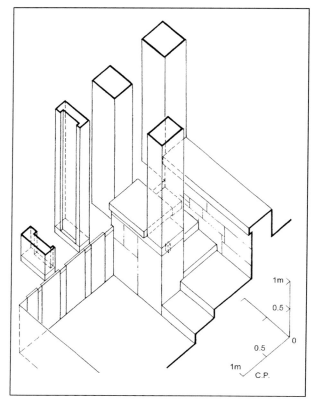

Fig. 166. Xeste 3, the lustral basin. Isometric drawing.

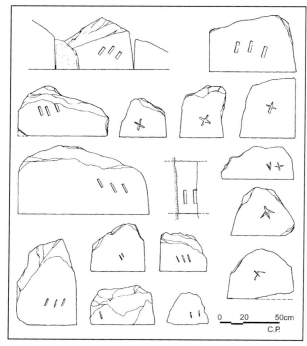

Fig. 167. Mason's marks from Akrotiri.

Fig. 168. Mason's marks on a block in situ, Xeste 4.

Another typical instance where mortises are used is the staircase. The two ends of the middle wall are bordered by dressed stones with a typical trapezoidal form. A pair of mortises is usually cut on the upper face of each stone in order to fasten the timber frame of the staircase (Fig. 109). This detail is so characteristic, and exclusive, that one can predict the existence of a staircase by the presence of such a stone alone: the entrance of the house abutting to the southeast corner of the House of the Ladies has such a stone in the debris, as does Room Delta 17.

Mortises are also found on ashlar frames of windows (Alpha-West) and other instances, such as the pier in the lustral basin of Xeste 3 (Fig. 166) and the pier in Room Delta 1a. A related issue is the special treatment of the outer zone on the upper face of the dressed stones in order to provide an even bedding for the wooden beam. It is a kind of *anathyrosis* and is more common on the sills of large windows.

Mason's marks are well known from Crete, and they are so scarce elsewhere that it came as a big surprise to count at least 80 at Akrotiri; there are surely many more (Figs. 167, 168). They derive mainly, though not exclusively, from Xeste 4 and they are of only a few types, the most common being the three oblique parallel lines and the X sign.

One trident comes from Xeste 3 (Fig. 169). Whatever the meaning of these marks—and there are various theories in this respect[17]—their abundance at Akrotiri speaks of a direct and privileged connection between Thera and Crete, as discussed in Chapter 12.[18]

The south facade of Xeste 3 is roughly hammered (Fig. 65). The wall includes a systematic timber frame of pairs of horizontal and vertical posts. The outer face of the wall is made of rather small stones, approximately 0.30 m thick and 0.20 m high, set in a relatively orderly manner. The face has been roughly leveled with a stone hammer, while smaller stones and pebbles fill in the gaps. This wall was plastered with a very strong lime mortar that was

Fig. 169. Mason's mark in the form of a trident from Xeste 3.

Fig. 170. Mudbrick walls from Alpha-East. Two mudbricks are still standing on edge.

painted in a pink-orange color, perhaps to match the color of the ignimbrite used in the other walls of the building.

Mudbrick walls are used in two ways for wall construction: either with the bricks placed flat (main walls) or set upright (light partitions). Both ways are quite common in Crete, but only the latter is attested at Akrotiri, probably because stone was abundant. Such walls are found inside the buildings as thin partitions, approximately 0.20 m thick (Fig. 170).

Mudbricks are hand made, as is attested by their rounded edges, and judging from their varying sizes, they were made at the work-site, to accommodate the needs of each individual building. The bonding material and the coating of the wall is the same clay. These walls rely on a dense timber frame to carry the loads, and it is clear that the mudbricks are inserted after the construction of the frame. The distance between two posts is usually 0.45 to 0.65 m, corresponding to the width of a mudbrick.

These walls have two great advantages. Because they are thin, they occupy little space, so they are a perfect means for dividing a room into smaller compartments. Also, they are relatively light and are therefore ideal for upper stories where they can be inserted anywhere, with no need for a stone wall underneath. A sturdy floor beam suffices to carry the frame. If the main floor beams have a different direction from what is desired, then an extra transverse beam is added underneath the mudbrick wall. This is well attested at the West House, Room 4 (lavatory) and is yet more proof of the high degree of prediction—i.e., design—involved in the building operation.

The two most common types of wall construction, rubble and mudbrick, are systematically reinforced with timber. Wood has perished, leaving

little if any trace behind, and this circumstance has led to an underestimation of its contribution in building technology. The unique state of preservation at Akrotiri, however, offers ample evidence for this contribution in the form of numerous imprints of wooden elements on the mud mortar or the fine volcanic ash encasing the wood. The meticulous study of this information has led to a re-assessment of the participation of wood in Aegean Bronze Age architecture and to a better understanding of the building technology of the time.

The most common type of timber reinforcement in rubble walls is the incorporation of branches, often in their natural crooked form, within the wall structure (Fig. 171). These beams form a horizontal grid consisting of two longitudinal elements, one on each face of the wall, joined at intervals by transverse beams (sometimes set obliquely, depending perhaps on the length of the available piece of wood). Such grids are incorporated within the thickness of the wall at various levels, starting usually

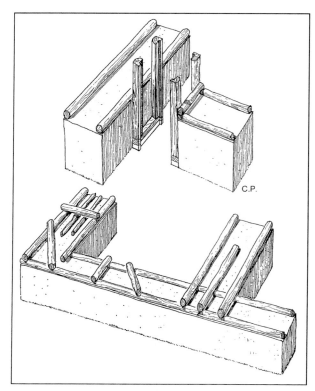

Fig. 171. Horizontal timber reinforcement showing typical structural details.

Fig. 172. Sector Delta, western exterior wall. The holes correspond to the timber reinforcement of the wall. The three holes belong to the transverse wall behind, separating rooms Delta 1 and 1a.

about 0.20 m from the ground floor. Typically two more grids are at each story, one at the level of the window sill and the other at the level of the lintel. No clear evidence of a timber frame exists at ceiling level, as one might expect, with the exception of Xeste 2. This grid is not always perfect, and the beams do not necessarily cover the entire length of a wall. Gaps may be present, or overlapping of two adjacent beams, depending on the availability of timber and the tendency to save time and effort.

In key positions such as the corners of the buildings, the joint of two walls in the form of a T, and the points where the timber reinforcement of the wall meets the wooden case of an opening, extra reinforcements ensure an even greater consolidation of the edifice. The most common practice is to extend all beams so that they overlap or fit each other with special cuttings (in corners especially). In a T-shape junction, an extra beam may be placed in the middle of the transverse wall (Delta 1 and 1a; Fig. 172). Tie-beams, finally, are joined with almost every window and door frame.

In at least two instances, diagonal bonds of the timber reinforcement are attested at the corners of the buildings (House of the Anchor, northwest corner of Delta 1a). They are of special importance, because they ensure the collaboration between the

two walls at the corner in case of lateral movement, typical in earthquakes. Prehistoric architecture, on the whole, is based on rectilinear forms; therefore, the presence of diagonal elements is striking in itself. In these two extraordinary cases, we are probably witnessing an experiment made by an intelligent individual who was at the verge of breaking through tradition; in other words, an "invention" was being born. From "invention" to "innovation" (that is to a generally accepted practice), however, it is a large step.[19] This specific builder understood the significance of diagonal bonding as a way to ensure the rigidity of the corner and to absorb the tensile force enacted in the event of a seismic load. The fact that the two examples belong to two different buildings—yet facing each other—may indicate either that the same mason was involved in both cases or that one copied from the other, probably during construction, because this detail is not visible after the building is completed. One more case of diagonal bonding is attested in a floor construction (see below). Interestingly enough, it belongs to the West House, in the same area as the two previous examples. The fact that Akrotiri was rebuilt after a mass *seismic destruction* may have facilitated the proliferation of this structural detail.

In a limited number of walls, a system of timber reinforcement involving vertical posts is attested. The best example is the north facade of Xeste 2 (Figs. 132, 133). The wall stands to a height of about 7 m, and the timber reinforcement extends in an orderly formation, starting from ground level and covering all three stories of the building. The timber grid stops at the west end of the facade, where the wall changes from rubble to ashlar. The beams we see in cement today probably have counterparts at the other side of the wall, and at the points where horizontal and vertical beams cross, transverse beams must join the two faces of the wall. This timber grid has several interesting details: the vertical posts, 0.17–0.20 m thick, are placed at a distance of 2.15–2.30 m, and one of them corresponds to an indentation of the facade, not more than 0.20 m deep. The vertical beam, in other words, coincides with the corner of this shallow indentation. The horizontal beams are placed at the level of the sill of a window (0.88 m and 0.95 m from ground level and upper floor level respectively) and the ceiling (2.00–2.10 m).

Another case is the south wall of Xeste 3 (Figs. 65, 173). Here, the wall is partly preserved to the height of two stories, and one can study the timber reinforcement in detail. It consists of pairs of upright posts, placed at intervals of approximately 1.50 m, starting from the southeast corner of the building. Each pair rests on a transverse beam set within the thickness of the wall. Dressed stones are incorporated in the wall to receive this transverse beam, at a height of 1 m above the ground. This way the wood is protected from the humidity of the ground (in Xeste 2 the wooden posts seem to continue below the floor of the street). The upper ends of the vertical posts were also bonded with transverse beams at the level of the ceiling of the first floor. The grid is completed by pairs of horizontal beams running along the south wall. Due to the peculiar structure of this wall—made of stones roughly hammered—the exterior horizontal beams are not visible, because they run behind the front stones (approximately 0.30 m).

The timber frames were not self sustainable, because they depended on the surrounding masonry for their rigidity. In other words, this is a composite load bearing structure, where wood and masonry work together to provide structural efficiency. Timber elements add elasticity to the masonry and ensure the cooperation of the various parts of the structure. Thanks to the high tensile strength of wood, these tie-beams can undergo significant deformations by bending. At Akrotiri, some remarkable examples of extreme cases of wall deformation did not result in collapse (e.g., West House, south wall of Room 4; Fig. 53). It is more than apparent that an important concern of the architects of these houses was to achieve the best possible earthquake-resistant result.

One timber wall is a unique structure involving an intricate construction made of load bearing wooden posts. It is found in Xeste 3, next to the entrance lobby, and it functions as a support for the staircase (see Xeste 3; Fig. 70). A number of strong vertical posts have been placed one next to the other to form a wall carrying the upper part of the staircase. These posts are semi-circular in section (a trunk cut in half), and they rest on slabs embedded in the floor. The small gaps between them have been filled with mud plaster, creating the impression of an ordinary wall separating the entrance lobby from the adjoining Room 4. This is one of the most daring and extreme structures not only at Akrotiri, but in the Aegean world in general.

Fig. 173. Xeste 3, south wall and isometric drawing of the timber frame.

Floors

Fig. 174. Floor pavement of large orthogonal slabs (Xeste 3, Room 3, ground floor).

The floors at ground floor level are usually made of packed soil mixed with gravel and other materials of small dimensions (charcoal, chips of stone and obsidian, sherds, shells, fragments of lime plaster, bones, etc). Tiny black pebbles are often scattered over the clay plaster while it is still damp, to reinforce the final surface. Such clay floors are about 0.10 m thick, and they are applied over a substructure of packed stones and soil, in many cases using the artificial layer of the *seismic destruction*. A common practice in many ground floors made of packed soil is the incorporation of slabs, in the form of a paved zone along the wall, probably for placing large vessels.

Almost all the entrance lobbies are paved with volcanic slabs. This kind of pavement is otherwise rare for ground floors in ordinary houses. Xeste 3, on the other hand—an atypical house—has several paved floors at ground level: Room 3 has a beautiful pavement made of rectangular slabs arranged in an orderly layout (Fig. 174); the lustral basin next to it has a similarly paved floor made of very large slabs (Fig. 73); and so does the small Room 12. The interstices are sealed with lime plaster over a layer of pebbles (lustral basin), and they are sometimes painted red. The schist-like slabs have a natural flat surface, with no signs of further treatment. The edges are roughly chipped with a stone hammer, and the resulting shape is approximately rectangular. Some of them are remarkably large (Xeste 3, lustral basin: 1.00 by 1.70 m).

The House of the Ladies (most probably also an atypical house) has a room on the upper floor (Room 7) paved with beautiful gypsum slabs cut in perfectly rectangular shapes. The ground floor of the same room is paved with marble slabs with large pebbles in between (Fig. 115). A few marble slabs are also placed casually on the floor next to the auxiliary staircase of Sector Beta.

In Alpha-East, Room A2, there is a rare case of a floor made of smashed shells of *porfyra* (Fig. 175). It is quite damaged, and it is most probable that this

Fig. 175. Floor made of smashed shells and lime plaster (Alpha-East, Room 2).

was the sub-layer, and the final surface was the usual mixture of clay and pebbles (this is detected at the edges of the floor where it is better preserved). It would be difficult to use a floor of this kind with no covering, because the angular fragments of the shells are easily detached.

Upper Floors

The construction of an upper floor is fairly typical: the load-bearing elements were horizontal beams, usually round in section (i.e., roughly dressed trunks) and sometimes rectangular, spanning the shorter side of the room. The beams were placed at a distance of about 0.60 m from each other. They were at least 0.12 m thick, and they were encased in the walls approximately 0.30 m deep (Room Delta 16, for example, had beams 0.15–0.18 m round, set every 0.50 m). Branches and twigs (0.05–0.07 m thick and 0.50–0.70 m long) were laid across the main beams, and when the gaps among the branches were too large, they were covered with flat stones (Fig. 176). A layer of clay mortar followed, about 0.20 m thick, and on top of that came the final finish of the floor, which varied according to the use of the room.

In small spaces, such as the middle landing of the staircase in Xeste 3, Room 5, the main beams were set closely next to each other. The clay mortar was laid over the beams with no intermediate layer of twigs or stones. Such floors are detected by the undulating upper edge of the wall plaster at the point where it meets the ceiling (Fig. 177).

The builders sometimes took extra precautions in the construction of the floors. Two techniques are of special interest. In some cases, vertical posts were fixed at the corners of the rooms, outside the walls. They were probably intended to carry horizontal beams that would run under the main beams of the floor at the point where they met the wall. Such an arrangement would relieve the walls from the extremely heavy loads of the floor and would also hold the upper floor in case of wall collapse.

The other technique is the reinforcement of the corner of a room with a diagonal beam (West House, Room 5; Beta-South, Room B1). The West House example can be studied in detail (Fig. 178). The diagonal beam is 0.12 m in section and 2.10 m long. Another one, perpendicular to the former, is fixed in the corner of the walls. The two extra beams run under the main beams of the floor and ensure the

Fig. 177. Wall plaster with an undulating upper edge that corresponds to the ceiling beams (Xeste 3, Room 5).

Fig. 176. The structure of the floor: the main beams are spanned with twigs (their imprints are visible) followed by a thick layer of clay and the pavement slabs (Beta-South, room Beta 1).

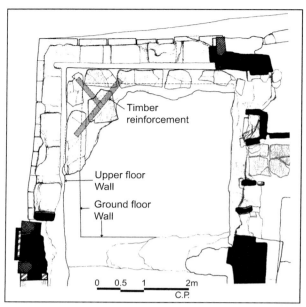

Fig. 178. West House, Room 5: plan of the upper floor. The corner is reinforced with diagonal beams.

rigidity of the corner in case of lateral movement, typically caused by earthquakes. They have the same logic as the diagonal bonding of the timber reinforcement of the walls, mentioned above. The fact that they are both unique instances shows that these were experiments of individual builders and not part of the building tradition of the time.

Two more cases of extra reinforcement of the floor have been attested: one is the large transverse beam added above the main beams of the floor in order to hold a mudbrick wall (West House, between Rooms 4 and 4a), and the other is an extra large beam inserted under a built bench with pithoi situated on the upper floor (Xeste 3, Rooms 10 and 12; West House, Room 6). In the case of Xeste 3, Room 10 (Fig. 74), it is interesting to observe that the extra beam held the heavy bench above but, as a result, it transferred all the loads to the surrounding walls, which were found badly deformed. These details prove the advanced structural conception of the time and the anticipation of the forms and the loads of the upper floor.

The auxiliary rooms of the upper stories have floor surfaces made of packed soil, similar to those on the ground floor. A few rooms of special importance, on the other hand, have their floors covered with lime plaster. This is not very common, because such floors are very fragile (Beta-South,

Room B1a; West House, Room 4; Xeste 4). In these cases, the walls are also covered with the same lime plaster, and the joint between the wall and the floor has been rounded. An incised line sometimes marks the transition between the two planes.

Many upper floors are paved. The slabs are of volcanic origin and are usually fairly rectangular in shape (Fig. 179). They are approximately 0.05 m thick and extremely heavy. It seems that the arrangement of the slabs started from the periphery of the room, in the form of a peripheral zone that was gradually filled with larger slabs moving toward the center. Pavements are also made of more or less uniform rectangular slabs, such as in Beta-South, Room B2, and the House of the Ladies, Room 7. The latter is quite unique. It is made of well cut slabs of gypsum from the Knossian quarries. The gaps between the slabs are filled with pebbles and clay and are sometimes sealed with lime plaster painted

Fig. 179. The paved upper floor has subsided (Delta-West, Room 9.1).

Fig. 180. Terracotta slab.

red. The red paint usually spreads over the slabs as well, in a manner reminiscent of the overflow of plaster in the interstices of the ashlar walls.

Other forms of floors include clay mixed with pebbles and stone chips of black and red lava (Delta-North, Rooms 18 and 19), smashed shells in lime plaster (Xeste 3, Room 3), a beautiful mosaic made of colorful stone chips and well polished lime plaster (Delta-North, Room 8), and possibly terracotta slabs (Fig. 180). Two such slabs (0.34 x 0.47 x 0.42 m) were found perfectly preserved in the area of Beta-South. Certain landings of staircases had a wooden floor (West House, Xeste 3).

Ceilings

Ceilings were either left with no treatment (usually on the ground floor) or were covered with reeds upon which a strong lime plaster was attached. Within the debris of the buildings, many fragments of lime plaster bearing a detailed imprint of the ceiling construction have been detected.

Even the string holding the reeds together can be seen (Figs. 181–183). Ceilings at Akrotiri can be as high as 3 m (Table 1). It is only logical to assume that in fully painted rooms the ceilings may have also been painted.

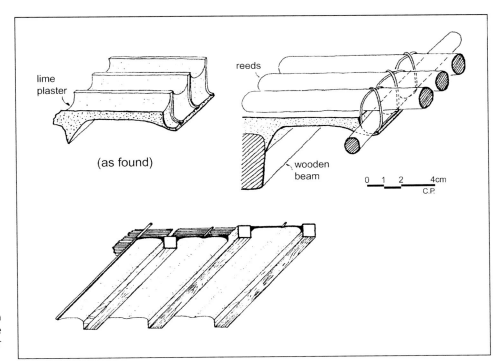

Fig. 181. The construction of a ceiling with lime plaster applied on a layer of reeds (Xeste 3).

Fig. 182. Fragments of lime plaster with imprints of reeds from ceilings (Xeste 3).

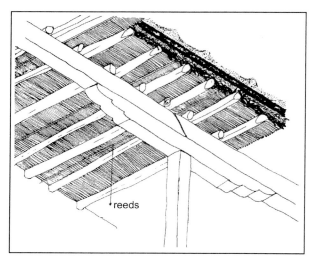

Fig. 183. Ceilings made of branches and reeds in Aegean vernacular architecture from the island of Skyros (Ελληνική Παραδοσιακή Αρχιτεκτονική 1983, 1: 204, fig. 42).

Ground Floor Rooms	Height	Upper Floor Rooms	Height
Beta-South 1	1.90 m	Beta-South (wall painting)	2.70 m
Beta-South 2	2.00 m	West House 4a	1.95/2.15m
Delta-East 2	2.50 m	House of the Ladies (wall painting)	2.10 m
West House 1/2	2.30 m	House of the Ladies (wall painting)	2.24 m
West House 4	3.00 m	House of the Ladies (wall painting)	2.70 m
		Xeste 3.3a (wall painting)	2.50 m
		Xeste 3.9 (wall painting)	2.05 m

Table 1. Indicative room heights.

Roofs

Fig. 184. A large piece of the roof with at least 8 different layers of clay (West House).

The roofs in Aegean houses were flat and accessible, and they played a very important role in the life of the house. Information concerning the roof structure, however, is extremely rare, even at Akrotiri. It is usually indirect, in the form of fragments of the roof found in the debris. These fragments show a structure similar to the typical floor: above the beams and the branches is a layer about 0.20 m thick of packed soil,s and on top are several layers of well packed fine clay, each 0.01–0.025 m thick (Fig. 184).[20] The different colors indicate a different type of clay for each layer.

To the south of Xeste 4, in an area that has been only partially excavated, the roof of a single story room is showing (Fig. 185). It has been preserved intact: its upper surface is made of fine, well compacted clay, and it has a strong inclination (25%) toward one of the corners of the roof, where a terracotta spout conducts rainwater to the street. This part of the roof was obviously not meant for use, due to the inclination, and the parapet of the wall is only 0.10–0.20 m high. One can see the projecting cornice made of slabs embedded in the exterior walls. This cornice turns at a right angle inside the gap of the parapet where the spout is fixed. It is a very interesting example—unique so far—of the construction of the roof.

In the area of Xeste 3, a large number of plaster fragments have been found in the upper levels of the destruction layer, obviously deriving from the roof (Fig. 186). They are of lime mortar, about 0.04 m thick, and are mixed with pebbles and stone chips. These plasters are very strong, and they formed an impermeable layer.

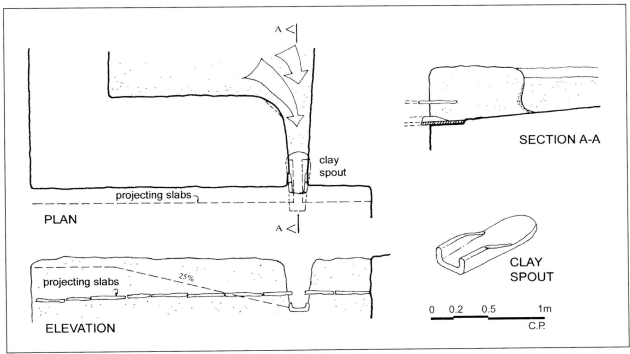

Fig. 185. Details of a well preserved roof with a clay spout and projecting slabs from an unexcavated building next to the South House.

Fig. 186. A thick and hard fragment of lime plaster in the form of "mosaic" from the roof of Xeste 3. The upper surface was polished, whereas the underside is rough and shows traces of its contact with clay mortar.

Columns and Piers

Columns are a common feature of the palatial architecture of Minoan Crete, but they are scarce in town houses. Similarly, at Akrotiri, they appear only as central supports of large, almost square rooms (Figs. 187–189). Our knowledge of these vertical supports derives mainly from the dressed stone bases that have been found within the settlement. Two of them were found in situ, in ground floor rooms, while the others come from rooms of the upper stories.

Stone bases are made of hard lava and are dressed with stone tools (tiny cavities made by the picking of the hammer are discernible on their surface). A typical base consists of two parts: the lower part is broader and roughly dressed, and it is embedded in the floor to function as a foundation; the upper part

HOUSE	COLUMN BASE			ROOM	
	PLAN	ELEVATION	DIMENSIONS	PLAN	DIMENSIONS
Alpha-East	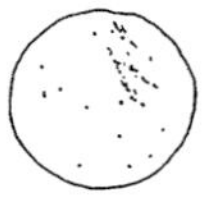	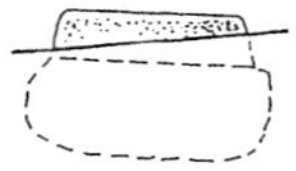	a: 0.39m b: ? c: —	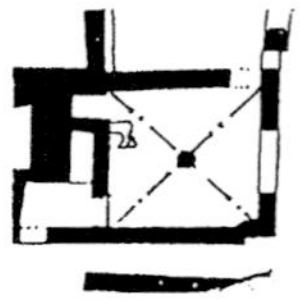	4.90X5.10m (25m²)
Alpha-East (1st floor)	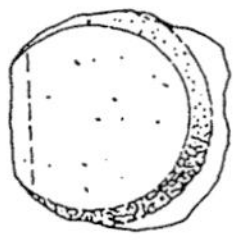	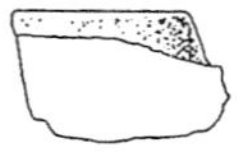	a: 0.40m b: 0.12/0.16m c: —		4.90X5.10m (25m²)
Beta-South (1st floor)	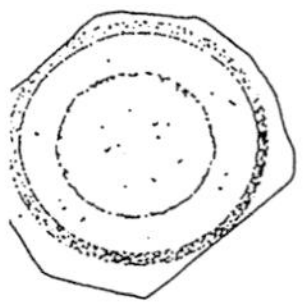	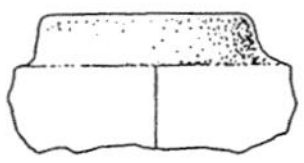	a: 0.49m b: 0.12/0.20m c: 0.34m	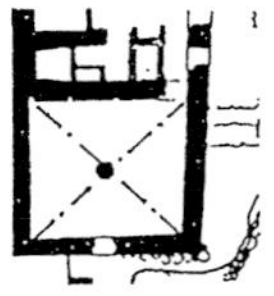	4.90X5.35m (26.20m²)
Delta-South (1st floor)	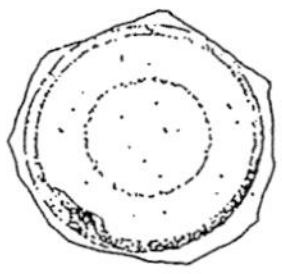	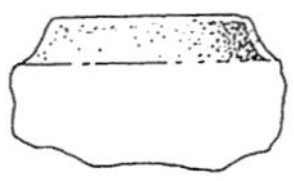	a: 0.45m b: 0.09/0.24m c: 0.26m	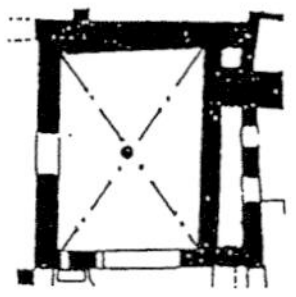	4.90X7.10m (34.80m²)
West House (1st floor)	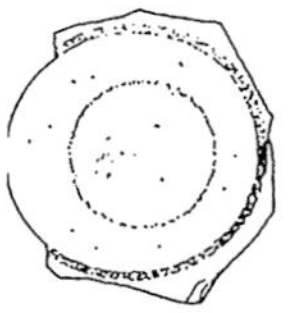		a: 0.51m b: 0.18/0.20m c: 0.30m	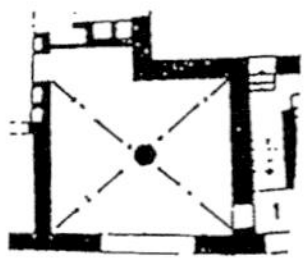	5.55X6.10m (33.90m²)
Xeste 4 (1st floor)	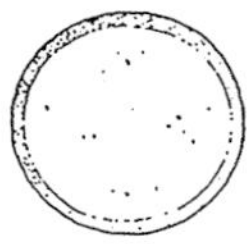	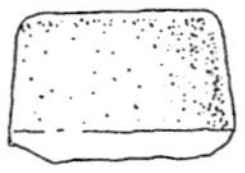	a: 0.43m b: 0.26/0.05m c: —		4.80X5.45m (26.10m²)

Fig. 187. Columns from Akrotiri: a) diameter (upper); b) height (upper/lower); c) shaft diameter.

Fig. 188. Column bases: a) Beta-South, Room 2; b) Gamma-South, Room 7 (?); c) Alpha-East, Room 1, ground floor and upper floor; d) West House, Room 3.

Fig. 189. Alpha-East, Room 1. The base of the column and its foundation.

is finely dressed and projects above the floor about 0.10 m. The lower part has a polygonal shape, and it shows how the mason was gradually approaching the round shape of the base. The upper part is semi-conical with all its edges smoothly rounded. A variation of this model is present on a base with almost no foundation from Xeste 4. The upper part is 0.26 m high, while the lower part has been reduced to only a few centimeters. Perhaps this base belongs to a room with a high ceiling. If its wooden column shaft could not exceed a certain height, it was the stone base that had to be taller.

Faint brownish traces of the wooden column are detected on the upper surface of three bases. These indicate that the columns had a smaller diameter than the stone bases (base to shaft diameters: Beta 2, 0.49 m/0.34 m; Delta 16, 0.45 m/0.26 m; West House, 0.51 m/0.30 m). Because there is no special treatment of the surface of the base to receive the shaft, it simply rested on the stone base, and it was stabilized by its weight and friction.[21] The upper part of the column is only known through its depictions in art. Wooden capitals were probably used, and one or two ceiling beams would rest on top.

Because the room with a central column has a large window on the exterior wall, it is assumed

that the main beams of the ceiling run parallel to this wall in order to avoid transferring too much load to the wooden lintel of the window. This is also attested by the beam holes on the walls of Delta 16. The dimensions of these rooms are close to an ideal square, 5 by 5 m. One side is actually 4.90 m while the other is 5.10–5.45 m, with the exception of Delta 16 which is 7.10 m long (the longest at Akrotiri). The typical span of 4.90 m seems to have been well calculated, as is evident in Beta-South, Room B2, where the new wall that was added in order to create the room with a central column was built exactly 4.90 m away from the existing wall.[22]

Only one pier has been identified at Akrotiri. It is found in Room Delta 1a; this is a large room, 3.50 by 7 m (Fig. 103). The pier consists of two superimposed large blocks of ignimbrite, each 0.55 by 0.70 m and 0.67 m high, and they rest on a foundation made of a slightly larger block (0.75 by 0.75 m) projecting a few centimeters from the floor. Two mortises (0.04 by 0.04 m and 0.05 m deep) are cut on the upper surface of the pier where a pair of ceiling beams were fastened with the aid of wooden pegs. This pier is situated on the long axis of the room, close to one of its narrow sides. Another pier was probably at the east, in a symmetrical position. Only the foundation block exists, embedded in the floor. The upper part of this support—if there was one—has to be assumed to be wood. It is not clear if a second pier was actually needed to support the ceiling, from the static point of view. Perhaps the initial idea was to have two supports, but the builders realized that one was enough. A pier on a low base is also reported from Therasia;[23] it, too, consists of two large blocks, 0.50 by 0.50 m. It is very close to a wall, which means that its position may have been dictated by the form and the structural needs of an upper floor.

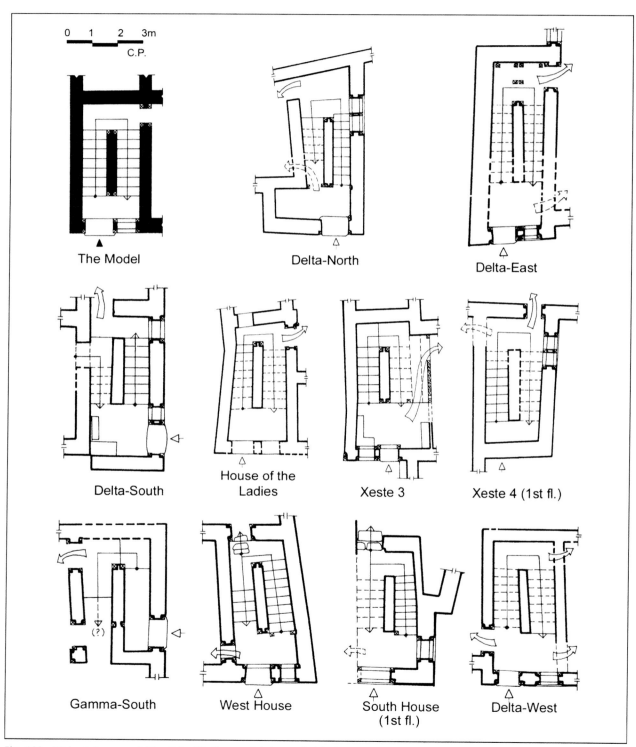

Fig. 190. Main staircases of Akrotiri with the model shown in black.

Staircases

Staircases are essential to Aegean Bronze Age architecture, not only because upper floors are very common, but also because roofs are a vital part of the house, so even one story houses need a staircase. Another reason why staircases are important is the extraordinary circulatory patterns attested almost everywhere on the site, involving an intricate vertical intercommunication. The numerous staircases at Akrotiri, most of them well preserved, can be divided into two categories, main staircases and auxiliary staircases.

Main staircases can be readily understood when walking around the site because they are the standard treatment for the entrance system in almost all the houses (Fig. 190). The staircase is approached through the front door. It is Π-shaped, with two parallel flights and two landings, one of which is broader and is also the entrance lobby. This form is so typical that while excavating such a staircase from above, one may anticipate the position of the entrance by the size of the landings (see, for example, Xestes 4 and 5). These staircases are spacious and well designed. They usually have steps of

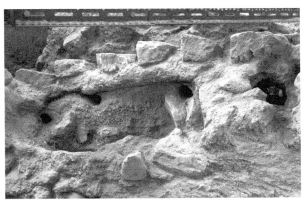

Fig. 192. West House, main staircase: view from the east.

dressed stones, and they are sometimes decorated (Xeste 3 and 4; the steps in both cases are of ignimbrite plastered and painted red). Their key position in the circulatory pattern of the house justifies their definition as main staircases.

Although the form of such a staircase has an innate symmetrical character, the actual result is usually trapezoidal in plan, and the two flights are not of the same width. The reasons for these deviations are both formal and functional. The first flight up, leading to the main quarters of the house, is more important and therefore broader, while the longer of the two narrow sides in the trapezoidal plan corresponds to the entrance because it must accommodate both a door and a window.

The remarkable construction of these staircases, leading two and three stories up, depends largely on wood (Fig. 191–193). The loads of the superimposed flights of steps, as well as those of the middle landings, are transferred to the ground through a robust timber frame encased in the walls. Timber is the prime element in this system, which explains the slender stone walls of the staircase. This frame consists of two pairs of posts fastened on dressed stones with dowels and mortises at the two ends of the middle wall. Horizontal beams tie the posts together on both sides of the middle wall. Pairs of beams also tie the ends of the middle wall with the corresponding side walls. A strong transverse horizontal beam is at the point where the two flights meet. It joins with the timber frame at the end of the middle wall, and its two ends are fixed in the walls encasing the staircase. Thus, a very sturdy frame is produced, embracing all the elements of the staircase. The stone walls, slender though they may be, help to give rigidity to the system.

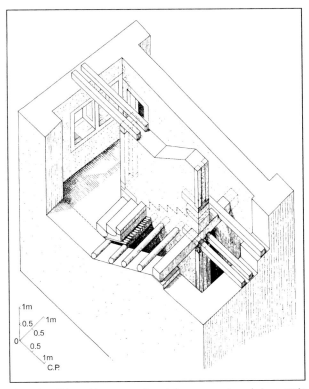

Fig. 191. West House, main staircase: restored isometric drawing showing the method of construction.

Fig. 193. A model of the West House: view of the main staircase.

The construction of the individual flight, on the other hand, is not as sophisticated. It follows the logic of the floor, but in an inclined position. No diagonal beams are present. The loads are carried by horizontal beams fixed transversely into the walls at intervals. Above the beams are twigs and branches, followed by a thick layer of compact soil. The dressed stone steps are put in position last, as a kind of veneer similar to the slabs of a floor pavement. The stone steps are distinctly triangular in section: the oblique surface is the bottom side that is placed on the inclined layer of compact soil. These steps are, of course, independent of the wall, and they are built quite often of two or more stones each. This construction explains the picture of a destroyed staircase as we see it today: the beams are the first to be detached from the side walls, thus leaving the walls intact, while the stone steps and their substructure have subsided (Fig. 194).

The topmost flight of the staircase and the corresponding landing are sometimes constructed entirely out of wood, as in the case of the West House, presumably to relieve the structure of extra weight. The lower flight of steps, on the other hand, is built on a compact substructure of soil and stones. The timber structure starts from the second flight onward, and the space underneath functions as a sotto scala.

Fig. 194. Delta-North, the first flight of the main staircase.

Designing a staircase presupposes a great deal of calculation (see Chap. 10). Depending on the function of the staircase (main or auxiliary), the dimensions vary, but they remain within a certain range. The builders obviously learned from experience that approximately 16 steps suffice to cover the height of a typical story. The first flight from the entrance is, thus, constructed with a standard number of 8 steps, and the remaining 8 steps are given to the other flight. This way the builders can control the construction of a staircase that may have to meet different needs (and heights) from one story to the other. The second flight will have enough space underneath it for storage or for an access to other parts of the house. In most cases an extra step on the middle landing, at the continuation of the middle wall, adds more space beneath the second flight.

It is interesting to note that all staircases are well lit. This is a basic requirement for staircases, even today, because their use can be precarious, especially when one is carrying bulky objects. Windows are in all landings, including the first one, which is the entrance. Most certainly these strict lighting regulations produced the unique light well of the House of the Ladies, because one of the sides abuts to a staircase. Quite often one can detect the presence of a staircase from the outside of an unexcavated building by the intermediate level of a window: if it is placed half way up the height of a floor, it can only correspond to the middle landing of a staircase (see Xeste 3, north facade; Xeste 4, south facade; and Xeste 5, west facade).

The entrance/staircase system is another of the many practices borrowed from Crete. The fact that it is applied in almost all the houses—typical and atypical—implies that it was generally accepted as the most effective way to deal with the requirements of access, both circulatory and structural. The symmetry of the system offered a great deal of flexibility to adjust to varying levels, especially in the case where the debris of the *seismic destruction* accumulated outside the house had created a much higher entrance level than that of the ground floor rooms inside.

Auxiliary staircases exist in most buildings (Fig. 195). They are situated in the interior, and they are usually smaller and of an inferior construction. They vary greatly, depending on the needs and available space. Their structure, on the other hand, is simple: they are narrow and steep, and they are built on a compact substructure (they usually join only two levels). The height of the steps varies greatly, ranging from 0.15 to 0.30 m.

This simplified construction offers great flexibility in the design of the staircase. Some extravagant forms are thus produced, as in Delta-North where four flights are involved (Fig. 110), and in the West House (Fig. 196), where the staircase is narrow and steep. The latter has very interesting details showing the effort of the builders to gain space: the very narrow steps are oblique in profile, so that the foot may find more space to step as one climbs up (on our way down we use only the heel in such steep staircases). Moreover, the surface of the steps is slanted so as to gain height. Another interesting case is the auxiliary staircase of Beta-South (Fig. 197): in their effort to accommodate the steps in a narrow space the builders have almost invented the spiral staircase!

The presence of one or more secondary staircases is obviously imperative for the function of the house. This is why they are sometimes accommodated

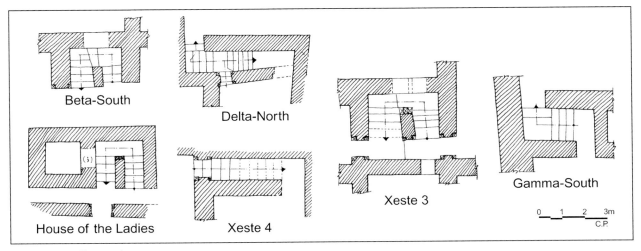

Fig. 195. Auxiliary staircases.

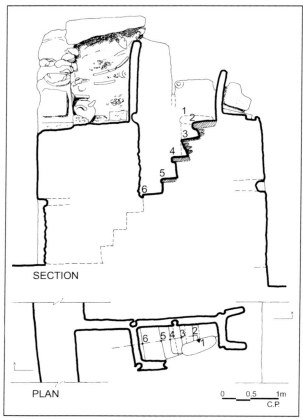

Fig. 196. West House, Room 7. The auxiliary staircase, plan and section.

Fig. 197. Beta-South, auxiliary staircase.

within what was thought to be a closet. In the more elaborate buildings, certain auxiliary staircases are large and follow the structural model of the main staircases (Xeste 3, Xeste 4, House of the Ladies). Because they accommodate more than two stories, they had to follow the structural model of the main staircase.

The existence of many staircases in a building is a common feature in Aegean Bronze Age architecture (see Kea, House A, for example[24]). In Crete, the distinction between main staircases, situated near or at the entrance, and auxiliary ones can be applied only to McEnroe's Types 2 and 3 buildings and not Type 1.[25] Yet, from the technical point of view, Theran staircases are much closer to those found in the elaborate Type 1 buildings.

within the most unlikely and inconvenient narrow spaces, as in the case of the West House where an auxiliary staircase was found, quite unexpectedly,

Doors

The large number of openings in a building, both doors and windows, is one of the most impressive elements of Aegean Bronze Age architecture. From the structural point of view discussed in this chapter, we should emphasize the fact that this is quite a bold style because the proportion and distribution of mass versus void is a fundamental issue regarding the stability of a building.

Doors and windows follow very much the same structural logic. They consist of a box-like timber frame well anchored within the wall. All frames are load-bearing elements; their dimensions, profiles, and joins are, therefore, carefully selected. For further security, the frames are sometimes stabilized

on ashlar stones with mortises and dowels. In addition, the timber cases of all doors and windows are carefully joined with the timber reinforcement of the walls. The overall goal is to ensure stability for the building by the systematic collaboration of all its wooden elements.

Entrance doors are focal points. A casual tour around the site shows the standardized and elaborate form of the entrances at Akrotiri (Fig. 198). The door is normally situated at a corner of the building with a window by its side. It has a huge threshold and is bordered by ashlar masonry. From the structural point of view, the presence of two adjacent openings of such large dimensions so close to

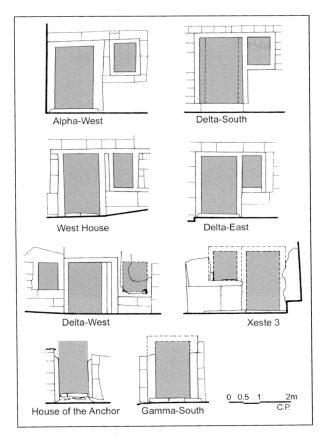

Fig. 198. Entrance doors.

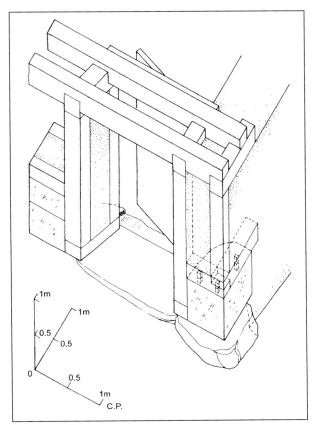

Fig. 199. Restored isometric drawing of the entrance door (Delta-North).

a corner of the building is a threat to its stability. The builders were obviously aware of this, because they took extra measures to stabilize and protect this part of the edifice (Fig. 199).

The two openings have a common timber frame: the dimensions of the beams (usually around 0.18 m), their careful joint with tenons and mortises, and the systematic encasement of the timber structure into the surrounding masonry are all well considered. A huge monolithic threshold, usually made of andesitic lava, functions as the foundation for a heavy timber frame for the door, and the two pairs of posts rest at its two ends. The stone projects slightly above street level, but it has a large invisible part underneath. There are, of course, deviations from this model (Fig. 200): the House of the Anchor has a marble threshold found badly broken (the price of the deviation from the rule), and the Porter's Lodge has a rather small threshold made of ignimbrite, but it is bordered by separate dressed stones that bear the loads of the timber frame. Most thresholds project outward a few centimeters and have their edges rounded, obviously for protection. Delta-South has a very pronounced

rounded projection: the threshold is high in this case (0.35 m), and perhaps the rounded shape facilitates its use.

The treatment of the upper face of the threshold clearly shows the form of the door: it consisted of a single wooden door leaf hanging from a wooden pole. This is attested by the curvilinear incisions on the stone threshold (Fig. 201) and also by the imprint of the door itself in one instance (Delta 19; Fig. 202). The two narrow ends of the threshold are slightly recessed to hold the transverse beams of the wooden frame (Gamma-South and Delta-North). The inner long edge of the threshold is also a few millimeters lower, forming a distinct zone 0.11–0.18 m wide. One end of this zone has a cavity (0.05–0.06 m in diameter and 0.02–0.04 m deep) where the wooden pole was fixed. The length of this zone—approximately 1 m—indicates the width of the door leaf (Table 2).

The wooden case consists of two pairs of posts resting on transverse beams and held together with a similar transverse beam on top (Fig. 199). These two frames define the jambs of the door and are spanned with two or more large horizontal beams

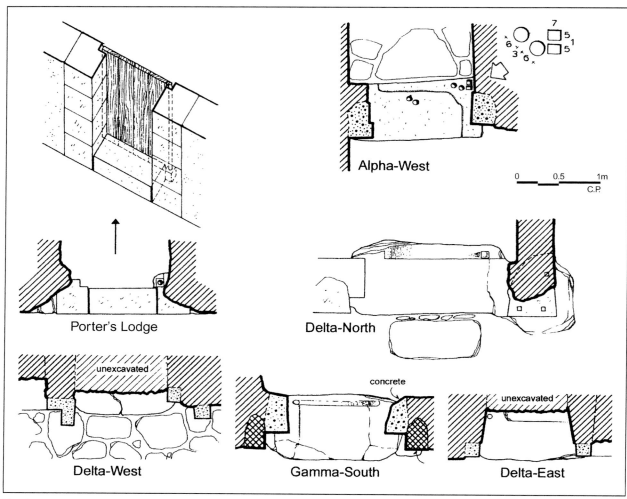

Fig. 200. Entrance doors: thresholds.

that form the lintel. The jambs are filled in at the end with clay mortar. We should emphasize once more that this frame, along with the similar frame of the adjacent window, bears the exceedingly heavy loads of two or three stories above. For this reason, the builders have gone to great efforts to stabilize the whole system: short horizontal beams are tied to the posts at sill level and fixed on the ashlar corner stones of the wall with mortises and dowels. They keep the posts in place, preventing them from buckling, and absorb lateral forces in case of a seismic event. In two instances, the West House (Figs. 203, 204) and Xeste 3 (Fig. 205), an interesting detail ensures further stability. Beside the threshold, inside the building, was a strong horizontal beam partly embedded in the floor (today one can see the groove and a row of thin slabs at the bottom). The pole of

the door obviously rotated in a cavity carved in the wood, but the main structural value of this beam lies in its function as a wedge, keeping the vertical posts of the door in position. This detail may have been more common than one can judge from the archaeological data, and it could explain the structure of the door in cases (especially in Crete) where no signs exist on the stone threshold.

In Delta-East, the door leaf left an excellent imprint on the volcanic ash (Fig. 202): it shows that it was made of two planks, held together with transverse horizontal beams at the bottom and the top. There must have been a way to lock the door, like the bolt identified at Knossos,[26] but it has left no traces. Only in Alpha-West is a double cavity in the center of the threshold that was probably for this purpose (Fig. 200).

Fig. 201. Delta-North, the threshold of the entrance door from the inside showing the recess for the door leaf and the pivot hole to the left.

Fig. 202. Delta-East: the imprints of the wooden planks of the door leaf are discernible.

Fig. 203. West House, the entrance.

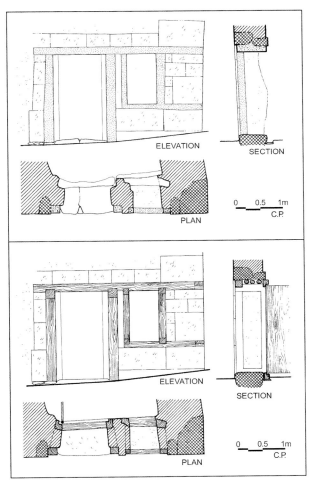

Fig. 204. West House: the entrance as found and restored.

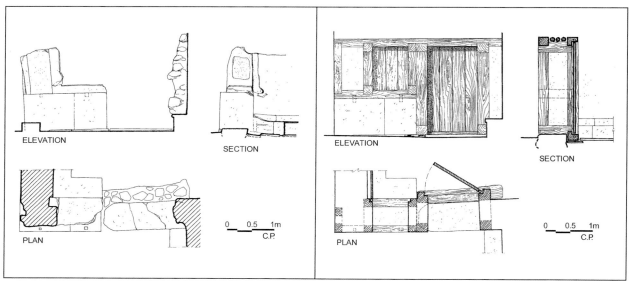

Fig. 205. Xeste 3: the entrance as found and restored. A beam holding the wooden pivot of the door was sunk in the floor right next to the threshold.

House	Width-a	Width-b	Height
Alpha-West	1.15	0.90 m	1.90 m
Gamma-South	1.20	1.00 m	1.90 m
Delta-South	1.25	?	2.15 m (*)
Delta-West	0.95	?	?
Delta-North	1.40	1.00 m	?
Delta-East	1.15	1.10 m	2.00 m
West House	1.15	1.00 m	1.95 m
Xeste 3	1.20	1.00 m	1.70 m (*)
H. Anchor	1.20	0.95 m	?
Porter's Lodge	0.80	0.80 m	?

Table 2. Width of doors. Width-a: width of the opening in the masonry. Width-b: width of the door leaf, actual width of the door. (*) indicaytes uncertain dimension due to restoration or state of preservation.

INTERIOR DOORS

Within the ruins of the settlement at least 120 doors can be seen today, half of them at ground floor level and the other half on the upper 2 floors (Fig. 206; Tables 3 and 4). Many of these doors were restored by pouring cement in the place of the missing timber frame, while others are only partly visible. The construction is typical and follows, more or less, the box-like model described above, though the doors at ground floor level are often simpler (they may have only one post on each jamb).

The two frames forming the jambs of the door rest on stone bases (Fig. 207). They are either roughly shaped or well dressed bases with a projecting upper part about 0.10 m high, and an invisible lower part (larger and roughly dressed) embedded in the floor, a technique reminiscent of the treatment of the column bases. The form of the projecting part of the stone base can be:

a) a simple rectangle

b) rectangular with one antenna (L-shaped)

c) rectangular with two antennae (double L-shaped)

d) No bases at all; the posts rest on flat stones embedded in the floor

The shape of the antenna of the stone base is followed in the wooden post as well. The post is often cut from half a trunk, and a rabbet is carved, in order to serve as a stopper for the wooden double leaf, very much like modern door frames. The plaster covering the walls and jambs seems to cover the timber frame as well, leaving only the antennae visible, unless the timber frame is made of beams that are rectangular in section, in which case all the post is visible.

The timber frame consists of the same posts and beams described above for the entrance door, though in reduced dimensions. An interesting detail attested in door frames of the upper floors is the horizontal beam embedded in the threshold, with its two ends fixed at the antennae of the stone bases (Xeste 3, Rooms 4–7 [Fig. 208]; West House, Rooms 5–7). This technique is similar to what was described above for certain entrance doors, and the purpose is the same: the beam at the threshold bears the pivots for the door leaves and, at the same time, it provides an excellent means for stabilizing the door opening,

Fig. 206. The imprints of the timber frame of an interior door (Delta 1a) and a door jamb cast in gypsum (Xeste 3).

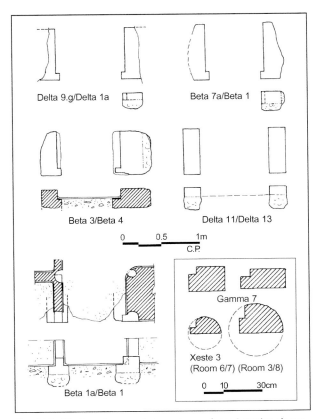

Fig. 207. Various forms of stone bases from interior doors.

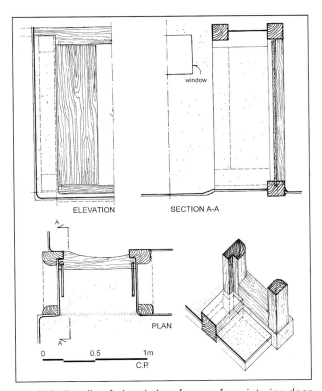

Fig. 208. Details of the timber frame of an interior door (Xeste 3, Room 7, first floor).

especially in case of the lateral forces of an earthquake. The threshold of the door is seldom paved, as is common in Crete. Usually, it follows the same veneer as the floor of the room that is entered from it.

The jambs of the door are covered with clay mortar and sometimes lime plaster (Fig. 209). In rare instances, the latter is painted (see, for example the West House: The Priestess). The lintel is bridged with smaller beams or slabs. Few traces survive of the door leaves. They all seem to be double and made of planks 0.02–0.025 m thick.[27] A number of stone pivots have been found, all of which derive from destruction layers from the upper floors (Fig. 210).The dimensions of the doors vary, as can be seen in Tables 3 and 4. Those at ground floor level tend to be shorter (1.40–1.60 m). Doors, as a rule, are placed at the corner of a room.

The construction of interior doors is very much the same in Crete. The characteristic dressed stone bases with one or two antennae seem to appear in Crete at the very beginning of the Neopalatial period, more or less simultaneously with their appearance at Thera. The door on the first step of the main staircase may be a Theran peculiarity (the first step is wider and functions as a threshold; Fig. 211). It is explained, however, by the fact that in Thera the staircase is identical with the entrance, and so there is no other way of controlling access to the upper stories. In Crete, the staircase sometimes is a separate room next to the entrance lobby, and so can be shut off with a proper door.

Fig. 209. Beta-North, Room Beta 1a. The lime plaster of the wall entirely covered the wooden door jamb.

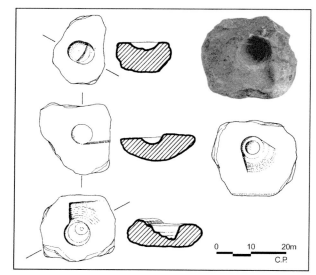

Fig. 210. Pivot stones found at Akrotiri.

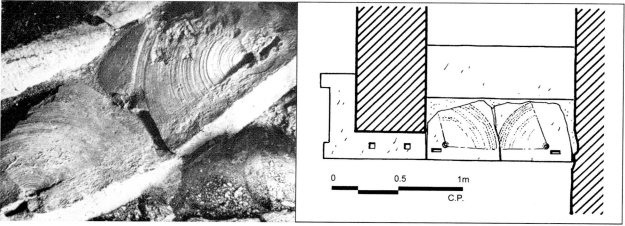

Fig. 211. Traces of a double door fixed on the first step of the staircase (Delta-North, main staircase).

House: Rooms	Width	Height	Bases
West House: 5/7	0.70 m	1.40 m	
West House: 1/3a	0.70 m	1.50 m	
West House: 3a/3b	0.80 m	1.45 m	
West House: 3b/4	0.68 m	1.35 m	
West House: 4/5	0.78 m	?	
Alpha-West: 2/1	0.75 m	1.52 m	+
Alpha-West: 2/3	0.60 m	1.60 m	
Beta-South: 1/7a	0.75 m	1.50 m	
Beta-South: 1		1.45 m	
Beta-South: 2		1.45 m	
Gamma-South: 1/2	0.97 m	1.60 m	
Delta-West: 1/1a	?	1.66 m	+
H. of Ladies: 6/south	0.68 m	1.60 m	+
H. of Ladies: 7/corridor	0.86 m	1.50 m	+

Table 3. Ground floor door dimensions.

House: Rooms	Width	Height	Bases
Alpha-West: 2/3			
Beta-South: 1/1a	0.80 m	>1.40 m	+
Beta-South: 1/7a	0.75 m	?	+
Beta-South: 2/3	0.67 m	?	+
Gamma-South: 4a/7	0.84 m	1.48 m	+
Gamma-South: 6/7	0.90 m	1.60 m	+
Delta-North: 8/8a	0.84 m	>1.76 m	?
Delta-West: 9.1/21	0.78 m	1.73 m(*)	
Delta-South: 12/13	0.83 m	1.70 m	+
West House: 1/3	0.85 m	1.70 m	+
West House: 3/5	0.75 m	>1.40 m	+
West House: 5/7	0.75 m	>1.50 m	+
West House: 7/6	0.70 m	>1.45 m	+
Xeste 3: 8/9	0.67 m	1.62 m	+
Xeste 3: 7/4	0.75 m	1.50 m	+

Table 4. First floor door dimensions. (*) means uncertain dimensions due to restoration.

PIER-AND-DOOR PARTITIONS

One of the most ingenious structural elements of the Minoan architects is the pier-and-opening partition (Fig. 212). It appears in the form of a series of doors, windows, cupboards, or a combination of the three, and it consists of a timber load bearing frame that usually substitutes for a wall. The Greek word *polythyron* has been used to describe this structure, but it also refers to a room with pier-and-door partitions.[28] Because there is some confusion in the exact meaning of the terms, it is better to give our own definition here: the term "pier-and-door/window partition" is reserved for the structure itself, implying a single row of openings, and the term "polythyron hall" will be used to refer to a room or a set of rooms using such elements.

The most sophisticated application of pier-and-door partitions is seen in Xeste 3 (Figs. 66, 70, 71); they are numerous (11 or 12) and are distributed on all three levels of the building. Those on the ground floor are very well preserved, and from the impressions left by the wooden elements, one can study their construction in great detail. What is striking is the amount of wood that has been used for these structures and, what is more, their almost exclusive role as load bearing elements for the eastern part of the building. In one case (between ground floor Rooms 4 and 7) the construction was clear: an opening was above one of the three doors (Fig. 213). The lintel formed a wooden shelf with several vases resting on it. This opening functioned as a window for the adjacent Room 7, situated in the heart of the building. It had no exterior walls and no other way of acquiring light and air.

From the technical point of view, little can be added; the wooden frame is the same as the ones described above, with all the elements well fixed to each other. Stone bases with antennae are the rule: they are either T-shaped or double-T-shaped (Figs. 214, 215). In Xeste 3, Room 3, the pier-and-door partition joining the central room with the lustral basin had bases made of wood (Fig. 166). This is a unique instance, and it probably has to do with the fact that this pier-and-door partition is situated at the edge of the sunken area of the lustral basin.

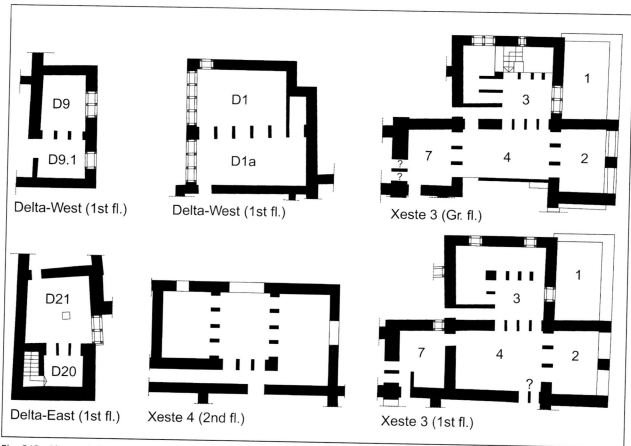

Fig. 212. Pier-and-door partitions.

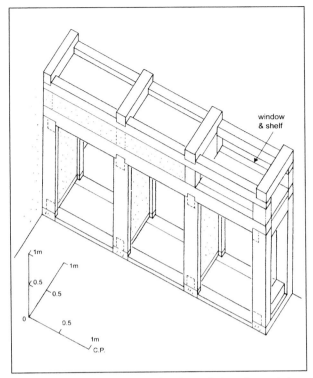

Fig. 213. Xeste 3: isometric drawing of the pier-and-door partition of the ground floor connecting Rooms 4 and 7.

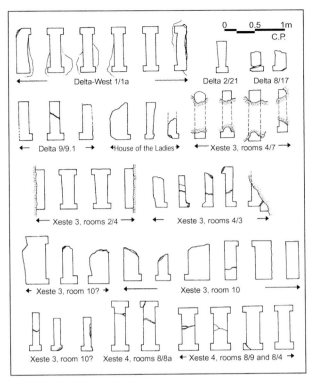

Fig. 214. Dressed stone bases of pier-and-door partitions.

While excavating the area by the pier-and-door partition joining Rooms 4 and 3 in Xeste 3, the excavators came upon an unexpected find: a large mass of pumice subsided, revealing the imprint of one of the leafs that had been detached from the door. It was 0.26 m wide and made of a well-dressed plank.

The shear number of pier-and-opening partitions found at Akrotiri is striking and can only be compared with those of the palaces and villas of Crete. The lavish use of timber technology at Akrotiri demonstrates vividly the high level of technical knowledge that the builders of the time possessed. Such bold and inventive applications, as those attested in Xeste 3 for example, can only result from a long experience and thorough acquaintance with wood as a building material, an experience dating back to the Middle Bronze Age in Crete.

Fig. 215. A pier-and-door base. The roughly dressed part was the foundation embedded in the floor.

Windows

More than 85 windows are visible today at Akrotiri—half of them on the upper floors. They attest to the unique state of preservation of the buildings (Fig. 216). They also speak of the high living standards and the sophisticated building technology of the time. Though at first glance they seem to vary greatly, on closer examination they belong to four distinct groups in terms of size, shape, and position in the building. The method of construction, on the other hand, is uniform for all

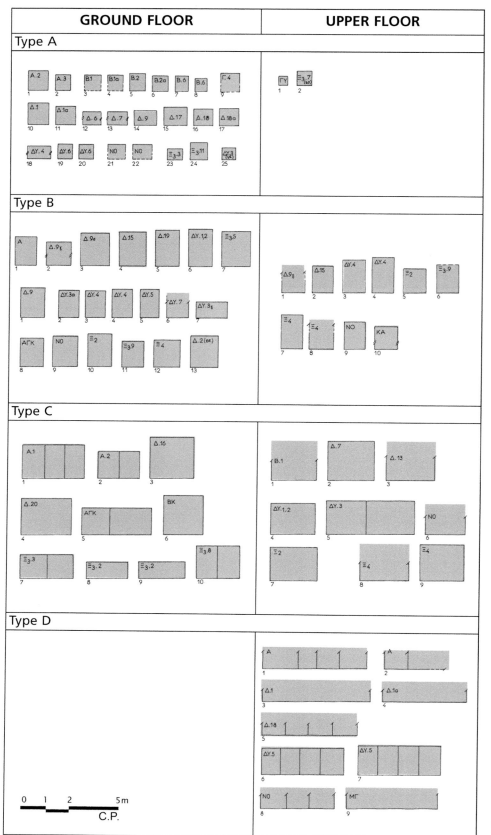

Fig. 216. The four types of windows at Akrotiri.

Fig. 217. Type A windows: Xeste 3, Room 9, ground floor.

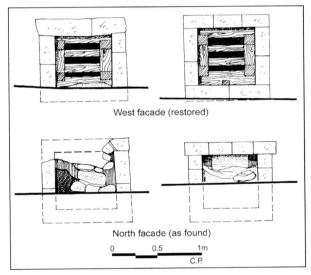

West facade (restored)

North facade (as found)

0   0.5   1m
C.P.

Fig. 218. Type A windows: Beta-South.

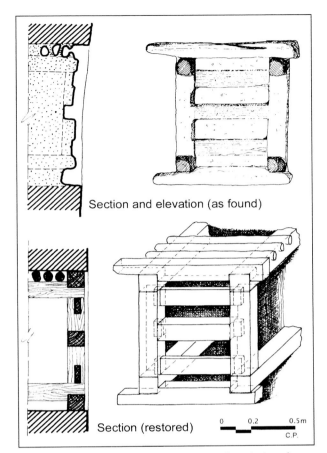

Section and elevation (as found)

Section (restored)   0   0.2   0.5m
C.P.

Fig. 219. Details from the construction of a window frame with lattice (West House, Room 5, ground floor).

windows and follows the same logic as that of the doors described above. All windows are placed in the center of the wall.

TYPE A: SMALL WINDOWS

Small windows are rectangular in shape with an average surface area of 0.50 sq m (Figs. 217–218). They occur almost exclusively at ground floor level, with few exceptions. The wooden frame is often simplified and, as a rule, no ashlar stones border the opening. The ground floor windows of Beta-South are exceptional in that they are framed with dressed stones. Moreover, it is clear that they existed before the *seismic destruction*, because they are partly covered with the debris accumulated in the streets after this disaster. Type A windows are placed high up on the wall, often right under the ceiling. The few interior windows are of this type (West House,

Rooms 3b–5, ground floor; Xeste 3, Rooms 7–8, first floor). These windows are minimal, in the sense that they function basically as air conduits and provide just enough light to move around. The rooms they serve are usually meant for storage.

TYPE B: VERTICAL WINDOWS

Vertical windows are rectangular in shape, with the longest dimension being the vertical one, and they have an average surface area of 1 sq m (Fig. 219). They occur at all levels and appear typically by the entrance door. Those of the upper floor are more elaborate in their construction and are bordered by dressed stones (a complete frame or only the lintel). In the West House, Room 3g, is an extreme variation of the type (Fig. 50). Though the opening has an elongated horizontal shape, it is meant to be a Type B window: the peculiar shape is derived from the priorities imposed by the lighting standards (the total surface of the opening) of the corresponding room. Because the vertical dimension was restricted by the low ceiling level inside and the high street level outside, the other dimension had to be enlarged. This led to the elongated horizontal form.

TYPE C: HORIZONTAL WINDOWS

Horizontal windows are large, with the longest axis being the horizontal one (Figs. 220–222). Their surface area varies greatly (1.43 to 4.35 sq m), and

because the typical height of the room and the height of the sill restrict the vertical dimension, it is the horizontal dimension that varies. The larger ones have one or two intermediate supports, not necessarily equally divided, and could be called multiple windows. They occur at all levels and are usually framed with dressed stones (with the

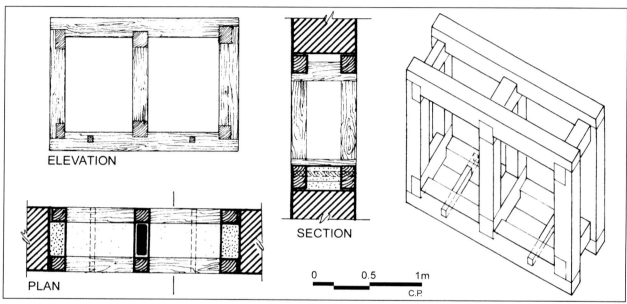

Fig. 220. Type C window from Xeste 3, Room 8, ground floor.

Fig. 221. Type C window from Xeste 3, Room 8, ground floor.

Fig. 222. Alpha-East, Room A1, the window before and after restoration.

exception of the ground floor Rooms A2 and D16). They occupy the center of the wall (not all its length, as is usually the case with the next category). The sill is approximately 0.70 m above floor level, as in most other windows. Multiple windows are usually found in the large rooms with central columns, hence their large sizes.

TYPE D: PIER-AND-WINDOW PARTITIONS

This class is a variation of the pier-and-opening technique. The pier-and-window partitions are usually divided in four parts, 0.60–0.80 m wide (Fig. 223), and they occupy the whole length of a wall (or a large part of it, as in the case of the West House; Figs. 224, 225). They have a characteristically low sill, 0.38–0.42 m, and an ashlar frame. In several corner rooms two pier-and-window partitions meet at the corner, as in the West House, Room 5, the South House, Alpha-East, and Delta-West. These rows of windows are found only on the upper floor. Like the pier-and-door partitions, their common lintel is below ceiling level, and the zone in between is built and sometimes covered with wall paintings in the

form of a frieze, as in the West House, Room 5. The sill has the same finish as the floor of the room. The intermediate jambs are made of mudbricks set on edge. Several such mudbricks are still lying on the sill of the pier-and-window partition of Delta 1a. Sometimes the sill beams at the inside of the room rest on slabs embedded in the wall. Those on the outside are usually set on the ashlar stones of the frame: the area they rest on is well dressed and slightly lower, forming a kind of *anathyrosis*. In the case of Alpha-West, the beams are fixed on the stone frame with dowels and mortises.

The timber frames of all the windows are load bearing elements (Fig. 226). The beams are 0.12–0.18 m thick and are either square in section or roughly rounded. They are fixed to each other with cuttings and perhaps wooden pegs. In a few instances (Xeste 3, Rooms 8 and 11; Beta-South, Room B1), a slender beam 0.04 by 0.04 m was inserted within the clay filling of the sill (Fig. 221). It obviously ran through the two main horizontal beams of the frame, and its purpose must have been to hold them together. There is a similar beam at the lintel of a door as well (Xeste 3, Room 11). The lintel is constructed either

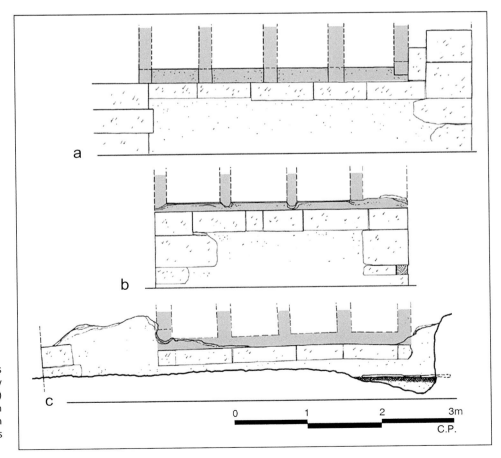

Fig. 223. Three examples of Type D pier-and-window partitions: a) Delta-East, b) the South House, c) an unexcavated building in the area of the Porter's Lodge.

0   1   2   3m
C.P.

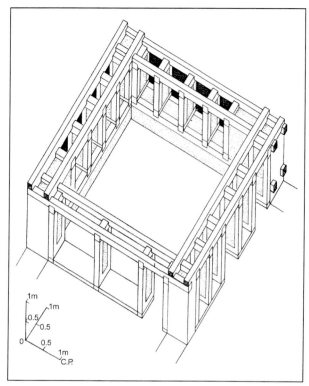

Fig. 224. Isometric drawing of pier-and-opening partitions (West House, Room 5, first floor).

Fig. 225. The timber frame of the pier-and-window partition left its imprint on the volcanic ash (West House, Room 5, first floor).

Fig. 226. Workers constructing a pier-and-window partition in Nepal, that closely resembles the Aegean Bronze Age technique (© Robb Kendrick/AURORA).

of timber beams laid side by side or of slabs spanning the gap.

In several windows on the ground floor level, detailed imprints of the wooden lattice have been preserved. It usually consists of two horizontal boards (0.02 by 0.10 m) fixed to the exterior window posts (Fig. 219, 227). The gaps between the boards are not more than 0.10 m in width, to ensure that no trespassing is possible. Sometimes a third horizontal beam is in between, with the same profile as the

posts. It functions as a reinforcement of the wooden case. Xeste 2 preserved the imprints of the lattice of an upper floor window (Figs. 132, 133, 228). The opening, 1.25 by 1.80 m wide, was divided into six parts by two vertical beams and one horizontal beam. These imprints were revealed in the early days of the excavation. Unfortunately, they were misinterpreted as the joints of ashlar masonry and were restored as such. In a few windows the wooden case has been omitted, and the lattice is fixed into square cuttings within the stone jambs (House of the Ladies, Xeste 3; Fig. 229).

A puzzling question that remains unanswered, despite the high state of preservation at Akrotiri, is the absence of shutters. No trace of shutters remains,[29] and the intricate wooden framing technique makes them quite improbable, at least for the multiple windows. With so many large openings, there must have been some way of regulating the weather conditions. Curtains made of mat or parchment are a possibility, but they leave no distinct traces.

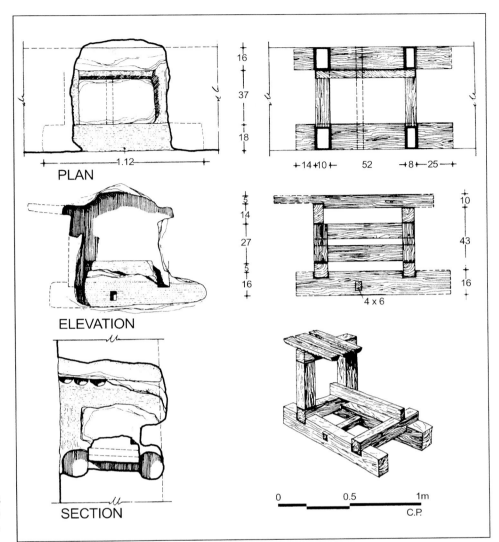

PLAN

ELEVATION

SECTION

16
37
18

14 10   52   8 25

5
14
27
5
16

10
43
16

4 × 6

0   0.5   1m
                        C.P.

Fig. 227. Structural details of a window frame with lattice (Xeste 3, Room 11, ground floor).

Regarding the windows, there can hardly be any comparison with other prehistoric sites, because of the state of preservation elsewhere. Nevertheless, it is clear that all four types occur in Crete, though only the larger windows are usually detected and reported. The latter are found in palaces and Type 1 houses, and they are usually related to ashlar walls. The pier-and-window partition is not a Theran innovation (see the Queen's Megaron at Knossos for example, or the earlier case at Malia, House Δγ[30]).

Windows are a conspicuous feature of Minoan architecture in art, and they are rendered in great detail as to their construction—even the lattice blocking the window opening is clearly visible in most cases, especially in the Archanes clay model of a house (Figs. 147, 230). Pier-and-window partitions

Fig. 228. Imprints of the timber frame and balustrade of a window (Xeste 2, first floor) that was mistaken for ashlar masonry (compare with Fig. 38).

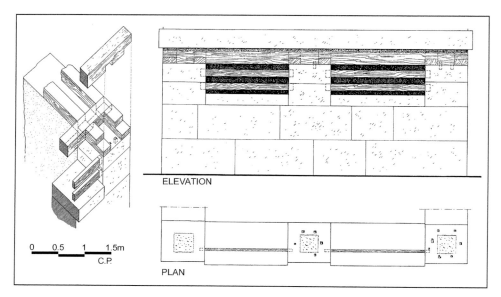

Fig. 229. Xeste 3, several structural details from the twin windows of Room 2.

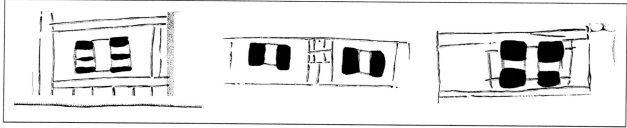

Fig. 230. Windows with lattices in the Archanes house model (Lebessi 1976: 19–21, figs. 5–7).

are also depicted: one in the Town Mosaic, and two interesting structures because of their early date (MM IIB) in the Shrine models from Knossos. Evans observes in astonishment the "extraordinary anticipation of modern civilized usage" of windows, and

L. Mumford points out that "the great novelty in Crete is the window, for here Knossos leaves behind the dark window-less dwellings of Sumer, lighted only from a narrow courtyard or a clerestory, if at all."[31]

Interior Fittings: Shelves, Cupboards, and Built Benches

Wooden shelves fixed in the wall were quite common. Their presence is often attested indirectly, by the manner in which the numerous objects resting on the shelves are found fallen within the debris of the room.[32] In several instances, the imprints of shelves were found intact. A well known example is the shelf running along the west wall of the room of the Spring Fresco (Delta 2), at a height of 1.85 m above the floor (Fig. 231). It is very broad, 0.71 m, and it is made of beams (0.07 by 0.10 m) fixed into the wall at a distance of 0.35 m from one another,

holding a layer of twigs set side by side and covered over with lime plaster.

Shelves were also detected in the West House. In Room 6, first floor, a large shelf (or two?) runs along the east wall (Fig. 232). It was a semi-autonomous structure held by wooden posts fixed in the floor. The adjoining Room 7 also had shelves. This small space included the auxiliary staircase and a cupboard next to it. Two shelves were in the cupboard, as attested by the imprints of the broken planks and the fallen vases.

Cupboards are very common at Akrotiri, either in the form of niches in a wall (Delta 10–13) or as pier-and-cupboard partitions (West House, Room 5). The latter are based on the concept of the pier-and-door partition with the addition of a clay wall to form the back of the cupboard. In the West House, Room 5, the interior of the cupboards was plastered and painted red, and each one had at least two superimposed wooden shelves. These cupboards could be shut with double doors, and planks with indented edges made to fit each other when closed left perfect imprints in the ash. Each cupboard had two separate pairs of doors, one for the lower and one for the upper part.

Another instance of a wooden shelf is found in Xeste 3, above one of the doors of the pier-and-door partition between Rooms 4 and 7, on the ground floor (see Pier-and-Door Partitions). This example has no precedent because all other pier-and-door partitions have a wall above the common lintel. Because Room 7 had no means of obtaining light and air, an opening was provided above one of the doors toward Room 4. The lintel of the door was spanned with planks so that it functioned as a shelf.

Vases were found intact upon the shelf which, however, was only recognized by its imprint on the volcanic ash.

Built benches are another commodity. The few sitting benches are all in the entrance lobbies (Xeste 3, the most elaborate in form; Delta 15; House of the Ladies). In the case of Xeste 3, a bench is also used outside the entrance door. Built benches are also used as working surfaces for mill installations (Delta 15, West House, Alpha-West). A different kind of built bench is attested in relation to storage: a number of pithoi set in a row are built within a rubble structure, as in Beta 1 (Fig. 84). What has come as a surprise is that such particularly heavy benches are also erected on the upper story, resting on the wooden beams of the floor (West House, Room 6; Xeste 3, Rooms 10 and 12; Fig. 74).

Built chests are another kind of interior fitting. They are usually made of clay bricks set upright and plastered over, dividing a space into small compartments (Xeste 3, Room 2; Beta 1, upper floor; Delta-North, Room 8a; House of the Ladies, Room 1).

Fig. 231. Imprints of a wooden shelf in room Delta 2.

Fig. 232. Cups and vases fallen from a shelf (West House, Room 6, first floor).

Chapter 9 Notes

1. This chapter is a synopsis of the author's book *Ακρωτήρι Θήρας. Η Οικοδομική Τέχνη*, Athens 1999 (see also Palyvou 1992). The book is an analysis of the building materials and techniques used at Akrotiri, where the reader may find a detailed account of individual cases, with many references to parallels from Crete, the Cyclades, and other places in the eastern Mediterranean. The translation of this work to the form included in this chapter was made with the financial support of INSTAP.

2. Rapoport 1969.

3. Evans 1927, discussion. Marinatos and others after him however, reported a lack of wood at Akrotiri (Marinatos 1968–1976, III: 10; Doumas 1974b: 201; Rackham 1980: 758).

4. Kinds of wood attested on Thera through the study of fossils are: *tamarix, Pistacia lentiscus* L., *Olea europaea, Phoenix dactylifera* I., *Chamaerops humilis* L. (Friedrich 1978; Rackham 1980).

5. Friedrich 2000: 105–113.

6. Touliatos 2000: 27–36.

7. Touliatos 2000: 27–36. The citation from Homer is *Odyssey* 9.129.

8. Einfalt 1978. Einfalt's work is the main source of information in this chapter.

9. Marinatos 1968–1976, VI: 7, pl. 1a.

10. Einfalt 1978: 527.

11. Marinatos 1968–1976, II: 49–51; III: 43, 45; IV: 16; Doumas 1994: 161, pl. 88a. For Crete, see Shaw 1971: 44–75.

12. Doumas 1983: 114–115; 1974a: 365–370; Moundrea-Agrafioti 1992; Devetzi 1992.

13. A wall built upon a layer of red pumice (of an earlier eruption) has been regarded as seismic protection (Doumas 1993: 169).

14. See also Delta-North, the exposed foundation of the ashlar wall by the entrance, Doumas 1996: 251, fig. 108a.

15. Shaw 1971: 99.

16. At Knossos, the north ramp leading to the Central Court is bordered by an ashlar wall including vertical timber. This is an exception that is probably related to the structure of the upper story.

17. See Palyvou 1999a: 161–163, with many references, especially n. 284.

18. A probable mason's mark is reported also from Therasia (Sperling 1973: 58).

19. Renfrew 1984: 390.

20. Shaw counted 7 to 8 layers in a large fragment from the roof of the West House. He observes, however, that "it is possible that we have a number of renewals of the waterproofing over a period of years" (J. Shaw 1977: 231).

21. A different type of column base was found recently in the area of Sector Gamma. It has a tall upper part with a large mortise on the upper face.

22. Palyvou 1984. Similar dimensions are attested at Therasia and in Crete (Hagia Varvara, Mochlos, and Malia).

23. Sperling 1973: 60–61.

24. Cummer and Schofield 1984.

25. McEnroe, 1982: 3–13.

26. Graham 1972: 175–177.

27. Part of a door leaf was detected in the House of the Ladies, Room 3 (Doumas 1990: 228 and pl. 138a).

28. For references to the varying uses of the terms "polythyron" and "pier-and-door partition" see Palyvou 1999a: 343, notes 557–561.

29. There is only one, rather vague and indirect reference to a shutter in the Excavation Daybooks: according to the excavators, the window next to the entrance door of Xeste 3 "was found shut."

30. Demargne et al. 1953: 53.

31. Evans 1921–1935, I: 303; Mumford 1961: 145.

32. Michailidou 2001.

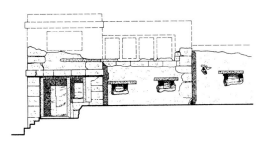

10

Design and Morphology

A Design Process: Models and Variations

The sophisticated architecture of Akrotiri speaks clearly of a very complex and demanding design procedure. Architectural design implies anticipating, programming, evaluating, cross-checking and, finally, optimizing a large number of parameters. The construction of a building is a one-way process: the form, function, and structure of each part have to be planned well ahead because they determine the building operation from the very beginning, when laying out the foundations and calculating the loads to be transferred to the ground, and one cannot come back to change things as construction proceeds.

The large size of many buildings (Xeste 4, for example, has a total surface of 957 square meters), the presence of two and three stories, and the fact that the room arrangement of the upper floors differs from that of the ground floor make things even more difficult in terms of design procedure. Even more remarkable, however, is the design of the intricate system of horizontal and vertical communication. The latter accommodates a large number of levels, and in several cases it also provides intercommunication between adjoining staircases,

through their middle landings! The design procedure implied by such a distribution of staircases shows a remarkable control of the 3-dimensional space.

Theran builders clearly exhibit great skills in conceiving and designing their buildings. It is difficult to judge how this design was made and how it was consequently executed, especially in the kind of architecture we see at Akrotiri where rooms are seldom strictly rectangular, corners are rarely at right angles, and very few walls are straight for some length. The techniques for designing and laying out the palaces and large mansions of Minoan Crete suggested by Graham, Preziosi, and others[1] do not readily lend themselves to Akrotiri, though they should not be excluded.

Many buildings actually consist of a simple juxtaposition of rooms along a structural pattern defined by the appropriate spanning system (see Xeste 3, for example; Fig. 233). This grid-like pattern—albeit in a latent form—incorporates all the basic walls, thus ensuring the stability of the structure while also simplifying and greatly facilitating the laying-out procedure. The interior of the building is then

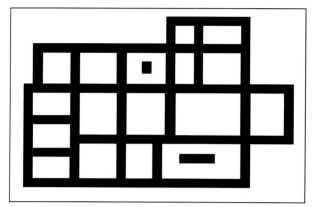

Fig. 233. The structural concept of crossing walls in Xeste 3.

divided and refined by the ingenious use of architectural elements such as the pier-and-opening partitions and the thin mudbrick walls.

It may be assumed that the design process of a typical Theran house was also facilitated by the use of "building regulations:" that is, by the repetitive use of well established formulae that had proved their efficiency in the long run of time.[2] Such "regulations" are implied by the high degree of standardization of room arrangement and structural details. This procedure—typical in anonymous architecture—is described by Rapoport as a system of models and variations.[3] The model consists of a set of generic forms and techniques arrived at collectively, through trial and error, and accepted by the community as the optimal solution—i.e., most efficient in terms of operation and costs—to standard requirements. These models do not exist as prototypes that should be copied; they are, rather, a set of guidelines that will help the builder find his own way through to the solution of each specific problem. The entrance system is a good example (Fig. 200): the "rule" is clear, yet each case is the outcome of the adjustment of the rule to a set of specific parameters. Another example would be the room with a central column (Fig. 189).

The Quantitative Aspect of Architecture: Measurements and Units

Architecture has an inherent quantitative aspect related either to structural needs (load bearing capacity, resistance to lateral movement, etc.) or to ergonomic requirements (the height of a door, the dimensions of a staircase, etc.). The former is translated into dimensions and proportions of timber elements, thickness of walls, inclination of drainage channels, and so on, whereas the latter are dimensions related to the human body. Both are by their nature universal and diachronic (see, for example, Le Corbusier's *Modular Man*, Fig. 234).

Whatever the design procedure at Akrotiri, calculations and measurements were surely applied, even if in a rough manner using one's own foot or palm as a unit. Measuring, after all, was an important practice of everyday life.[4] The system and the unit(s) applied in building operations, however, are difficult to estimate for two reasons. Firstly, problems exist with the approximation of the construction and the ruinous state of preservation. Secondly, many unknown parameters are at play, such as the identity, training, and equipment of the people working in the building industry and the relationship between the worksite and the place of provenance of the building materials (quarries of stone, for example). It may be that different groups of architects used different measuring units, especially if they worked as itinerant artisans. This possibility is implied by the varying sizes of the mudbricks throughout Akrotiri, for example. The bricks remain quite standard within the same building, however, which means that each worksite was more or less autonomous.

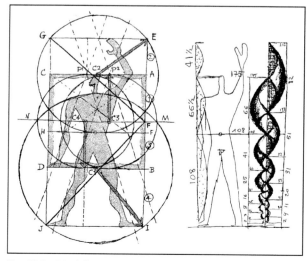

Fig. 234. *Modular Man* (Le Corbusier 1951: figs. 18 and 100).

The ashlar walls are perhaps the best places to look for measurement techniques and the possible application of a specific unit. Xeste 4 offers a good example because the ashlar facades are well preserved and stand to a great height (Fig. 235). Two points have already been discussed:

a) the blocks have only the front face dressed in a clear orthogonal shape (so this is the only surface one may examine for specific dimensions)

b) the rows of blocks tend to diminish in height from bottom to top.

It should be emphasized, however, that many irregularities exist in these walls. Thick plaster spreads over broken edges at the joints, and small slabs are used as wedges, filling in gaps and divergences from the ideal height of a block (some of the blocks seem to be in secondary use).

An analysis of the dimensions of the north facade of Xeste 4 shows that a clear numerical rule existed in the layout of this wall: the lowest row is 0.57 m, then follow two rows of 0.52 m each, and two more of 0.46 m each. The next row is the cornice, 0.40 m high (farther to the west the cornice is slightly smaller in height, 0.38 m, because it is at a slightly higher level). A similar sequence of diminishing heights of pairs of rows is repeated on the upper floor, above the cornice: two rows of 0.36 m and at least one of 0.345 m. The ground floor rows, in other words, diminish by 0.06 m each time, whereas the upper floor rows diminish by 0.02–0.025 m. This in itself is a clear indication of metrical calculations. Observations of this sort, however, are not always as clear as that: on the other facades of Xeste 4, the rule is more freely applied, and the same may be said for Xeste 3 (the south wall of Room 2, also has diminishing rows of blocks from bottom to top: 0.80 m, 0.67 m, 0.50 m, 0.41 m, though there is no consistent difference).

Among the shortest stones the most common height is 0.27 m (the topmost rows in situ for Xeste 4). Many blocks of this height are found within the debris, and it is also the size of several cornices and frames: Xeste 2 (north wall), Alpha-West (frame over entrance), Delta-East (frame over entrance), West House (frame over entrance). Interestingly enough, on the Xeste 4 facades one can see blocks 0.27 m high inserted in a row 0.30 m high; these are obviously in secondary use, and thin slabs were added to fill in the gap. There are, however, shorter blocks as well: Delta-South (0.18–0.20 m, above the entrance). It is interesting to note that the dimension 0.27 m coincides with the "short" value of the Minoan foot proposed by Preziosi.[5]

Apart from the height of the rows, no clear indication of a unit determining the long side of the block or the overall length of a wall exists, though it should be said that ignimbrite blocks are generally longer than those made of tuff (some are as long as 1.80 m at Xeste 3). It would be easy to assume that the length of the north wall of Xeste 4 (23 m) is approximately 85 units (85 x 0.27 cm = 22.95 m), but there are so many discrepancies involved, both in the construction of the wall and the measurements one can take today because of the deformations, that it would be a very unsafe assumption. One could actually construe the results in almost any desirable way. On the other hand, it is of great interest that the north wall of Xeste 2 is approximately of the same length, 23 m.

There is evidence that the blocks were shaped in situ, at least in their final form (chips of stone are

Fig. 235. Xeste 4, north facade showing the heights of the ashlar rows.

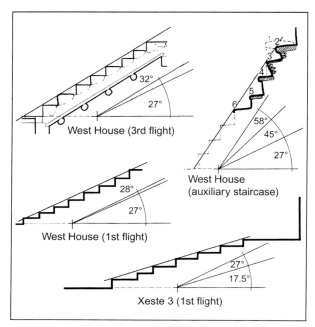

Fig. 236. Stairs with varying inclination values.

often found in the bonding material among the blocks), which means that their size could have been adjusted ad hoc to the situation, according to the available piece of stone and the general rule of avoiding intersecting vertical joints from one row to another. Mason's marks, very common in Xeste 4, may be related to the position or the dressing of the blocks (see Chap. 9).

Metrical calculations are implied in other instances as well. The square room with the central column has one dimension—4.90 m—that is almost standard. In at least two cases (Beta 2 and Delta 16), the rooms resulted from a rearrangement, and it is clear that this dimension dictated the exact interventions to the existing building. This dimension most probably derives from the maximum length the builders could span with one intermediate support. It may also be assumed that it derives from 18 times the unit 0.27 m (0.272 m more precisely).

Staircases are another instance where measurements and calculation play an important role. The width of a flight and the dimensions (height and width) of a step are sizes that derive from the proportions of the human body. By modern standards, a main staircase should have steps 0.14–0.20 m high and 0.26–0.32 m broad, while the flight must be at least 0.55 m wide for one person or 1.10–1.20 m for two. The inclination should range between 23–34°. A comfortable staircase has steps 0.155 m high and 0.31 m broad and an inclination of 27°. An auxiliary staircase should not exceed 45° inclination. Beyond that, it is of the "ladder" type. Such anthropocentric rules have a timeless effect. At Akrotiri (Fig. 236), the main staircases, especially the first flights, tend to be of a low inclination (this makes access slower and somewhat more formal), while the auxiliary staircases tend to be of a stronger inclination (therefore not as comfortable in their use). Furthermore, all the steps must be of the same height (only the first or the last may differ). This rule is not always attested at Akrotiri, especially in auxiliary staircases where the height difference between two adjacent steps may be quite big.

An Approximate Geometry and the Elusive Effect of Symmetry and Order

Most buildings exhibit a latent geometry in their general layout: straight lines and right angles are approximate, while a grid-like modular design concept attested in several cases is only roughly identified as such. In some Xeste buildings, however, a more defined geometry is present, along with indications of a metrical system. On the whole, Bronze Age architecture is characterized by approximation, as opposed to the precision that imbued the monumental architecture of the Greco-Roman world that followed. Even the palaces and the large mansions of Minoan Crete exhibit a degree of approximation, despite the fact that they are obviously designed on a much stricter geometry.

Symmetry does exist in Theran architecture, albeit in a latent manner. The simple rule of positioning each window in the center of the wall, for example, is in itself a rule of symmetry deriving nevertheless from structural requirements—best distribution of the void in the masonry—and also functional—best distribution of light (Fig. 237). Yet, as a morphological feature, it is largely obscured on the total facade of the building because the sum of the individual symmetries is not a symmetrical result per se. This is due to the interference of other parameters, such as the fact that some walls are thinner on the upper floor, so the "middle" of the wall is different from one story to the other. Therefore, two superimposed windows (each one symmetrical in regard to its own wall) may end up off axis.

The model of the main staircase is another example: its form (resembling Π) has an inherent symmetry (Fig. 192). The actual staircases, however, are never entirely symmetrical. On close inspection one observes numerous deviations, described in detail and interpreted in Chapter 9.

Order is produced in several instances through the use of a repetitive element, such as the even distribution of the vertical timber reinforcement of Xeste 2 and Xeste 3 (Figs. 65, 133). The numerical aspect of this order is once more very approximate. The reason for the elusive result is that the builder was not very concerned with the final overall effect of his structures, but worked his way step by step, applying his "rules" to each part of the building separately, as necessary. It takes much more premeditation for an effective application of such morphological goals. Most importantly, however, these were structural rules (the even distribution of the timber reinforcement, for example, is clearly a technical requirement), and their aesthetic values may not have been in the minds of the builders at all.

Morphological aspects may be better understood through the depictions of architecture in contemporary art.[6] The Town Mosaic shows that the artist conceived the built environment in a more abstract manner, thus bringing out the underlying rules of

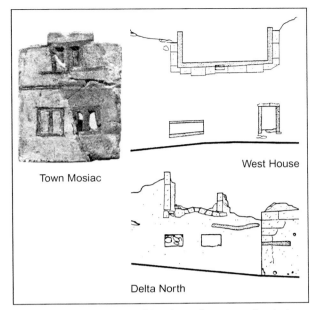

Town Mosiac

West House

Delta North

Fig. 237. The typical combination of two small windows below and a large one above in art (Town Mosaic, Evans 1921–1935, I: fig. 223) and at Akrotiri.

order and symmetry—windows are symmetrically distributed, and ashlar facades are so perfect that they resemble the isodomic masonry attested only in Classical architecture.

The Gridiron Pattern

In Crete, symmetry and order are most conspicuous in the Minoan Hall system, and even more patent in the later Mycenaean Megaron. This type of room arrangement is absent at Akrotiri. The Polythyron Halls, on the other hand, though they do involve a certain amount of symmetry, are basically organized on a different scheme: that of the grid.

The use of a gridiron pattern in several instances is one of the highest expressions of the sophisticated design system attested at Akrotiri. The grid is closely related to the pier-and-opening partition that became characteristic of Neopalatial architecture, because it imposes the concept of a grid in its own right. The modular unit is the width of the door or the window: 0.60–0.80 m. The eastern part of Xeste 3, with its numerous pier-and-door partitions, is an example of this sort (Fig. 70), and so is Room 5 on the upper floor of the West House (Fig. 54). The latter is a superb example of the use of the modular grid: a timber framework extends on all

four sides of the room and is kept in place by four stone pillars at the corners. Each side is divided by intermediate posts into four-plus-one parts: four openings (windows, doors, or cupboards) and one massive part (wall). The grid pattern is further developed by the artist who painted the room: by painting yellow vertical stripes below each jamb of the pier-and-window partitions, and also by continuing the horizontal lines of the sills and lintels with colorful bands, he completed the grid in all three dimensions. Thus, he achieved an overall effect of unity and coherence, further emphasized by the Miniature Frieze running all around the room. From the metrical point of view, dimensions are largely approximate, hence the different width of the walls at the two ends of the pier-and-window partitions. The divergence, however, was no problem to the artist who intended to draw two similar figures on both ends (this being a further emphasis of symmetry): he simply folded up the arms of one fisherman so as to fit the narrower wall. In this beautiful room, one can easily appreciate how the gridiron pattern has helped to integrate all the parts, architectural and artistic, into one overall concept of space. The timeless quality of discipline and the modernity of such a design process—a true predecessor of the 20th century A.D. Bauhaus School—can hardly escape us (Fig. 238, Pl. 3A).

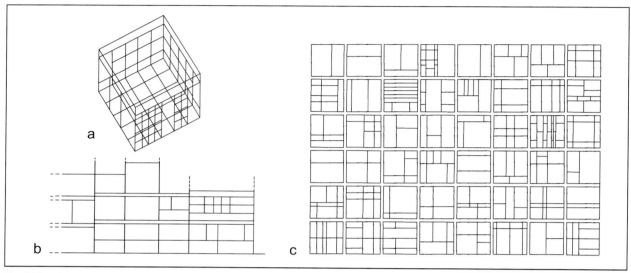

Fig. 238. a) West House, Room 5; b) Xeste 2; c) *The Panel Exercise* (Le Corbusier 1951: 92–93, fig. 39).

Boxes, Zones, and Frames

In most cases the upper story of a building covers the whole area of the ground floor, and it is only on the highest floor (if there is one) that verandas are likely to exist. Many buildings, therefore, have a cubist effect and a massive bulky appearance—see the West House, for example (Figs. 47, 48). The houses of the Town Mosaic emit very much the same effect, and it is only the projecting structure of the main staircase on the roof—both in art and in reality—that reduces the box-like picture to a certain extent. The overall effect, however, is differentiated largely by two simple techniques: the indentation of the facades and the projecting cornices defining the floors. The former adds a perpendicular undulation to the facade that breaks up the initial box into a series of smaller ones. Light and shadow would have further enhanced the effect. The latter—i.e., the division of a surface into horizontal zones—is a well established and popular concept in Bronze Age art, attested also in vase painting and wall painting (see below). Both these elements seem to have been appreciated largely for their morphological value— one may even assume that they were applied for precisely this reason. We should add, of course, that the large number and variety of windows piercing these volumes diminished to a great degree the otherwise heavy and compact aspect of these buildings. Openings tend to be much larger on the upper floors, adding to the differentiation of the overall structure and emphasizing the static aspect of the edifice: solid lower parts versus lighter upper parts. One may even add that the diminishing rows of blocks on the ashlar facades would have helped in the same direction, enhancing the perspective (higher up is farther away, therefore smaller). Possibly sheltered verandas on the roof, of the type seen on the Archanes model, or even balconies, would further relieve the building from the box-like effect.

Projecting cornices are applied on both ashlar and rubble walls, and from the way they are constructed (they are not related to the construction of the floor; Fig. 158) it is clear that they function largely as morphological features (they also protect the timber beams underneath). Cornices project the interior division of a multi-story house, but they do not necessarily coincide with the floors. At Xeste 4, for example, judging from the way the upper cornice cuts through certain windows, it is safe to assume that it does not accurately follow the different levels inside the building. The same may be true for Xeste 2. It seems more likely that the facades were arranged in tiers according to how they looked from the outside; that is, starting from street level (not necessarily the same as ground level inside) and working upward. If this is true, then it proves beyond a doubt that the projecting cornices were basically a morphological element.

The framing aspect is implied by two techniques. Ashlar corner stones delineate the periphery of each building, defining the edges of each individual facade. Ashlar stones bordering openings, on the other hand, delineate the areas where the mass of the wall has been perforated. The framing effect, however, has again a latent aspect, because it is weakened by the color differentiation of the four sides of the frame (Beta 1, window of north wall seen in Fig. 80, has a black sill and white jambs) and even more by the way the timber frame interrupts the stone frame at the corners, discussed in Chapter 9.

The Wall Paintings

Clay plastered walls, common in auxiliary rooms, produce poorly illuminated spaces because they do not reflect much light. The white lime plaster, on the other hand, creates a perfect background, reflecting adequate light and providing a clean and calm space in which to live. It is also a challenge to the eye: forms are projected on the white surface, attaining a sharper outline and allowing for their own colors to show. Moreover, every contact with this surface leaves visible marks, from the incidental touch of a hand and scratch of a finger nail to the casual splash of all pigments that nature could provide.

Color was applied on the white surfaces already in the building phase before the *seismic destruction*.[7] Polychrome bands were common, but spirals have also been reported from the House of the Ladies. In the West House, underneath the wall paintings of Room 4, a sponge-like design or splashes were detected, as if imitating incidental splatter.

Lime plastered walls of the last phase are either monochrome—white, yellow ocher, or red—or painted. Red plasters were actually quite common throughout the early phases of the Bronze Age, and they seem to mark specific spaces. The power of red as a color (blood; life) may explain the reason why red plasters are associated with rooms that tend to have some special significance related to rituals: Xeste 4, Room 14 may be such a case.[8] The fine layer of lime plaster seems to cover parts of the wooden elements: in most cases, door posts, sills, and lintels would only show their outer edges, more like planks and not beams, and sometimes no wood would show at all because it was covered with lime plaster (Fig. 209).

Wall paintings were well established by the Neopalatial period, both in Crete and Thera. This new art and the sophisticated style of architecture characteristic of the zenith of Minoan civilization are intricately bonded and interrelated. Wall paintings are enhanced and at the same time restricted by architectural space, and they are experienced not in their own right (regardless of the context), but as part of the experience of being within a building. In the following paragraphs, the basic concepts of space, as expressed both through architecture and art, are discussed.[9]

Concepts of Space

Two different and virtually opposite concepts of architectural space are equally reflected in wall treatment, depending on the proportionality of mass versus void:

MASS EXCEEDS VOID

Extensive wall surfaces are interrupted by minor voids—small windows, cupboards, or a single door (Figs. 239, 240; Pl. 4B). Space is enclosed, wrapped in a uniform membrane. The structural aspect is decreased, and the walls act as a continuous barrier surrounding the spectator. Compactness and continuity are transmitted to mural treatment and are further enhanced by creating panorama effects: corners and minor voids are completely ignored, as in the Spring Fresco and the Blue Monkeys, and a global effect is achieved. Such a treatment may be applied to all four sides of a room or only to adjacent sides that share this characteristic. Because the theme of Aegean wall paintings is often taken from nature, it may result in a symbolic abolishing of walls as boundaries and insulation from nature,

Fig. 239. Delta-East, showing the room with the Spring Fresco spread on three of the room's four walls. Three figures are added for scale.

Fig. 240. Beta-South, the Blue Monkeys. The corner of the room is ignored.

thus relieving the rather claustrophobic effect of a room with very few openings.

VOID EXCEEDS MASS

The structural aspect of architectural space is dominant. The framework is conspicuous, and voids play the most significant role, often dictating an overall grid system for the articulation of space (Pls. 3A, 4A). Wall masses are not substantial, and they look as if they were added only after the wooden framework was erected (and this may well be the case in some instances). This concept of space is characteristic of Neopalatial architecture, both in Crete and Thera, and it creates an ambience almost peculiar to the Minoan feeling of space where indoor and outdoor blend in one integral entity.

Mural surfaces consist of a number of individual panels, standing separately and in juxtaposition to one another. Each piece of wall surface is treated as an autonomous part, and structural elements such as sills, lintels, and jambs are incorporated as guide lines to create borders and frames for the pictures. The framing effect is further achieved through the composition of the picture, by the axiality or autonomy of the theme: e.g., the two antelopes and the two boxing children facing each other. The fisherman with his hands outstretched also conveys the framing aspect, while the other fisherman, with his hands folded on one side, evokes the idea of movement breaking through the borders of the frame.

The Unifying Elements: Continuity and Horizontality

The ultimate goal in all cases is unity, and this is achieved by two basic principles that relate the various parts into an overall composition:[10] the uniform horizontal zoning of all surfaces and the iconographical correlation of all pictures involved. Horizontality prevails in most instances, and space is sliced into a tripartite arrangement corresponding directly to the three basic elements that follow.

ZONE A

The lower zone of a wall painting represents the base, either artificial (a floor) or natural (the earth). It can be reduced to only a few centimeters (Xeste 4, procession of men) or extended to a broad band, straight (House of the Ladies) or undulating to depict a rocky landscape (Spring Fresco, Pl. 4B). In the first case the illusionary base of the picture on the wall painting is almost identical with the real one— i.e., the floor of the room—while in the latter it is detached. Accordingly, the subject of the central zone (Zone B) is brought close to the spectator or removed from him, dictating to a large extent his involvement with the happenings depicted on the walls.

The plain, less significant lower part also acts as a protective zone that may be obscured by furniture—bed, table, stool—or damaged by wear, as for example with the relief wall painting of Xeste 3 that has a broad lower zone of plain red color that is quite worn.

ZONE B

Zone B is the main area. It corresponds to the boundaries of the human body, adhering to its scale and verticality and defining the area of action. The openings act as breaks within the barriers and conduits of communication (for air, view, sound, bodily contact, etc.). Action is either "seen through" the wall or "projected" on its surface; in other words, it takes place either outside the room or within it.

When the ground level is raised, the main theme is naturally raised also. Yet, it is interesting to observe that the iconographic horizon adheres to the actual horizon of a man standing in the room— i.e. 1.50–1.60 m above floor level. This way the viewer can appreciate the picture naturally and intimately. If the iconographic horizon were higher and the viewer had to raise his head, then his attitude toward the picture would be that of subordination, and if the other way around, then the viewer's feelings would be those of superiority. This eye-to-eye contact explains why figures on a raised base end up approximately two-thirds of natural size (West House, House of the Ladies, and Xeste 3; Figs. 241–243).

The upper limit of this zone is usually at the level of the lintel. The lintel defines the average height of a standing man with raised arms, so it is the effective height of a picture that can be read at ease. In auxiliary spaces, this level is often the height of the ceiling, but in living areas more upper space is needed to avoid a claustrophobic effect, and the ceiling is higher up, resulting in a substantial topmost Zone C.

ZONE C

Zone C corresponds to the area beyond the scene of action. It is the upper limit or "the sky." It varies in width and treatment, its most common form being a narrow band above lintel level that defines the upper limit of the wall and the transition to the ceiling. The band is either a set of multicolored strips, or a painted frieze running all around the room. The continuity of the frieze is ensured by the thematic correlation of its parts—if figurative—or by the decorative motif—e.g., a garland of ivy leaves (Pl. 4A).

A popular motif is the running spiral, itself an interminable design. The circle, however, is not compatible with the angles and corners of a room. In the room with the Blue Monkeys (Beta 6), this deficiency is overcome by adding large quantities of plaster at the corner until the angle is transformed into a curve. This crude solution to the problem shows that the structural aspect of architecture is subdued to the artistic principle of unity. Other types of decorative motifs may simulate architecture: the ivy leaf, for example, may be a reminder of the top of a wooden pergola supporting such an ivy leaf plant on the roof of a house, not unlike the Archanes model.

Sometimes there is more wall surface above this zone, usually painted yellow to match the natural color of the wooden ceiling beams. This yellow area accommodates all the irregularities and undulated lines at the top of the walls and visually belongs to the ceiling, allowing for the wall to end at a uniform straight line at the top of the frieze. Such yellow bands are common in rooms that have the ceiling beams exposed—hence the undulated upper limit of the wall—whereas in rooms that have plastered ceilings held on reeds attached to the rafters, they are not needed.

The urge to clearly mark the transition between two perpendicular surfaces (floor-wall, wall-ceiling) is strong, and it is present even in cases where no wall paintings exist. Where a monochrome lime plaster covers all the surfaces, this distinction is made by a simple incised line, hardly visible from some distance (Xeste 3, Room 7; Xeste 4, Room with a Central Column). Yet the artist who plastered the surfaces, thickening the plaster at the joints between floor, wall, and ceiling into a curved and rather ambiguous mold for extra strength, felt the compulsive need to draw this line as a symbolic marker of the transition from one plane to the other.

In conclusion, the zoning concept is a most powerful principle of design in mural treatment. It is in itself a manifestation of continuity and horizontality, the very same horizontality that prevails in architecture. The overall morphology of Aegean architecture declares horizontality through the

stepped terraces sprawling down the hillside, the horizontal timber zones of rubble walls, and the ashlar courses and cornices.

Southwest wall

Northwest wall

0   0.2   0.5   1m
C.P.

Fig. 241. The West House, Room 5. Eye-to-eye contact between a person standing in the room and the figures in the wall paintings.

Fig. 242. The House of the Ladies, Room 1. Eye-to-eye contact between a person standing in the room and the figures in the wall paintings.

Fig. 243. Xeste 3, two restored sections of Room 3 and the lustral basin.

The Illusion Effect: Simulating Architectural Elements

Simulating architectural elements aims at imitating materials and techniques so as to enhance the appearance of the real architecture. This is often

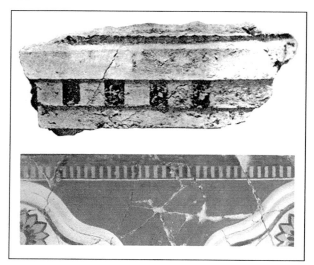

Fig. 244. Rectangles depicted on a wall painting from Xeste 3 and in stucco, Knossos (Evans 1921–1935, III: fig. 359).

done when there are inadequate means of actually constructing these elements. Simulated elements are depicted in full scale and in close relation with the architecture and so should be distinguished from architectural elements depicted on a wall painting as part of the setting of a scene. The latter elements belong to the narrative of the picture, and they are not related to the actual architecture of the room. Their scale is commonly reduced to that of the figures included in the picture, for example, the facade of a shrine in the "Crocus Gatherers" in Xeste 3.

Architectural simulations are usually elements of decorative value, such as cornices, dadoes of variegated stone, and friezes.[11] Dadoes are depicted in the West House, Room 5, interspaced with vertical yellow bands imitating the wooden beams holding the slabs onto the wall (Pl. 3A). The sill of the window of Room 4 is also painted to simulate variegated stone as a veneer of the horizontal surface of the sill, obviously imitating the kind of sill stones existing in other windows (Alpha 1, for example).

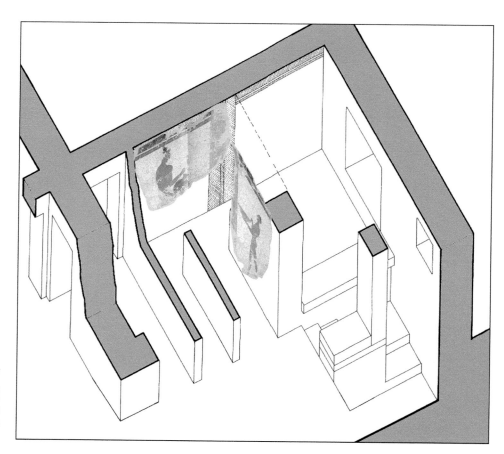

Fig. 245. A computer reconstruction of Xeste 3, Room 3b. The vertical bands at the ends of the wall paintings simulate timber jambs.

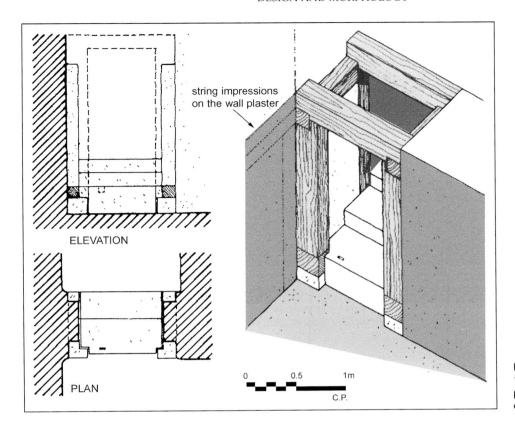

string impressions
on the wall plaster

ELEVATION

PLAN

0   0.5   1m

C.P.

Fig. 246. Xeste 4, Room
14: incisions on the wall
plaster simulating timber
elements.

A band with rectangles in alternating colors, black and white or blue, simulating a frieze sculpted in stone or molded in stucco, borders the upper part of the relief wall painting from Xeste 3 (Fig. 244). The architectural prototypes of this depiction are moldings in stucco.[12]

A similar concept lies behind the plain yellow vertical bands incorporated in certain wall paintings. These correspond to existing wooden elements within the room and function as the painted counterparts of missing door jambs and pilasters. Two examples, from the House of the Ladies and Xeste 3, are well attested because the architectural details of the rooms to which they belong are well known (Figs. 242, 245).

Another way to simulate architectural elements is by incising lines on the surface of a monochrome plaster. An example is found on the first floor of Xeste 4 (Fig. 246): the room with a central column has walls—and probably the floor, also—covered with lime plaster painted red. Part of the north wall next to the doorway leading to the auxiliary staircase shows vertical and horizontal incised lines imitating posts and beams. They all correspond to alignments dictated by the structural elements of the existing door jambs and lintel, and they relate to real architectural members as if they were their continuation. These lines are not very prominent, because they are thin and shallow incisions on a dark monochrome surface, but they seem to be important in conveying space, because instead of a uniform red skin enveloping the room, the walls are now articulated in an architectural manner.

The "Projection" Effect

It has been suggested that actions and rituals possibly taking place within the room are projected on the walls like a photograph, capturing a momentous event. Nanno Marinatos believes that this was a major function of the wall paintings of Thera because "by painting these scenes the Akrotirians made the power of the ritual effective forever."[13]

The processional figures are good examples of the projection technique: either walking along a corridor or climbing up a staircase (Xeste 4), they are shown in the act of participating in a procession. The base line is minimal, hardly distinguished from the actual floor or the step, and the figures are depicted in full scale. These pictures convey a very strong feeling of involvement: one could almost recognize oneself among the figures in the procession.

Objects are also depicted this way: a typical example is the flower pot on the jambs of a window in the West House, simulating a real vase standing on the sill of the window (left side of the window on the right in Pl. 3B). To make this even clearer, the picture on the jamb includes painted "jambs" and a "sill" of variegated stone inclined in an upright position. The overall effect is a kind of "architecture within architecture."

The X-Ray Effect

This technique implies that the wall surface is treated as being transparent, showing its inner structure. There is no clear evidence of such treatment, but it is suggested through architectural representations in art.

A popular element featured in many house facades drawn in miniature—e.g., in the Town Mosaic—is the rows of circles interpreted by most scholars as beam-ends. The only life-sized example of such a painting comes from Pylos.[14] The drawing is very realistic, because the wood has grains and even knots, but its position on the wall is unknown, so one cannot tell whether it functioned as an X-ray or as a simulation of a real beam.

Akrotiri offers a possible architectural prototype, though unfortunately the color is faded, and the motif remains somewhat ambiguous: it is a fragment of a stone frieze found in the debris of Xeste 3. Its surface is plastered and painted with what seems to be a row of blue circles. Such a frieze was most certainly placed on the top of a wall, in which case the design was an X-ray of the ceiling beams lying behind the wall. Judging from the Town Mosaic, the circles correspond either to floor beams or to the transverse beams of the timber reinforcement of the wall, depending on their position on the facade. Their dense arrangement seldom represents reality—especially in the latter case—and the actual beam ends are never visible from the outside. If such paintings did not exist on real facades, then what we see in the miniature depictions is the X-ray technique applied in art.

The Temporal Effect of Color and Light

Color is omnipresent in the Theran landscape, and it is only natural that it would find its way into architecture either directly through the use of natural resources or indirectly as a source of inspiration (Pls. 1A–1C). The colors of the building materials are so powerful that they fundamentally affect the buildings.

The volcanic rocks of Thera provided architects—past and present—with stones of exquisitely vivid colors: red, black, gray, brown, white, green, and purple. Dressed stones of such colors were used at the corners of the buildings, as cornices at floor levels, as frames around doors and windows, and as pavements and dadoes inside the houses. In all cases, colors are carefully matched to create intentional effects: corner stones alternate from black to red (the visual effect is similar to what one sees in the houses depicted on the wall paintings), frames have different colors for each side, while cornices usually retain one color throughout.

The color of the exterior walls is also quite intense. A majority of the houses are plastered with a bright yellowish clay mortar. Lime plaster has been applied in only a few instances. In the case of Xeste 3, south facade, the plaster was painted in an orange/pink color. The ashlar walls are very impressive in terms of color. Only two buildings have extensive ashlar facades, Xeste 3 and Xeste 4. The former has the dark brown/black color of the ignimbrite, and the latter has the bright cream-white color of tuff. Interestingly enough, the interstices are stuccoed and painted in such a way as to simulate the color of the stone–dark red in Xeste 3 and white in Xeste 4.

Inside the house, color is especially marked in the rooms with the wall paintings. It is also present in other ways: certain floors, for example, were of an exquisite appearance, especially those paved with dark gray slabs with shiny particles and stuccoed with a dark red lime plaster. The mosaic floor of Delta 8 is also a delight to the eyes, with its multicolored limestone gravel. Ceilings, too, were probably colorful (though only white plaster has survived), especially those of the rooms with wall paintings. Last but not least, one should mention the dominating warm ocher-yellow color of wood lavishly applied in the buildings.

The colorful effect of the rooms with painted walls was projected outward, to a certain degree, through the wide windows common in such rooms. The pot of flowers painted on the window jamb on the upper floor of the West House (Pl. 3B) was obviously meant to be enjoyed both by the residents and the passers-by (though not easily seen through the narrow alley outside). This is an interesting juxtaposition of private versus public experience. Walking through Akrotiri would have been an experience strongly imbued with color; a fact suggested moreover by the colorful depictions of towns in art. But we must also keep in mind that color was everywhere, and that it participated in the built environment in many ways; through the beautiful vases standing on tables, shelves, and window sills; the textiles, hides, and mats hanging around as rugs, covers, and curtains; and even the dresses people wore. We must further keep in mind the temporality of color in nature and its analogy in architecture. Thera in spring time has an incredibly rich range of colors, so different from those in summer. As in nature, so in architecture colors react to the environmental conditions accordingly. When stones are wet, for example, their colors become deep and bright, and sometimes they actually acquire hues

that were not discernible before. Today, the ruins under the shelter are kept permanently dry, and dust settles on their surface without any hope of being removed either by rain or wind. As a result the uniform yellowish beige of the volcanic dust is the only color at the site. It took some years to observe the simple fact that ashlar stones piled outside the shelter (Pl. 1C)—in other words, kept clean from the dust—had bright colors; and, of course, so did the stones on the houses.

Light is the most important agent in conceiving space and surface articulation because it accentuates or softens the effects, brings out latent qualities of texture and form, and enhances color. The architecture of Akrotiri—and Minoan architecture in general—is an architecture of openness, the prevailing concept of space being that of "void exceeding mass." Light, therefore, penetrates deeply into the fabric of the buildings from a large number and variety of openings. Doors, however, had doorleaves, and the majority of windows—if not all—had composite lattices, and some may have had shutters. Light, therefore, was controlled to some extent (there was a need for temperature control as well). But most importantly, light would filter into the building through a dense web of vertical and horizontal wooden elements, as for example, in Xeste 3 (Fig. 247). As a result, it would reach the inner surfaces decomposed into alternating strips of light and shadows. This effect would create impressive wall patterns, and when hitting painted surfaces, it would enhance their appearance (or perhaps disturb it).

Fig. 247. Model of the eastern part of Xeste 3. Light penetrates through the multiple doors and windows.

Light varies constantly according to the hour, the day, and the season, and it depends on the orientation of the openings and the surfaces it reflects upon. When daylight is gone, oil-lamps are lit. Placed on high stands, hanging from above, or carried around, they would create sharp contrasts and dark peripheries that would bring out surface textures and irregularities on the wall paintings that were not there during the day, and the colors will emit an entirely different range of shades. These fascinating cycles of living tissues of architecture often escape our imagination when dealing with ruins from a purely archaeological point of view.

Dark spaces are in some cases adorned with wall paintings, as in the narrow spaces of Room 3, Xeste 3; their context is the main issue for their symbolic function, even if they are not easily discernible in the dim light. Most wall paintings, after all, were seldom seen as a whole, the way we see them today in a museum exhibition; usually one saw only partial views between door jambs, columns, furniture, and people moving around.[15]

The Artist and the Architect

Strictly speaking, mural treatment comes after the erection of an edifice. The artist arrives when the building is practically finished; the surfaces he will deal with are defined, and the manner in which his art will be experienced by the users of the building (access, light, visibility) is predetermined. He can intervene on architecture only superficially, by molding and shaping the final layer of lime plaster; for this layer was presumably left to the artist to prepare. The suppleness of the plaster allows the artist to adjust and organize the final surface as he thinks best by incising lines with a taut string on the wet plaster and sketching his themes with sharp tools. This small advantage can prove quite redeeming, as in Room Beta 6 with the Blue Monkeys, where the artist added an exceedingly thick plaster at the corner of the room, rounding it up into a cylinder in order to accommodate the circle of a running spiral that would be impossible to draw had he worked on the kind of sharp corner that the architect left behind.

But who decides which rooms should be painted and in what way? By answering the first part, the answer to the latter is only one step further. At Akrotiri, where observation is facilitated by the excellent state of preservation, there is evidence of a standard pattern of room arrangement that points to an overall "house model." Lyvia Morgan extends this observation to Kea, pointing out that, as in Thera, next to the room with miniature paintings is another room with paintings in panels, concluding that this pattern is specifically Cycladic.[16]

The Aegean "house model" (with its idiomatic variations in the Cyclades and in Crete) was presumably the outcome of a long tradition and was well known to all members of the community. Mural treatment was part of this model, along with the entrance system, the circulatory pattern, the distribution of storage areas, and the stone that was appropriate for a threshold or a column base. The rooms that ought to be painted, therefore, were well known from the beginning, and obviously so was the reason for painting these rooms, i.e., their function. Mural treatment, after all, aims at providing each room with the kind of ambience appropriate to its function. This common knowledge guided the artist just as much as the architect. In a type of architecture with high standards of design, as the Minoan, the pictorial program assigned to each building could have been known in advance, and we may well imagine the artist working together with the architect in conceiving space long before the walls were there for him to paint.

Chapter 10 Notes

1. Graham 1960; 1967; 1969: 222–229, 254–255; Preziosi 1983; Cherry 1983.

2. See Palyvou 1990.

3. Rapoport 1969.

4. Michailidou, ed., 2001. The sophisticated measurements applied in weighing and recording speak of well established and widely used systems.

5. Preziosi 1983: 490.

6. Architectural representations are abundant, and many of them show an amazing awareness of structural details. This awareness shows a strong affiliation between artists and architects and a knowledge of building technology shared by a more general public. See C. Palyvou, *Architecture in Aegean Bronze Age Art: Facades with no Interiors* (in press).

7. Beta 1, underneath the antelopes of the north wall (Marinatos 1968–1976, VII: 17); West House, Room 4 upper floor, Beta 6 Monkeys (Doumas 1992a: 30, n. 63–65).

8. Fragments of red painted plaster of an earlier date were found underneath the antelopes, Beta 1 (Marinatos 1968–1976, VII: 17).

9. This part is based largely on the author's article, Palyvou 2000.

10. See, for example, Iliakis 1978; Morgan 1983.

11. See Graham 1972: 199–205.

12. Fyfe 1902; see also Evans 1921–1935, III: 513–514, fig. 359 though not exactly an architectural fragment but a painted stucco base supporting a frieze of sphinxes and columns.

13. N. Marinatos 1984: 49–51.

14. The beam-ends have a diameter of approximately 0.32 m, placed on top of a wooden beam. See Lang 1969: 131–136; Lang comments that there are no parallels from Crete (p. 28).

15. See N. Marinatos, 1986, on the significance of the polythyra in controlling access, visibility, and light in ceremonial areas.

16. Morgan 1990: 258.

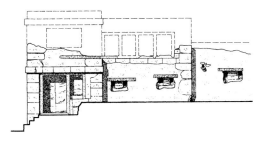

11

Reconciling with the Wrath of Engelados

An Organized Community Confronts Seismic Hazards

The Aegean is one of the most seismically sensitive regions of the world, and 50% of the seismic energy on European ground is emitted here. Scientists confirm that this activity goes far back in time. Earthquakes—especially when seriously disastrous—make a great impact on the people who live through them, and it is no surprise that after writing became a possibility they were meticulously recorded in various texts. Literature testifies to this and provides valuable information for some of the most severe earthquakes in antiquity, as far back as the 6th century B.C.,[1] while certain details even suggest the intensity of an earthquake. Beyond this time—before the benefit of written records—scientists are on their own in their effort to detect and date earlier seismic events. Archaeological data often proves to be a major source of information in this respect.

McCoy points out that seismic energy in the southern Aegean in historic times was related more to tectonic activity than to volcanism.[2] There is no evidence that the Bronze Age people of the Aegean distinguished between volcanic hazards, as such, and tectonic activity, but they certainly knew about seismic hazards. In Greek mythology, Engelados, who was responsible for the earthquakes, is also related to a volcano, because he was buried under Sicily by the wrath of Athena.

Thera has a long history of seismic events, some of which were very destructive.[3] The 1956 earthquake, with a Richter magnitude of 7.8 and an epicenter between Amorgos and Astypalaia, caused extensive damage and drove the majority of the population away from their homeland. Memories of this frightful event are still very vivid in the minds of the eldest citizens. The story of Thera is indeed a story of extremities of nature and of man's struggle to cope with them. In doing so, he has to balance between boldness and prudence, to experiment and to improve by learning fast from his mistakes and, above all, to observe carefully the signs of danger. Such a constant threat is bound to affect the mentality and the architecture of the peoples who choose to live in the Aegean region, as Evans observed very early in his explorations at Knossos,[4] comparing the situation to that in Japan. The fascinating thing about the Aegean Bronze Age people is that despite the high seismic risk, they developed a very bold architectural style, almost on the verge of being provocatively dangerous for such a troubled land. Yet, in an era as prolific as the Late Bronze Age, it seems that difficulties of this sort were turned into a challenge and a stimulus for further exertions and new technological achievements. This is, indeed, the architecture of an affluent society sparing no time and labor in improving its environment, a society that exhibits a free spirit exhorting able artisans to invent and innovate. In times as opulent and creative as these, the dialog between style and technology can only find a happy outcome and trigger a feedback process that will enhance both.

The town of Akrotiri was extensively rebuilt after such a *seismic destruction*. The anti-seismic technology applied in this rebuilding operation speaks vividly of the threat that was lingering during that period. There are conscious and deliberate improvements in this technology, while its unanimous adoption points to some kind of "building regulations" followed by all the inhabitants, very much like the "building codes" enforced on Thera after the disastrous earthquake of 1956.

Earthquake resistant concern is an integral part of the ultimate goal to build safe and long-lasting structures. It is often difficult to tell, therefore, if the builders were aware of the earthquake resistant contribution of certain structural details they adopted. One of the factors that may have accelerated technological developments in this direction is the frequent recurrence of catastrophic events. If a builder had the unfortunate opportunity to live through a number of severe earthquakes and judge for himself how the structures he built behaved under such extreme circumstances of stress, he may have better understood the mechanisms of strain and the weak points of the edifice. It would have been, thus, easier for him to develop ideas to correct and improve his own techniques. This could be the case for the few diagonal timber bonds described above, as they were an excellent anti-seismic technique.

Building in a safe, anti-seismic manner starts from the very beginning, while constructing the foundations (or even before that, when choosing the site on which to build). The archaeological records offer ample information on this issue, because it is, after all, mostly the foundations that have survived. This data, however, has been widely misunderstood, and it has been said that "Traditional Minoan construction paid little heed to the strength of foundations."[5] One reason for this misconception is that quite often no distinction exists between the foundation and the upper part of a wall. Only the elaborate ashlar facades have broader foundations, projecting above street level. A. Zois revised this picture,[6] pointing out several features that show a conscious effort to consolidate the foundations, such as the levelling of rock surfaces, the formation of terraces, the incorporation of rock-cut ledges as socles of rubble walls, and especially the addition of bracing-walls to consolidate the foundations of a structure. The latter have been often misinterpreted either as remains of earlier building phases or as walls forming small subterranean compartments accessible from above with trap doors. This is the case at Gournia, for example, as Zois points out. Yet, it is the strong inclination of the land that dictated these extra walls. Their possible use for underground storage space is only a side-effect.

True basements did exist and were quite popular in the Aegean from early times (e.g., Christiana, an islet close to Thera; Phtellos on Thera; Hagia Eirene on Kea[7]). One may even go as far as to suggest that they may have been appreciated for the seismic protection they offered. After all, it is the basements that the inhabitants of Akrotiri trusted mostly to hide their belongings when they abandoned their settlement, hoping to find them intact when they returned. In many cases they were, indeed, found intact by an unexpected intruder 3,500 years later.

Multistory architecture, on the other hand, has a long tradition in the Aegean. Two-storied houses appear as early as the middle of the third millennium B.C. (Early Cycladic II–III), as we now know from the finds on the island of Ios.[8] This is of special interest, because an additional story above ground raises extra demands for the stability of the structure. The Aegean builders, therefore, had all the motivation and the time to develop the sophisticated multistory technology we see during the Late Bronze Age. By that time, two-story buildings were the norm, and even a third story was added to certain structures of special significance. It is very interesting to observe that the structural concept often differs from one story to the other: the ground floor is usually massive, with thick walls and only a few small openings, while the upper floors are wisely made of lighter construction including many openings, to the effect that some rooms look more like semi-open verandas.

The answer to the quest for building in an earthquake resistant manner, however, was given primarily by the extensive use of timber. From the data presented in the previous chapters, it has become clear that this was a half-timber building technology, where timber and stone supplement each other. A sophisticated timber technology is applied everywhere: in the reinforcement of the stone walls, horizontal and vertical, in the elaborate construction of openings, where wood is the main load bearing element, and in the staircases, where timber frames embrace all the surrounding walls, carrying the loads of two and three stories down to foundation level. The pier-and-opening (door, window, or cupboard) structure (a true invention of the south Aegean people) is the boldest manifestation of this timber technology (see Xeste 3, for example).

Wood adds elasticity to the building (see Chap. 9) and thanks to its high tensile strength, it can withstand significant deformations. The example of the West House is most telling: the south wall of Room 4 was marginally saved from collapse thanks to the timber reinforcement that kept the deformed wall in place (Fig. 53). This means that the people inside the house could leave the house safely. The way the timber elements in a building relate to each other is also indicative of the anti-seismic concern. This concern is best demonstrated by the special reinforcements discussed in Chapter 9, especially the diagonal bonding and the way timber elements are fixed on ashlar stones with wooden pegs inserted in mortises. These techniques show that the builders were aware of the consequences of lateral thrust (typical of earthquakes) and the way to deal with the problem by stabilizing the timber parts with pegs and also by ensuring the collaboration of all the parts of the building in all directions (this is achieved by the diagonal bond and the rigid corner). Ashlar stones offer extra stability, especially at the corners, the most vulnerable parts of an edifice. All these details, discussed at length in the relevant chapter, show that the architects of Akrotiri were very advanced in their understanding of the static behavior of the multistory structures they were erecting.[9]

Apart from the technical point of view, the extraordinary circumstances of preservation at Akrotiri give us an unexpected glimpse of the behavior of the prehistoric inhabitants during a seismic event (or volcanic for that matter), from the very first days following the earthquake to the final evacuation. So, let us retrace the last days at Akrotiri, according to the archaeological data.[10]

It was summer time, around 1525 B.C. (or was it 1646?), and the city was living through its daily routine enjoying a period of affluence and economic development. Nothing could foretell the catastrophic events that were to follow. An initial coughing of the volcano gave good warning, and the first crumbling walls chased the people out of their houses. A thin layer of ash soon covered the streets and the debris of the fallen walls. They had managed to leave in time, however, saving their lives and some of their most valuable belongings (gold and precious metal objects are rarely found among the excavated debris).

The evacuation was timely and effective, a clear indication that it was ordered and organized by a central authority. The word was quickly passed to all the inhabitants who then had to prepare to leave their houses, not knowing for how long. We can only imagine the turmoil and the anxiety of the people having to decide quickly what to do with their households: objects were moved around, the most valuable belongings were packed—the value estimated in terms of necessity, cost, and easy transfer but also on a personal sentimental basis. What stayed behind was carefully stowed in places believed to be more secure (Fig. 248). Numerous objects were placed on the sills of windows (actually, almost all of them have something standing on their sills, often intact for that matter). Larger objects were placed under the lintels of doors (such as the pithos found in the doorways of the pier-and-door partition of Delta 1–1a, blocking the access completely; Fig. 249). Vessels were also packed around the column of Beta 2. It is clear that the people knew from previous experience that the frames of the openings and the area surrounding a column were safer and more liable to protect their belongings than if they had left them lying in the middle of the room. Deep basements were also trusted, and valuable vessels

Fig. 248. Vases carefully stored in the corners of the room before departing (West House, Room 5, ground floor).

Fig. 249. Delta-West, a large pithos was placed within the doorway of the pier-and-door partition between Rooms 1 and 1a.

were stored there, some wrapped up for extra protection (Fig. 250). Delta 13 has such a basement found packed with vases and a hoard of bronze vessels. Small spaces were also thought to be safer (the ceiling beams were more liable to resist in a small roof span), as in the case of Delta 18–18a, where an amazing number of objects, including fine pieces of furniture, had been stowed. The houses were thus tidied up, the doors were sealed,[11] and the town was evacuated in a systematic and timely manner.

The people did not give up that easily, however, because they were accustomed to the sudden wraths of the volcanic land they had inhabited (severe earthquakes, at least, must have been common). When things calmed down, they came back to look for casualties and check their houses. It seems that things were quiet enough to make them feel they could start preparing their return. They formed

rescue parties that spread all over the town, working simultaneously at various points. These were men who knew well how to organize such an operation: where to camp and what the priorities were. After opening rudimentary paths for access, the human casualties, if any, were the first to be dealt with. Most probably, however, the evacuation that preceded saved the lives of the people. They started clearing the debris from the streets, putting aside the stones to be reused. The picture shows that they had time enough only for the basics: they demolished dangerous ruins[12] and provisionally blocked doors and windows that were on the verge of collapsing (Fig. 251). This was mostly a collective work dealing with communal problems, and if they entered the houses at all it was to bring out necessities, such as food supplies, cooking pots, and beds, all of which have been found lying outside on thick layers of debris. Three such beds were found standing on accumulated debris to the north of Sector Gamma (Fig. 252). They knew well that it was not safe to stay indoors, and they camped outside.[13] This, unfortunately, is a painfully familiar picture for those who live in regions of high seismic risk.

All this proved in vain, however, because they soon realized that the monster sleeping in the depths of their land had been awakened for good. There must have been clear signs of a paroxysmal event in

Fig. 250. The imprint of a mat placed upright between a vase (now removed) and the wall for protection.

Fig. 251. The entrance to Gamma-South was blocked provisionally during the rescue operation.

Fig. 252. Beds placed on the debris of a ruined house to the west of Delta-South.

process unlike anything they had experienced before (the poisonous gases coming out of a volcano suffice to make life unbearable). They knew that they had to leave their town again, and perhaps the island as well. Scattered as they were all over the ruined town, it was probably a central authority in charge that once more ordered their departure.

The only human skeleton found to date is that of an old man in a remote rural installation on Therasia—a lonely figure, trapped under the ruins of his house, a few meters from the front door.[14] Far from the protective mechanisms of the urban environment, and perhaps reluctant to leave his land anyway (there are so many parallels of this behavior throughout history), he paid the consequences with his life.

Judging from the reaction of the people in similar situations throughout history, it can be said that the Therans functioned in a very efficient manner, a clear sign that they belonged to a well organized community and were experienced in such disaster events. All evidence points to an obedient and collective response to the commands of a trustworthy authority that was deciding and organizing the way and the means of this mass escape.

When and how they left, and where they went, we really do not know. Did they rush toward the harbor and embark on their boats—those elegant boats we see on the wall paintings of the West House? If so, did they escape the tsunami waves (surely they should have known about them from previous experience)? Did they depart in time to avoid any such consequences? Or perhaps they never left. Maybe they are still buried under the thick layer of volcanic ash that covers the island. Scholars have long been trying to trace the signs of their escape. Some believe that they survived, and that they gradually scattered all over the eastern Mediterranean—Crete, mainland Greece, Cyprus, Asia Minor, even the Syro-Palestinian coast. This is inferred by minute signs, such as a distinct artistic preference that may indicate the presence of able Theran craftsmen in foreign services far away from their homeland.[15]

Earlier Seismic Activity

This was certainly not the Therans' first or only experience of severe earthquakes. At least one more instance can be detected from the archaeological evidence. It is dated approximately 50 years prior to the final destruction and has been labelled conventionally the *seismic destruction* to distinguish it from the volcanic destruction that put an end to life on the island for many centuries.

The main archaeological evidence of this overwhelming destruction is the thick layer of debris and the extensive rebuilding of the settlement. The mass rebuilding that followed was not merely the act of each individual repairing his house, because it involved communal decisions at a large scale, such as the clearing of all public spaces, the permanent demolition of dangerous structures (parts of buildings became open public spaces after that, as in the Square of the Mill House and Delta 20), the deposit of the debris, the construction of new street pavements, and the rebuilding of the sewage system.

Handling the large masses of debris accumulated from the houses that were destroyed, as well as those that had to be demolished, was no easy task. One of the problems that arise in such situations is what to do with the material that cannot be reused. The Therans resorted to a well known solution to the problem: the debris was laid on the streets and public open areas and a new street pavement was constructed 1 to 2 m above the earlier street level. This debris has been found in many places within the site, in the form of an artificial layer consisting mainly of well compacted soil and sherds (Figs. 50, 96, 104). Stones were removed from the destruction layer and reused. This is a normal practice in similar situations, because it is very difficult and costly to transfer the debris outside the town.

Many of the ground floor rooms that survived this destruction were incorporated in the rebuilding of the houses. Due to the thick artificial layer outside, most of the lower rooms became semi-basements. The entrances, however, had to be entirely rearranged, or rebuilt, in order to adjust to the new street level. The typical staircase incorporated in the entrance was an ingenious solution to the problem of accommodating various levels. In Sector Delta, parts of buildings were demolished and buried under their debris, and public spaces took their place. Moreover, new entrances were built in many houses, and rooms were added in several cases. All the works, however, adhered to the rules of good neighborliness and communal laws, the latter being especially evident in the way the new building (Delta 15) follows the existing indentation of the neighboring facades (Fig. 32). A similar sequence of events was about to begin after the last destruction, had it not proved so fatal.

What does all this imply in terms of land ownership, public management, and communal laws? The picture that arises is that the people of Akrotiri were enjoying the benefits of a well organized community. Such drastic measures can only be understood as communal decisions made and enforced for the benefit of the common welfare. So, though the relics of Akrotri may seem to us untidy or erratic today, they actually show a remarkable effort of a community as a whole coping with a complex system of variants. The effort was rendered even more difficult by the ever-raging volcanic heart of the Theran homeland.

It is not only in times of danger that the community exhibits its orderly function. The repetition of a house model, ranging only in size and complexity, reflects a corresponding social unit of varying degrees of size and significance. Judging from the large number of houses sharing architectural elements indicative of affluence (ashlar masonry, large amount of timber, wall paintings, lavatories), it seems that this was a truly prosperous harbor town. It is not easy to assess from the architecture alone the kind of family that was housed in these buildings, but surely evidence exists for a social unit involving people engaged in numerous household activities and industries. The atypical houses, on the other hand, point to specialized communal activities. The same is true for certain larger public open spaces, such as the Square of the Cenotaph.

Many parallels throughout the pre-industrial era point to communities functioning on the basis of unwritten laws, formed through time and tradition and enacted by the fear of public opinion and superstition. This very common attitude goes far back in time and is reflected in a Mesopotamian omen text that reads: "If a house blocks the main street in its building the owner of the house will die; if the house overshadows (overhangs) or obstructs the side of the main street the heart of the dweller in that house will not be glad."[16]

Chapter 11 Notes

1. Papazachos and Papazachou 1997.

2. McCoy and Heiken 2000: 61.

3. On the volcanic history of Thera after 197 a.d., see Vougioukalakis 2001: 37–50.

4. It is interesting to note his own remarks after having himself lived through such a severe earthquake in Crete (Evans 1927: discussion).

5. Graham 1972: 149.

6. Zois 1990.

7. Marthari 2001.

8. Marthari 1990a.

9. E. Tsakanika, a civil engineer, is currently working on the *Earthquake Resistant Timber Structures in Prehistoric Greece*, Ph.D. in progress (National Technical University of Athens).

10. See also Nikolakopoulou 2003.

11. At least four doors were found closed: Delta 19, West House, Xeste 3, and House of the Ladies. In these cases, that is, the imprints of the door leaves were preserved.

12. See Doumas 1974a.

13. Doumas 1993: 180.

14. Sperling 1973: 59. The site at Therasia could be reached either by land, in a round about way, or by sea, though the high cliffs forming the coast line in this area would impede this access.

15. See, for example, Cameron 1978: 580. Televantou 1994: 378–383.

16. Frankfort 1950: 111.

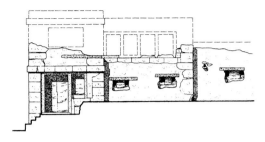

12

Thera and Her Neighbors in a
Time of Opulence

Life in the Aegean has always revolved around seafaring and trade. These powerful driving forces led early people to a remarkable evolution from rural to urban life. Crete became the focal point of these developments: she was a large, self-sustainable land, rich in resources, which dominated within this broad sea. Urbanization here led to unprecedented socio-political developments and the subsequent creation of the palace as the hub of urban life. The palace—more a building compound than an edifice in its own right—was inextricably bonded with the surrounding town and housed institutions that initiated a new era for the Aegean world.[1] A distinct style of Minoan architecture was born.

The first palaces were destroyed (by earthquakes?), but they were rebuilt soon after in a more luxurious manner and with advanced building techniques, albeit along the lines of their predecessors. This event marks the beginning of the "golden age" for the Minoan world. One of the novelties of this era—the Neopalatial era—was the wide dissemination of the architectural vocabulary of the palaces—and the lifestyle for that matter—to the majority of sites on Crete as well as many sites on the southern

Aegean islands. Moreover, a sophisticated building technology, involving time and labor consuming techniques and craft specialization, was now available to a broader public. Large well-built mansions—the so-called "villas"—appear all over Crete, either in an urban context or in the countryside. It is a period of great prosperity, creativity, and opulence for Crete and her neighbors in the south Aegean. It is within this roughly outlined framework that we seek to understand the place and identity of Thera and her privileged position in the developments of the time.[2]

Since the discovery of Akrotiri by Marinatos, the relationship between Crete and Thera has been open to debate. The affinities between the two places are so overwhelming—especially when compared to the other Cycladic islands—that the question of the Minoanization of Thera has hardly retained the question mark at the end. In the late 1960s scholars had already crystallized their ideas, often in a dogmatic manner,[3] about the identity of the Minoan civilization on Crete versus the contemporary civilizations of the Near East and the Cyclades. They embarked on a strongly biased debate of the Minoanization of Thera, and the tug of war between Cretan dominance and Cycladic autonomy (or Minoan "imperialists" and Cycladic "nationalists," as Davis succinctly described it[4]) was pulled according to the viewpoint of each scholar.[5]

The word "influence," commonly used in this debate, often echoes earlier theories of "diffusion" which, as Renfrew points out, imply that "change comes from outside," and that it is "infectious," i.e., spreads through contact.[6] New features, however, are accepted by a community—"inventions" become "innovations," in Renfrew's words—only if and when the overall circumstances favor such choices by the individuals. "Just because man can do something does not mean that he will," writes Rapoport.[7] In this discussion, therefore, it is important to examine carefully the notion of influence. For this purpose, it will prove useful to distinguish between the three main constituents of architecture (and of all artifacts for that matter): structure, function, and form (*firmitas*, *utilitas*, and *venustas*, to quote Vitruvius[8]). "Influence" or "affinities" in each one of these areas has a different significance when examining the relationships between the associated members. A time and labor consuming technique, such as ashlar masonry, for example, may have

been disseminated from Egypt to all the eastern Mediterranean as a technology, but the forms and the functions it served in each case varied greatly—from fortification walls to tombs, palaces, and town houses.[9] In other words, only the practical aspects of the architectural tradition of Egypt were copied and used to create forms (and serve functions) completely foreign to Egypt. When an architectural form is copied, on the other hand, the kind of relationship implied is much stronger and of a different nature. Such is the case, for example, with the lustral basin, a highly idiomatic architectural form related to rituals in Crete. Its presence on Thera implies the same function as well. Even stronger are the affinities when popular architectural forms with a long tradition in one place are copied in another—from Crete to Thera, again—as in the case of the room with a central column. These examples are discussed in detail below.

Starting the comparative analysis with structure, we could safely state that the affinities between the two places are overwhelming in this respect: building technology is practically identical in Crete and Thera. The distinctive features of this technology are ashlar masonry and timber framing.

Ashlar Masonry

Although the art of carving stone has a long tradition in the Cyclades in small-scale glyptic art, ashlar walls are unknown at Akrotiri before the Late Bronze Age. In Crete, on the other hand, dressed stones appear as early as MM II in the first palaces of Knossos and Phaistos and in the palatial architecture of Quartier Mu at Malia.[10]

These early ashlar structures already have the main characteristics typical of the Neopalatial period: only the face of the block is finely dressed, whereas the back of the wall is built with rubble; dowels are cut on their upper surface to secure wooden beams fixed on the stone with wooden pegs, etc. This technology remained more or less the same throughout the 200 years from its first appearance in Crete to the time of Akrotiri. What did change in the Neopalatial period (the time of Akrotiri), is the extent of its application. It is no longer an exclusive feature of the palaces, but it appears in many other buildings and town houses as well.[11] This change has nothing to do with technology, because masons knew their job long before and added little through the years.[12] The clientele

changed. The town houses using this technique may be only 10–15% of the total, but their distribution all over the island, from Chania to Palaikastro, and from rural villas to urban mansions,[13] shows that the section of the Cretan society using ashlar masonry for its houses cannot be easily distinguished from the rest of the community.

The Theran ashlar walls are of excellent quality, and they seem to outnumber the uses in many Cretan sites, with the exception of Knossos. Ashlar stones are reported from other sites on Thera, also.[14] Moreover, ashlar blocks found within the artificial layer of the debris accumulated after the *seismic destruction*[15] indicate that they were in use even before this horizon, that is before, or right at, the beginning of LM IA. This means that the proliferation of ashlar masonry in domestic architecture happened almost simultaneously in both places.

At Akrotiri, dressed stones incorporated in rubble walls at key positions are very common. Ashlar frames around openings and ashlar projecting cornices are not well preserved in Crete, so a comparison would not be safe. For corner stones, on the other hand, there is no question of preservation. Though all three cases exist in Crete, it may be said that the systematic way they are applied at Akrotiri is a Theran trait.

The concluding point is that ashlar masonry is a technology with a long history on Crete, but its application to domestic architecture is as new for Crete as it is for Thera. This means that the events that triggered changes in Crete during the Neopalatial period affected Thera simultaneously and in a similar way. It is interesting to push this line of thought a little further: part of the technology of ashlar masonry used in both places is the incision of mason's marks on the surface of the blocks. In Crete mason's marks appear in MM II, at the same time as the first ashlar walls. In the Neopalatial period, however, although dressed stones are now also used in houses, mason's marks remain a feature typical of palace architecture, with the palace of Knossos far ahead of the others.[16]

What should we infer then from the 80 or more mason's marks found at Akrotiri?[17] Akrotiri comes right after the three major palaces of Crete in number of mason's marks. These statistics may change as excavations proceed and reports are published. Preservation, on the other hand, is not an issue, because mason's marks can be found on blocks unearthed from the debris, as in the case of Galatas. Moreover, just as each site on Crete has its predominant mason's marks, so does Akrotiri with its prevailing three parallel lines and cross. I believed the former to be peculiar to Akrotiri, but recent excavations on Crete have revealed many such mason's marks: at Knossos, Petras, Galeni, Galatas and elsewhere.[18]

To emphasize the significance of their presence at Akrotiri even further, we should point out that in the rest of the Aegean world and on the mainland of Greece, mason's marks are extremely rare: two mason's marks found at the impressive Tholos Tomb I at Peristeria, Peloponnese (a double axe and a branch) have been suggested as evidence of a Cretan architect.[19] Whatever the meaning of these marks—and there are theories of all kinds—their presence at Akrotiri speaks of a direct and privileged connection between Thera and the palace of Knossos.

Timber Framing

Timber reinforcement, in the form of horizontal grids, has a long tradition in Crete, going back to the beginnings of the Bronze Age, as at Vasiliki.[20] It is also common in Thera and Therasia,[21] yet it is rare in contemporary Hagia Eirene and Phylakopi. During the Late Bronze Age, timber reinforcement becomes more sophisticated through the use of vertical posts. This technique may derive from the construction of mudbrick walls, where the contribution of timber is essential.[22] The Hypostyle Crypte at Malia is an early example (MBA) of timber reinforcement of mudbrick walls in the form of vertical post pairs. The system exhibits a high degree of regularity and, as van Effenterre has shown,[23] it is reminiscent of the structural concept of the pier-and-door partition.

Vertical timber reinforcement of stone walls, however, is believed to be a Neopalatial feature.[24] The cases attested at Akrotiri (Xeste 2, Xeste 3, Beta 1) are well constructed and cover two or three stories. The parallels on Crete are all found either in the palaces or in the large mansions of McEnroe's Type 1 houses,[25] such as Tylissos and Sklavokambos. This technique, on the other hand, is not attested elsewhere in the Cycladic settlements. It becomes a typical feature, however, of Mycenaean architecture in the Greek mainland,[26] as well as in places such as Cyprus and Ugarit, probably through Mycenaean influence.[27]

A notable structural difference between the Theran and the Cretan timber techniques is that the former is based on a three-dimensional framing concept, while the latter is more commonly in the form of individual pairs of posts that are not bonded with longitudinal beams (this is the case especially at Tylissos, Hagia Triada, Zakros, and Nirou Chani).[28] All other details are otherwise common in both places.

Timber reinforcement is conspicuously absent in ashlar walls, as mentioned above. This is well attested in the numerous ashlar facades that have survived on Crete and Akrotiri and is also demonstrated vividly in the architectural representations of ashlar walls in Aegean Bronze Age art. Timber framing would, indeed, disrupt the regularity of the courses and the interlocking of the blocks. Timber reinforcement of rubble walls, on the other

Fig. 253. The Grand Staircase at Knossos: an intricate timber system carried the loads of three stories to the ground.

hand, is commonly depicted in art (see, for example, the Town Mosaic and the Archanes clay model of a house).[29] In the latter, incisions reveal not only the horizontal and vertical beams but also the transverse beams, which show as beam ends on the face of the wall.

The "timber wall" of Xeste 3 is one of the boldest structures not only for Akrotiri but for the Aegean world in general. It may only be compared to the even more daring and larger construction of the Grand Staircase at Knossos, where superimposed wooden columns carry the loads of three stories (interestingly enough, staircases are involved in both cases; Fig. 253).

Similar conclusions are reached when one compares the architecture of Crete and Akrotiri in terms of form and function. Let us examine three cases of special interest:

THE ROOM WITH A CENTRAL COLUMN

This room can be easily recognized by its almost square plan, its stone base at the center, and its direct relationship with the entrance (Fig. 254). It

has a long history in Crete, going back to the beginnings of the Middle Bronze Age. It has always been the hub of the Minoan house and served a variety of purposes as a common room for everyday activities and informal social contacts. Michailidou's work on the origins and function of this room type is most illuminating.[30] This room is typical of town houses (Types 2 and 3 by McEnroe), while it is absent in the large Neopalatial mansions (Type 1) or may have existed in an upper story with a different functional significance. It is one of the oldest and most persisting architectural forms, and it remained the predominant living space of the Cretan house throughout the Minoan era—i.e., for approximately 400 years.

At Akrotiri six such rooms have been excavated, all easily identified by their dimensions, the dressed stone base in their centers, and their position in the house. What is striking is that in most cases, if not all, this room is a later addition or has resulted from remodelling of pre-existing rooms. The "room with a central column" was incorporated into the existing buildings during the extensive rebuilding operation that took place after the *seismic destruction* of the town at the beginning of LM IA. This is especially evident in Sector Beta, as discussed above, where a room at ground-floor level had to be sacrificed to this end. In conclusion, a traditional Cretan room, the hub of the Cretan house, was introduced into Theran architecture at a specific time.

THE LUSTRAL BASIN AND THE MINOAN HALL

The lustral basin is a highly idiomatic space in Minoan architecture. It has a long history in Crete: a room sunk in the ground in Quartier Mu is believed to be the earliest known example.[31] Most of the lustral basins we know of, however, are of the second palace period. Outside the palaces, the number of lustral basins throughout Crete is very limited, and they all belong to elaborate Type 1 buildings.[32] Sometime within LM IA, many lustral basins went out of use or were remodelled (filled in). This change was associated, according to Driessen, with the introduction in domestic architecture of another palatial type of room, the Minoan Hall.[33]

The Minoan Hall, as known in Crete, is absent in Thera, but there is one unmistakable lustral basin in Xeste 3. It is related to a number of rooms interlinked with pier-and-door partitions. The pier-and-door partition, very popular at Akrotiri, should not be associated exclusively with the Minoan Hall, because it is applied as a structural element in many different ways.[34]

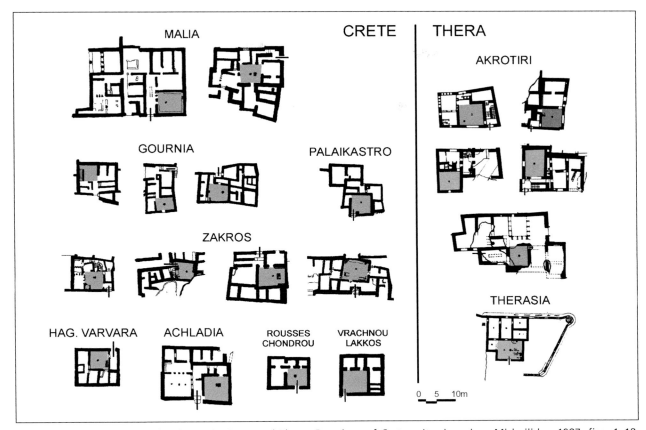

Fig. 254. Rooms with central columns in Crete and Thera. Drawings of Cretan sites based on Michailidou 1987: figs. 1–18. Therasia based on Sperling 1973: fig. 20.

Time, though elusive, is important in this case. The Theran lustral basin was in use at the end of LM IA, when the volcanic eruption took place, although its time of construction is unknown. Are we to assume that the still functioning Theran lustral basin, in combination with the absence of Minoan Halls, points to a time within LM IA but before the change that occurred in Crete? In other words, did the Minoan Hall appear in Crete in domestic architecture after the volcanic destruction of Thera, and is this why it is not present in Theran architecture? This question, intriguing though it may be, pushes archaeological interpretation beyond its limits. Can we really pinpoint "events" and "short times" in archaeological records when our time-table is arranged conventionally on the basis of 25 to 50 year-long periods? Whatever the case, such a room, with a peculiar and distinct architectural form and structure, and strongly imbued with ritual notions, can hardly have been transplanted from Crete to Thera stripped of its function. The scarcity of lustral basins, even in Crete,[35] makes the Theran lustral basin stand out as a very important element.

THE PIER-AND-DOOR PARTITION, THE MINOAN HALL, AND THE POLYTHYRON HALL

The large number of pier-and-door partitions at Akrotiri is very significant because this detail is an almost exclusive feature of Cretan architecture. Apart from Akrotiri, the only other examples reported outside Crete come from Trianda, on Rhodes,[36] a settlement believed to be a Minoan colony.

From a technical point of view, all the pier-and-door partitions follow the same structural concept. This conclusion is deduced from the characteristic stone bases rather than the timber frame (which has left little evidence in Crete). The construction of a typical jamb with three upright mudbricks is found in Crete also, in particular at the mansion of Sklavokambos.[37]

Evans' ideas concerning clerestories above the doors of pier-and-door partitions (Fig. 255) have been proven correct, thanks to Xeste 3 (see above). Yet, it was the exception and not the rule, and only appeared when its presence was imperative. In all other cases, the area above the common lintel of a pier-and-door partition is walled

Fig. 255. The Minoan Hall in the Royal Villa, Knossos, Crete (Michailidou 1981: fig. 60).

and often decorated with paintings in the form of a frieze. The discovery of such friezes may indicate the presence of a pier-and-door/window partition, as Cameron has already suggested.[38] The wooden bases of Xeste 3, Room 3, also have their parallel in Crete, in Quartier Mu, and the palace of Malia; the former is the earliest example of a pier-and-door partition (MM II period).[39]

Pier-and-door partitions are used for a variety of purposes and in a variety of combinations.[40] They occur mostly in central Crete, in palaces and Type 1 buildings, and their most common application is in the Minoan Hall, as a substitute for the exterior wall joining the room with the porch. In Thera, there are no Minoan Halls, and pier-and-door partitions are only applied inside the buildings, substituting for one or more interior walls. This type of arrangement, consisting of at least two rooms joined with pier-and-door partitions, the Polythyron Hall, is quite common in Crete, occurring at Zakros, Nerokourou, and elsewhere.

The Wall Paintings

The quantity and quality of the wall paintings found at Akrotiri is far beyond anything one could have hoped for or expected. Judging from the scanty remains of Cretan wall painting fragments, it came as a surprise that almost all the houses at Akrotiri, at least those more fully excavated, have one or more rooms with wall paintings. The "typical Theran house," in other words, seems to include a specific type of room with wall paintings. It is usually situated deep in the fabric of the house, far from the entrance. It is well lit, with a beautiful paved floor, and it is equipped with niches or cupboards. It also has one or more annexes (i.e., spaces allotted only to the service of this specific room). All this is typically found on the upper floor, with the few exceptions discussed above.

Crete has very little to show in this respect, and despite the fact that the upper floors are seldom preserved, one would expect some fragments to survive in the debris below. Given the hindrances in comparing Akrotiri with Crete, one is still left with overwhelming astonishment and admiration for what Akrotiri has to show. Restoration of the wall paintings is slow and still in progress (and will remain so for many years to come). Yet, there has been spectacular progress in the past few years, especially with the wall paintings of Xeste 3. This atypical house is most atypical in this respect as well: the number of walls decorated with paintings is increasing as the restorers progress with their work. It is estimated that over 50% of the 35 rooms of Xeste 3 had wall paintings. This is truly an invaluable treasure for Aegean scholars, who may now have the opportunity to study not only the information that these pictures provide, but also the relationship of the wall paintings to the architecture.

Size of Houses

If we broaden our scope to compare the townscape and settlement pattern, the similarities between Crete and Thera are equally striking (Fig. 15, 16). Numerous habitation sites of various sizes are dispersed all over both islands. As Davis and Cherry have pointed out, the settlement pattern of Thera is unparalleled on Kea and Melos, yet typical for Crete.[41] Moreover, the two Cycladic coastal towns of Hagia Eirene and Phylakopi were fortified, while Akrotiri seems to follow Crete in its absence of fortifications. The size and townscape of Akrotiri can hardly be compared to the Cycladic towns, as discussed in Chapter 5. Akrotiri was surely a large town, comparable only to the largest towns of Crete (Palaikastro, for example). In addition, the layout of the town shows functional zoning (large mansions to the south) and a high degree of organization in the open, public space.

The size of the houses is also comparable to the Cretan distinction between mansions and ordinary houses (Fig. 256, 257). The smaller size (96–100 m²) is similar to the average house at Gournia and suburban houses at Palaikastro. These are believed to represent low-class citizens, though Driessen and MacGillivray point out[42] that some of them seem to be simply later constructions that do not conform to the initial layout. At Akrotiri, the two small houses, Alpha-East and Delta-East, are by no means poorer than the rest. The most common size at Palaikastro[43] is between 130 and 180 m² (21 out of 36 buildings measured), and this is very much the case at Akrotiri as well (6 out of 11 houses fall between 139 and 187 m²). The large houses are limited and range between 200 and 300 m² at Palaikastro (6 out of 36) and between 269 and 367 m² at Akrotiri (Xestes 3 and 4, and possibly Beta-South). All these calculations, of course, are approximate and give a general idea of the size of the house. The true values lay in the size of the floor area, that is in the total floor surface of all the stories. Because the large houses tend to have three instead of two stories, the difference becomes even bigger (compare Alpha-East at 200 m² to Xeste 4 at 957 m²).

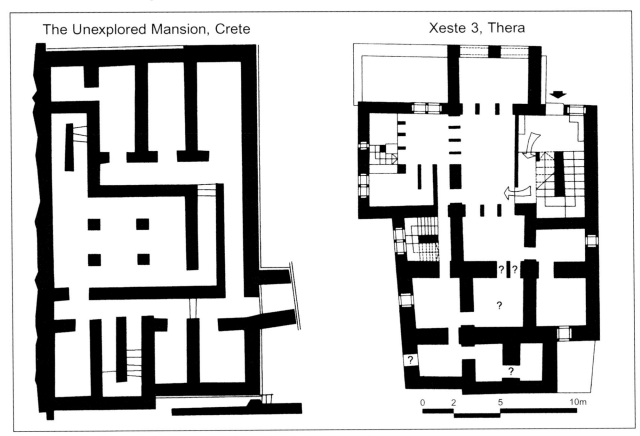

Fig. 256. The Unexplored Mansion from Crete (Popham 1984: pl. 2) and Xeste 3.

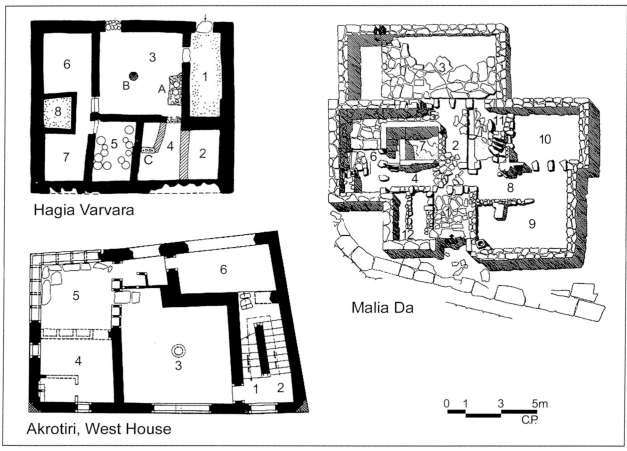

Fig. 257. The West House compared to Cretan houses at Hagia Varvara (Hood 1971: 63, fig. 31) and Malia House Da (Demargne and Gallet de Santerre 1953: pl. 63).

Concluding Remarks

In this comparative study, we have worked with one disadvantage: our data in the long run—the time needed to build up tradition—is far richer for Crete than it is for Thera. Most of what we see today at Akrotiri represents a short period, framed between two major events, both presumably triggered by nature; the terminus post quem was a seismic destruction at the very beginning of LM IA, and the terminus ante quem was the final eruption of the volcano that occurred approximately 50 years later. Both events are within the same chronological period.[44] As we know, such termina do not always help us understand the sequence of architectural development.

Perhaps it would help to approach the issue in a different way: are there any elements of Theran architecture missing in Crete? If so, they may belong to a local, non-Cretan, tradition that we have no other evidence for. The answer is: not really. Certain

details that I thought to be particular to Akrotiri in the past (e.g., ashlar corner stones, mason's marks with 3 parallel lines, the door-and-window entrance system) are now known from Crete.

One could argue that what we see in Thera is actually a variation of the Cretan prototypes. But are there any prototypes, as such? Is not variation the very essence of Minoan architecture? How are we to distinguish between a "non-Minoan element" at Akrotiri and a regional "Minoan variation" at Palaikastro,[45] not attested at Malia, for example?

Where has this comparison led us? First of all, there can be no doubt that the building technology applied at Akrotiri is of Cretan origin. All the techniques—and we are speaking of an elaborate and sophisticated technology—have a tradition of two to four hundred years in Crete, whereas in the Aegean islands all evidence points to a rather conservative and conventional building tradition. And this we know despite our incomplete information about Thera's architectural past. This does not mean that they were less able architects (a glance at the early Cycladic remains of Kea and those of Skarkos on the island of Ios would suffice for the opposite[46]); able craftsmen, indeed, are much better predisposed to adopt a higher technology.

The houses at Akrotiri were not built on a virgin land, except for a few cases; they were continuing a long sequence of habitation, attested under the ruins of the town, albeit in a fragmentary manner. Sometime around the very beginning of LM IA, the Therans were already using the Minoan building technology, in a sporadic manner. Then, the big earthquake (still within the first phase of LM IA) destroyed their town to a large extent. This dramatic event, far from detrimental, gave the Therans the opportunity to rebuild their town and to reform their houses by lavishly using the sophisticated technology they were already familiar with. They even went so far as to import building materials from Crete.[47]

The emerging picture is as follows: after the *seismic destruction*, the remains of a vague Cycladic past, already influenced by the Cretan building technology, blended with an innovative architecture of Cretan origin. In terms of form and function, the new look of the houses was comparable to those of many Cretan towns (e.g., Malia, Zakros, Palaikastro). In terms of building technology, however, Akrotiri differs from these Cretan towns because it is closer to the sophisticated technology used in Crete by the palace people and by 10–15% of the Cretan society. This new picture of Akrotiri alludes to the architecture of an affluent society.

It is important to remember that all this took place at a time when Crete was going through major reforms. The archaeological data speak of a proliferation of palatial privileges in the towns and of the rich rural installations in the countryside. In this process Thera, though outside Crete, is not only present from the very beginning, but receives a distinctly large portion of the pie that gives her an almost privileged place by the side of Knossos itself. This is the archaeological assumption; the political and historical implications are a much more complex issue that needs to be evaluated through a comprehensive and multivariable study.

The works of this "golden age" speak of bold and ingenious craftsmanship. The striking proliferation over an extensive region of the palatial architectural style shows that the people involved in building exchanged knowledge and experience freely, and formed, most probably, a body of specialized artisans and even itinerant builders. A situation like this leaves much space for experimentation and innovation. We witness an era of versatile thinking and uninhibited creativity, based, however, on a longlasting and firmly rooted Cretan tradition. This knowledge was gradually disseminated to Mycenaean Greece, an "Aegean koine" by then. After the abrupt end of Thera and the fall of Cretan power, the Mycenaeans took their architectural knowledge as far east as Cyprus and the Syro-Palestinian coast. These places were most certainly visited by the seafaring Therans long before the fatal events. It may not be implausible to suggest that some Therans migrated to harbor towns of the east Mediterranean after the destruction of their own homeland, bringing with them their craftsmanship and sophisticated life style. A cosmopolitan harbor town such as Ugarit, after all, would not have been too foreign a place to start all over again.

Chapter 12 Notes

1. See Driessen et al. 2002 on the Minoan palaces.

2. See also Palyvou 1999b.

3. See Zois 1996, for an excellent analysis of the interpretive labyrinth of the Knossian ruins; but also W.J. Graham's sharp criticism on dogmatic interpretations regarding the affinities between Cretan and Mesopotamian palaces (Graham 1964).

4. Davis 1992: 707.

5. For a comprehensive overview on the subject, see Wiener 1990; 1991.

6. Renfrew 1984: 390.

7. Rapoport 1969: 24.

8. Vitruvius, *The Ten Books on Architecture:* chapter III (Morgan, trans. 1960).

9. See Hult 1983.

10. J. Shaw 1971.

11. Driessen 1990.

12. Evans believed that earlier blocks were elongated and had deeply cut mason's marks (Evans 1921–1935: I, 347–348), a matter quite insignificant for technology, which is debated by Shaw (1971: 98). It was only in Classical times that ashlar technology truly changed: blocks were now dressed on all sides, bonding mortar was hardly used, and dowels/mortises

were used to tie together stone to stone and not stone to wood, as in Prehistoric times.

13. McEnroe 1982: 7.

14. Ashlar blocks are even reported from Therasia (Sperling 1973: 58).

15. Palyvou 1984.

16. For mason's marks in Crete see Sakellarakis 1967; Hood 1987; Driessen 1990, 8, n. 38; Tsipopoulou 1986.

17. Palyvou 1999a.

18. I wish to thank L. Platon, G. Rethemiotakis, and I. Sakellarakis for giving me estimates of mason's marks found in their excavations, and S. Hood, who has long been working on a corpus of mason's marks at Knossos, for our valuable discussions on this topic.

19. Hood 1984: 36, n. 23; the suggestion was put forward by O.T.P.K. Dickinson.

20. Shaw 1971.

21. Sperling 1973: 58.

22. Shaw 1971: 144; Blegen 1964: 118.

23. van Effenterre 1980: I, 126–128, n. 148.

24. Shaw 1971: 144.

25. McEnroe 1982: 12.

26. Blegen 1964: 33, 117, 119 and notes 4–11 with references; Küpper 1996: 67–94, figs. 177–209, pls. 34–45.

27. Callot 1983: 27.

28. Shaw 1971: 144–147; Palyvou 1999a: 115–116, notes 173 and 184.

29. Foster's groups 2 and 3 of the Town Mosaic plaques (Foster 1979: 108–109). For the Archanes model, see Lebessi 1976: 22.

30. Michailidou 1986: 522.

31. van Effenterre 1980: 177.

32. Lustral basins in non-palatial architecture: Knossos Chancel Screen, South House, and Little Palace; Amnisos; Tylissos A and C; Malia Za, Da, E, and Quartier Mu; Chania. Also possibly Knossos: Southeast House and Royal Villa; Nirou Chani; Malia Zb; see also McEnroe 1982: 5. Driessen 1990: fig. 10.

33. Driessen 1982: 27–92. See also Andreadaki-Vlasaki 1988; Platonos 1990.

34. Palyvou 1987: 198–201.

35. Driessen 1990.

36. Marketou 1988: 29–31.

37. Marinatos 1939a: 71–72.

38. Cameron 1976: 6–7 and n. 17, with references to wall paintings in the form of a frieze from Aegean sites.

39. Schmid 1983: 715, n. 23.

40. Palyvou 1987: 195–293, n. 575; Driessen 1982: 29.

41. Davis and Cherry 1990: 191–192.

42. Driessen and MacGillivray 1989: 106.

43. Cunningham 2001: 82.

44. Marthari 1990b.

45. See McEnroe 1990 on regional styles.

46. Barber 1987: 28; Marthari 1990a: 97–100.

47. See, for example, the gypsum slabs found in the area of the House of the Ladies and deriving from the Knossos quarries. Einfalt 1978: 527.

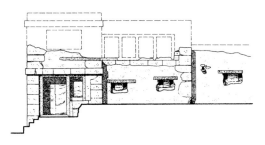

Bibliography

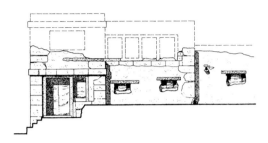

Bibliography

Abbreviations follow the conventions recommended in the *American Journal of Archaeology* 104 (2000), pp. 3–24.

Andreadaki-Vlasaki, M. 1988. "Ὑπόγειο Ἄδυτο ἡ Δεξαμενή Καθαρμῶν στα Χανιά," *AAA* 21, pp. 56–76.

Aston, M.A., and P.G. Hardy. 1990. "The Pre-Minoan Landscape of Thera: A Preliminary Statement," in Hardy et al., eds., 1990, II, pp. 348–360.

Barber, R.L.N. 1987. *The Cyclades in the Bronze Age*, London.

Bernabò-Brea, L. 1964. *Poliochni: Città preistorica nell' isola di Lemnos*, I, Rome.

Betancourt, P.P., V. Karageorghis, R. Laffineur, and W.-D. Niemeier, eds. 1999. *MELETEMATA: Studies in Aegean Archaeology Presented to Malcolm H. Wiener as He Enters His 65th Year* (*Aegaeum* 20), Liège.

Bietak, M. 1995. "Connections between Egypt and the Minoan World—New Results from Tell el-Dab'a/ Avaris," in Davies and Schofield, eds., 1995, pp. 19–28.

Blegen, C. 1964. "Architectural Notes from Pylos," in *Χαριστήριον εἰς Α.Κ. Ὀρλάνδον*, I, Athens, pp. 117–125.

Bosanquet, R.C., and R.M. Dawkins. 1923. *The Unpublished Objects from the Palaikastro Excavations 1902–1906*, Part I (*BSA Supplementary Paper* 1), London.

Boulotis, C. 1990. "Villes et palais dans l'art égéen du IIe millenaire av. J.-C.," in Darcque and Treuil, eds., 1990, pp. 421–459.

Branigan, K. 2001. "Aspects of Minoan Urbanism," in Branigan, ed., 2001, pp. 38–50.

Branigan, K., ed. 2001. *Urbanism in the Aegean Bronze Age*, Sheffield.

Callot, O. 1983. *Une maison à Ougarit. Étude d'architecture domestique: Ras Shamra-Ougarit* 1, Paris.

Cameron, M. 1976. "Savaki's Bothros: A Minor Sounding at Knossos," *BSA* 71, pp. 1–13.

Cameron, M. 1978–1980. "Theoretical Interrelations among Theran, Cretan and Mainland Frescoes," in Doumas, ed., 1978–1980, pp. 579–592.

Cherry, J.F. 1983. "Putting the Best Foot Forward," *Antiquity* 57, pp. 52–56.

Cummer, W.W., and E. Schofield. 1984. *Ayia Irini: House A*, *Keos* III, Mainz am Rhine.

Cunningham, T. 2001. "Variations on a Theme: Divergence in Settlement Patterns and Spatial Organization in the Far East of Crete during the Proto- and Neopalatial Periods," in Branigan, ed., 2001, pp. 72–86.

Danezis, I.M., ed. 2001. *Σαντορίνη, Θήρα, Θηρασία, Ασπρονήσι, Ηφαίστεια*, Athens.

Darcque, P., and R. Treuil, eds. 1990. *L'Habitat égéen préhistorique* (*BCH Supplément* 19), Athens and Paris.

Davies, E.V., and L. Schofield, eds. 1995. *Egypt, the Aegean and the Levant*, London.

Davis, J.L. 1977. *Fortifications at Ayia Irini, Keos*, Ph.D. diss., University of Cincinnati.

———. 1986. *Keos* V. *Ayia Irini: Period V,* Mainz am Rhine.

———. 1992. "Review of Aegean Prehistory I: the Islands of the Aegean," *AJA* 96, pp. 699–765.

Davis, J.L., and J.F. Cherry. 1990. "Spatial and Temporal Uniformitarianism in Late Cycladic I: Perspectives from Kea and Milos on the Prehistory of Akrotiri," in Hardy et al., eds., 1990, I, pp. 185–200.

Demargne, P., and H. Gallet de Santerre. 1953. *Fouilles exécutées à Mallia: exploration des maisons et quartiers d'habitation, 1er fasc.* (*Études crétoises* 9), Paris.

Devetzi, T. 1992. "Το λίθινα σκεύη εργαλεία," in Doumas, ed., 1992, pp. 119–128.

Doumas, C. 1974a. "Late Bronze Age Engineering in the Aegean," *AAA* 7, pp. 365–370.

———. 1974b. "Περί τῆς Μινωϊκῆς Ἀρχιτεκτονικῆς ἐν Θήρᾳ," *ArchEph* 1974, pp. 199–213.

———. 1976. "Ανασκαφή Ακρωτηρίου Θήρας," *Prakt* 1976, pp. 309–329.

———. 1983. *Thera: Pompeii of the Ancient Aegean*, London.

———. 1985. "Ανασκαφή θήρας (Ακρωτήρι)," *Prakt* 1985, pp. 168–176.

———. 1987. "Η Ξεστή 3 και οι κυανοκέφαλοι στην τέχνη της Θήρας," in *Ειλαπίνη. Τόμος τιμητικός για τον καθηγητή Νικολάο Πλάτωνα*, Herakleion, pp. 151–159.

———. 1990. "Ανασκαφή Ακρωτηρίου Θήρας," *Prakt* 1990, pp. 224–235.

———. 1992a. *The Wall Paintings of Thera*, Athens.

———. 1992b. "Ανασκαφή Ακρωτηρίου Θήρας," *Prakt* 1992, pp. 176–188.

———. 1993. "Ανασκαφή Ακρωτηρίου Θήρας," *Prakt* 1993, pp. 164–187.

———. 1994. "Ανασκαφή Ακρωτηρίου Θήρας," *Prakt* 1994, pp. 155–166.

———. 1995. "Ανασκαφή Ακρωτηρίου Θήρας," *Prakt* 1995, pp. 127–136.

———. 1996. "Ανασκαφή Ακρωτηρίου Θήρας," *Prakt* 1996, pp. 247–257.

———. 2000. *Die aktuellsten archäologischen Funde in Akrotiri auf Thera*, Munich.

———. 2001. "Η Θήρα της εποχής του Χαλκού: Πολιτισμικό σταυροδρόμι στην ανατολική Μεσόγειο," in Danezis, ed., 2001, pp. 87–96.

———. ed. 1978–1980. *Thera and the Aegean World I–II. Papers Presented at the Second International Scientific Congress, Santorini, Greece, August 1978*, London.

———. ed. 1992. *Ακρωτήρι Θήρας. Είκοσι χρόνια έρευνας (1967–1987)*, Athens.

Driessen, J. 1982. "The Minoan Hall in Domestic Architecture on Crete: To Be in Vogue in Late Minoan IA?" *ActaArchLov* 21, pp. 27–92.

———. 1989–1990. "The Proliferation of Minoan Palatial Architectural Style: (I) Crete," *ActaArchLov* 28–29, pp. 3–23.

———. 2001. "History and Hierarchy. Preliminary Observations on the Settlement Pattern of Minoan Crete," in Branigan, ed., 2001, pp. 51–71.

Driessen, J., and J.A. MacGillivray. 1989. "The Neopalatial Period in East Crete," in *Transition. Le monde égéen du Bronze Moyen au Bronze Recent*, R. Laffineur, ed. (*Aegaeum* 3), Liège, pp. 99–111.

Driessen, J., I. Schoep, and R. Laffineur, eds. 2002. *Monuments of Minos: Rethinking the Minoan Palaces, Proceedings of the International Workshop "Crete of the Hundred Palaces," Louvain-la-Neuve, 14–15 December 2001* (*Aegaeum* 23), Liège.

Einfalt, H.C. 1978–1980. "Stone Materials in Ancient Akrotiri—a Short Compilation," in Doumas, ed., 1978–1980, I, pp. 523–528.

1983–1990. *Ελληνική Παραδοσιακή Αρχιτεκτονική* 1–7, Athens .

Evans, A. 1921–1935. *The Palace of Minos*, I–IV, London.

———. 1927. "Work of Reconstitution in the Palace of Knossos," *AntJ* 7, pp. 258–267.

Foster, K.P. 1979. *Aegean Faience of the Bronze Age*, New Haven and London.

Fouqué, F. 1879. *Santorin et ses éruptions*, Paris.

Frankfort, H. 1950. "Town Planning in Ancient Mesopotamia," *Town Planning Review* 21, pp. 99–115.

Friedrich, W.L. 1978–1980. "Fossil Plants from Weichselian Paleosols, Santorini," in Doumas, ed., 1978–1980, I, pp. 741–744.

———. 2000. *Fire in the Sea. The Santorini Volcano: Natural History and the Legend of Atlantis*, 1st English ed., Cambridge.

Fyfe, T. 1902. "Painted Plaster Decoration at Knossos with Special Reference to the Architectural Schemes," *Journal of the Royal Institute of British Architects* 10, pp. 107–131.

Gale, N.H., ed. 1991. *Bronze Age Trade in the Mediterranean* (*SIMA* 90), Jonsered.

Giousouroum, N., E. Katsa, I. Tzahili, C. Palyvou, A. Sarpaki, and A. Douma. 1992. *Ακρωτήρι Θήρας: τα αμπέλια στη ζωή μιας κοινότητας, Proceedings of the Workshop Ιστορία του Ελληνικού κρασιού, 7–9 September 1990, Santorini*, Athens.

Graham, J.W. 1960. "The Minoan Unit of Length and Minoan Palace Planning," *AJA* 64, pp. 335–341.

———. 1964. "The Relation of the Minoan Palaces to the Near Eastern Palaces of the Second Millennium," in *Mycenaean Studies*, E.L. Bennett, Jr, ed., pp. 195–215.

———. 1967. "Further Notes on the Minoan Foot," *Πεπραγμένα του Β΄ Διεθνούς Κρητολογικού Συνεδρίου*, Athens, pp. 157–165.

———. 1972. *The Palaces of Crete*, 2nd edition, Princeton.

Grillo, P.-J. 1975. *Form, Function, and Design*, New York.

Hägg, R., ed. 1997. *The Function of the "Minoan Villa,"* Stockholm.

Hägg, R., and N. Marinatos, eds. 1984. *The Minoan Thalassocracy: Myth and Reality*, Stockholm.

———. 1987. *The Function of the Minoan Palaces*, Stockholm.

Hardy, D.A., C. Doumas, J.A. Sakellarakis, and P.M. Warren, eds. 1990. *Thera and the Aegean World III: Proceedings of the Third International Congress, Santorini, Greece, 3–9 September 1989*, I–III, London.

Heiken, G., F. McCoy, and M. Sheridan. 1990. "Palaeotopographic and Palaeogeologic Reconstruction of Minoan Thera," in Hardy et al., eds., 1990, pp. 370–376.

Hood, S. 1971. *The Minoans*, London.

———. 1984. "A Minoan Empire in the 16th and 15th Centuries B.C.?" in Hägg and Marinatos, eds., 1984, pp. 33–37.

———. 1987. "Mason's Marks in the Palaces," in Hägg and Marinatos, eds., 1987, pp. 205–212.

Hult, G. 1983. *Bronze Age Ashlar Masonry in the Eastern Mediterranean* (*SIMA* 66), Göteborg.

Iliakis, K. 1978–1980. "Morphological Analysis of the Akrotiri Wall-Paintings of Santorini," in Doumas, ed., 1978–1980, pp. 617–628.

Kariotis, S. 2003. "Ακρωτήρι Θήρας. Η στρωματογραφική ακολουθία στην Πλατεία Διπλών Κεράτων," in Vlachopoulos and Birtacha, eds., 2003, pp. 419–444.

Kruft, H.W. 1994. *A History of Architectural Theory from Vitruvius to the Present*, Princeton.

Küpper, M. 1996. *Mykenische Architektur: Material, Bearbeitungtechnik, Konstruktion und Erscheinungsbild, Internationale Archäologie* 25, Espelkamp.

Lang, M. 1969. *The Palace of Nestor at Pylos in Western Messenia II: The Frescoes*, Princeton.

Le Corbusier. 1951. *The Modulor*, London.

Lebessi, A. 1976. "Ο οικίσκος των Αρχανών," *ArchEph* 1976, pp. 12–43.

Manning, S.W. 1995. *The Absolute Chronology of the Aegean Early Bronze Age: Archaeology, Radiocarbon, and History*, Sheffield.

———. 1999. *A Test of Time. The Volvano of Thera and the Chronology and History of the Aegean and East Mediterranean in the Mid-Second Millennium BC*, Oxford.

Marinatos, N. 1984. *Art and Religion in Thera, Reconstructing a Bronze Age Society*, Athens.

———. 1986. "On the Ceremonial Function of the Minoan Polythyron," *OpAth* 16:6, pp. 57–73.

Marinatos, S. 1939a. "Το Μινωικόν μέγαρον Σκλαβοκάμπου," *ArchEph* 1939–1941, pp. 69–96.

———. 1939b. "The Volcanic Destruction of the Minoan Crete," *Antiquity* 13, pp. 425–439.

———. 1968–1976. *Excavations at Thera*, I–VII, Athens.

Marketou, T. 1988. "New Evidence on the Topography and Site History of Prehistoric Ialysos," in *Archaeology in the Dodecanese*, S. Dietz and I. Papachristodoulou, eds., Copenhagen, pp. 29–31.

Marthari, M. 1990a. "Σκάρκος: Ένας πρωτοκυκλαδι-κός οικισμός στην Ιο," in Ίδρυμα Ν.Π. Γουλανδρήν, *Lectures 1986–1989*, Athens, pp. 97–100.

———. 1990b. "The Chronology of the Last Phases of Occupation at Akrotiri in the Light of the Evidence from the West House Pottery Groups," in Hardy et al., eds., 1990, pp. 57–70.

———. 2001. "Η Θήρα από την Πρώιμη στη Μέση εποχή του Χαλκού. Τα αποτελέσματα από τις ανασκαφές στον Φτέλλο και τον Άγιο Ιωάννη τον Ελεήμονα," in Danezis, ed., 2001, pp. 105–120.

McCoy, F.W., and G. Heiken. 2000. "The Late Bronze Age Explosive Eruption of Thera (Santorini), Greece: Regional and Local Effects," in *Volcanic Hazards and Disasters in Human Antiquity* (*Geological Society of America, Special Paper* 345), F.W. McCoy and G. Heiken, eds., pp. 43–70.

McEnroe, J. 1982. "A Typology of Minoan Neopalatial Houses," *AJA* 86, pp. 3–19.

———. 1990. "The Significance of Local Styles in Minoan Vernacular Architecture," in Darcque and Treuil, eds., 1990, pp. 195–202.

Michailidou, A. 1981. *Knossos: A Complete Guide to the Palace of Minos*, Athens.

———. 1987. "Το δωμάτιο με τον κίονα στο μινωικό σπίτι," in *Αμητος. Τιμητικός τόμος για τον καθηγητή Μ. Ανδρόνικο*, Thessaloniki, pp. 509–526.

———. 2001. *Ακρωτήρι Θήρας: Η μελέτη των ορόφων στα κτήρια του οικισμού*, Athens.

———. ed. 2001. *Manufacture and Measurement: Counting, Measuring and Recording Craft Items in Early Aegean Societies* (*Μελετήματα* 33), Athens.

Morgan, L. 1983. "Theme in the West House Paintings at Thera," *ArchEph* 1983, pp. 85–105.

———. 1988. *The Miniature Wall Paintings of Thera: A Study in Aegean Culture and Iconography*, Cambridge.

———. 1990. "Island Iconography: Thera, Kea, Milos," in Hardy et al., eds., 1990, pp. 252–266.

Morgan, M.H., trans. 1960. *The Ten Books on Architecture* by Vitruvius, New York.

Moundrea-Agrafioti, A. 1992. "Τα λίθινα λαξεμένα εργαλεία—Μεθοδολογία μελέξης και θέματα κατανομών," in Doumas, ed., 1992, pp. 129–138.

Mumford, L. 1961. *The City in History*, London.

Nesbitt, K., ed. 1996. *Theorizing a New Agenda for Architecture: An Anthology of Architectural Theory 1965–1995*, Princeton.

Nikolakopoulou, E. 2003. "Ακρωτήρι Θήρας. Η πόλη σε κατάσταση έκτακτης ανάγκης," in Vlachopoulos and Birtacha, eds., 2003, pp. 554–573.

Palyvou, C. 1977. "Ανασκαφή Ακρωτηρίου Θήρας. Αρχιτεκτονική αποτύπωση στον προϊστορικό οικισμό Ακρωτηρίου Θήρας," *Prakt* 1977, pp. 392–399.

———. 1978. "Ανασκαφή Ακρωτηρίου Θήρας. Αρχιτεκτο-νικές αποτυπώσεις," *Prakt* 1978, pp. 225–228.

———. 1984. "The Destruction of the Town at Akrotiri, Thera, at the Beginning of LC I: Rebuilding Activities," in *The Prehistoric Cyclades*, J.A. MacGillivray and R.L.N. Barber, eds., Edinburgh, pp. 134–148.

———. 1986. "Notes on the Town Plan of Late Cycladic Akrotiri, Thera," *BSA* 81, pp. 179–194.

———. 1987. "Circulatory Patterns in Minoan Architecture," in Hägg and Marinatos, eds., 1987, pp. 195–203.

———. 1988. "Προβλήματα στερέωσες και προστασίας σε προϊστορικά μνημεία. Το παράδειγμα της Θήρας," in *Επεμβάσεις σε Αρχιτεκτονικά Μνημεία και Παραδοσιακά Οικιστικά Σύνολα*, Herakleion, pp. 29–41.

———. 1990. "Architectural Design at Late Cycladic Akrotiri," in Hardy et al., eds., 1990, I, pp. 44–56.

———. 1992. "Υλικά και τρόποι δόμησης στον υστεροκυκλαδικό οικισμό του Ακρωτηρίου," in Doumas, ed., 1992, pp. 35–42.

———. 1999a. *Ακρωτήρι Θήρας: Η οικοδομική τέχνη*, Athens.

———. 1999b. "Theran Architecture through the Minoan Looking Glass," in Betancourt et al., eds., 1999, II, pp. 609–615.

———. 2000. "Concepts of Space in Aegean Bronze Age Art and Architecture," in Sherratt, ed., 2000, I, pp. 413–436.

———. 2003. "Architecture and Archaeology: the Minoan Palaces in the Twenty-First Century," in *Theory and Practice in Mediterranean Archaeology:*

Old World and New World Perspectives, J.K. Papadopoulos and R. Leventhal, eds., Los Angeles, pp. 205–234.

———. 2004. "Outdoor Space in Minoan Architecture: 'Community and Privacy'," in *Knossos: Palace, City, State (BSA Studies* 12), G. Cadogan, E. Hatzaki, and A. Vasilakis, eds., London, pp. 207–217.

Papagiannopoulou, A. 1991. *The Influence of Middle Minoan Pottery on the Cyclades (SIMA* 96), Göteborg.

Papazachos, B.C., and Papazachou, C.B. 1997. *The Earthquakes of Greece*, Thessaloniki.

Platonos, S. 1990. "Νέες ενδείξεις για το πρόβλημα των καθαρτήριων δεξαμενών και των λουτρών στο μινωικό κόσμο," in *Πεπραγμένα του ΣΤ´ Διεθνούς Κρητολογικού Συνεδρίου* I (2), Chania, pp. 141–155.

Popham, M.R. 1984. *The Minoan Unexplored Mansion at Knossos*, London.

Preziosi, D.A. 1983. *Minoan Architectural Design: Formation and Significance*, Berlin and New York.

Rackham, O. 1978–1980. "The Flora and Vegetation of Thera and Crete Before and After the Great Eruption," in Doumas, ed., 1978–1980, I, pp. 755–764.

Rackham, O., and J. Moody. 1996. *The Making of the Cretan Landscape*, Manchester.

Rapoport, A. 1969. *House Form and Culture*, Englewood Cliffs, New Jersey.

Renfrew, C. 1972. *The Emergence of Civilisation*, London.

———. 1984. *Approaches to Social Archaeology*, Edinburgh.

———. 1985. *The Archaeology of Cult: The Sanctuary at Phylakopi (BSA Supplementary Volume* 18), London.

Sakellarakis, J.A. 1967. "Mason's Marks from Archanes," in *Europa, Studien zur Geschichte und Epigraphik der frühen Aegäis: Festschrift für Ernst Grumach*, Berlin, pp. 277–288.

Sakellarakis, G., and E. Sakellaraki, 1991. *Αρχανες*, Athens.

Sarpaki, A. 1992. "A Paleoethnobotanical Study of the West House, Akrotiri, Thera," *BSA* 87, pp. 219–230.

———. 2001. "Ο κρόκος της ζαφοράς. Φυτό κατέξοχήν της Σαντορίνης," in Danezis, ed., 2001, pp. 177–182.

Schmid, M. 1983. "Les portes multiples au 'Mégaron' du Palais de Mallia," *BCH* 107, pp. 705–716.

Shaw, J.W. 1971. *Minoan Architecture: Materials and Techniques (ASAtene* 49), pp. 7–265.

———. 1977. "New Evidence for Aegean Roof Construction from Bronze Age Thera," *AJA* 81, pp. 229–233.

———. 1990. "Bronze Age Aegean Harboursides," in Hardy et al., eds., 1990, I, pp. 420–436.

Shaw, J.W., and M. Luton. 2000. "The Foreshore at Akrotiri," in Sherratt, ed., 2000, pp. 453–466.

Shaw, M. 1985. "Late Minoan I Building J/T, and Late Minoan III Building at Kommos," *Scripta Mediterranea* VI, pp. 19–24.

———. 1986. "The Lion Gate of Mycenae Reconsidered," in *Φίλια έπή εις Γεώργιον Ε. Μυλωνά*, Athens, I, pp. 108–123.

Sherratt, S., ed., 2000. *The Wall Paintings of Thera, Proceedings of the First International Symposium, 30 August–4 September 1997, Thera*, Athens.

Sotirakopoulou, P. 1990. "The Earliest History of Akrotiri: The Late Neolithic and Early Bronze Age Phases," in Hardy et al., eds, 1990, III, pp. 41–50.

———. 2001 "Οι αρχαιολογικές μαρτυρίες για την πρώτη κατοίκηση της Θήρας," in Danezis, ed., 2001, pp. 97–104.

Sperling, J.W. 1973. "Thera and Therasia," in *Ancient Greek Cities* 22, Athens.

Televantou, C.A. 1982. "Θήρα, Καμάρι, Ορυχεία Μαυρομμάτη," *ArchDelt* 37 Part B, pp. 358–359.

———. 1990. "New Light on the West House Wall-Paintings," in Hardy et al., eds., 1990, I, pp. 309–326.

———. 1994. *Ακρωτήρι Θήρας: Οι τοιχογραφίες της Δυτικής Οικίας*, Athens.

Touliatos, P. 2000. "Timber in Shipbuilding in Prehistoric and Ancient Greece: The Early Influence on the Timber Structures," in *Restoration of Old and Modern Wooden Buildings*, A. Soikkeli, ed., Finland, pp. 27–36.

Tsipopoulou, M. 1986. "Τεκτονικό σημείο από τον Πέτρα Σητείας," *AAA* 19, pp. 171–177.

Tzachili, I. 1989. *Υφαντική και υφάντες στην ύστερη εποχή του Χαλκού στο Αιγαίο*, Athens.

———. 1990. "Τα σκουπίδα στο Ακρωτήρι Πεπτωκότα προϊόντα και απορρίμματα σε μία Αιγαιακή προϊστορική πόλη," *Archaiologia* 35, pp. 12–18.

———. 1994. "Αρχαίες και σύγχρονες κροκο-συλλέκτριες από το Ακρωτήρι της Σαντορίνης," *Ariadne* 7, pp. 7–33.

van Effenterre, H. 1980. *Le palais de Mallia et la cité minoenne*, I–II, Rome.

Vlachopoulos, A., and K. Birtacha, eds. 2003. *ΑΡΓΟ-ΝΑΥΤΗΣ. Τιμητικός τόμος για τον καθηγητή Χρίστο Γ. Ντούμα*, Athens.

Vougioukalakis, G. 2001. "Σύντομη ιστορία των Ηφαιστείων της Σαντορίνης," in Danezis, ed., 2001, pp. 37–50.

Warren, P.M., and V. Hankey. 1989. *Aegean Bronze Age Chronology*, Bristol.

Whitelaw, T. 2001. "From Sites to Communities: Defining the Human Dimensions of Minoan Urbanism," in Branigan, ed., 2001, pp. 15–37.

Wiener, M.H. 1990. "The Isles of Crete? The Minoan Thalassocracy Revisited," in Hardy et al., eds., 1990, pp. 128–161.

———. 1991. "The Nature and Control of Minoan Foreign Trade," in Gale, ed., 1991, pp. 325–350.

———. 2003. "Time Out: The Current Impasse in Bronze Age Archaeological Dating," in *METRON: Measuring the Aegean Bronze Age* (*Aegaeum* 24), K.P. Foster and R. Laffineur, eds., Liège, pp. 363–395.

———. forthcoming (a). "Chronology Going Forward (with a Query about 1525/4 B.C.)," *Bietak Festschrift*, Vienna.

———. forthcoming (b). "Times Change: The Current State of the Debate in Old World Archaeology," *Proceedings of the Second EuroConference of "SCIEM 2000", 28 May–1 June, 2003*, Vienna.

Zois, A. 1990. "Pour un schéma évolutif de l'architecture minoenne. A: Les fondations. Techniques et morphologie," in Darcque and Treuil, eds., 1990, pp. 75–93.

———. 1996. *Κνωσός, το εκστατικό όραμα*, Herakleion.

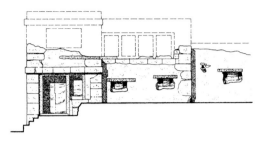

Index

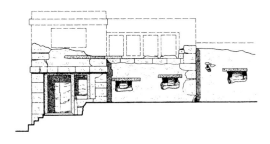

Index

Sumer, 152
symbol(ism)/symbolical, 61, 161, 163, 170
symmetry/symmetrical, 77, 131, 133, 135, 158, 159
Syropalestinian coast, 177, 187
Syros, 26

technology, xxiv, 43, 57, 104, 111, 121, 145, 171 n. 6,
    174, 175, 179–181, 186, 187 n. 12
tenons, 119, 137
tensile strength, 122, 123, 175
tephra, 4
terrace, 29, 35, 37, 38, 61, 75, 78, 79, 164, 174
terracotta, 127
        conduit, 40, 41, 53
        spouts, 39, 40, 129
textile, 40, 169
Therasia, 1, 9, 13 n. 1, 15, 16, 22, 29, 43 n. 1, 112, 132,
    154 nn. 18, 22, 177, 178 n. 14, 181, 183, 188 n. 14
threshold. *See* door
timber, 43 n. 24, 73, 111, 112, 119, 122, 123, 133, 134,
    136, 145, 150, 160, 166, 167, 174, 175, 178 n. 9,
    182. *See also* wood
        branch, 121, 125, 128, 181
        board, 150
        charcoal, 124
        construction, 50, 57, 115, 116, 121, 123, 133,
            134, 140, 144, 175, 181–183
        framework, 50, 59, 61, 71, 88, 115, 116, 119,
            120–123, 133, 137, 140, 141, 144, 149, 159,
            161, 175, 180, 181, 183
        plank, 50, 138, 139, 142, 145, 152, 153, 164
        reinforcement, 114, 115, 119, 121–123, 125,
            126, 136, 150, 159, 168, 175, 181
        trunk, 123, 125, 141
        twig, 125, 134, 152
        types of
            conifers, 112
            cypress, 112
            tamarisk, 112, 153 n. 4
            Pistacia lentiscus L., 153 n. 4
            Olea europae, 153 n. 4
            Phoenix dactylifera I., 153 n. 4
            Chamaerops humilis L., 153 n. 4
            olive wood, 112
        wall, 116, 120–123, 133, 154 n. 16, 156, 164, 181,
            182
torrent, 19, 25, 33, 39, 40, 65, 68, 74, 79, 82, 83, 85,
    86, 95, 113
townplan, xxiv, 17, 31, 34, 35, 38
townscape, 185
town mosaic, 119, 152, 159, 160, 168, 182, 188
trade, 10, 15, 179
tradition, 112, 122, 126, 170, 178, 180, 186, 187

traditional architecture, 25, 174, 180, 182. *See also*
    vernacular
traffic, 29, 115
trench, xxv, 40, 77, 91, 96, 114
Trianda, Rhodes, 183
Troy, 9
tsunami, 177
tunnel, 10, 12, 39, 72, 189, 190
Tylissos, 181, 188

Ugarit, 181, 187
underground chambers, 15, 174
upper class, 63, 86
urban
    look, 26
    mansions, 27, 174
    public, 104

Vasiliki, 175
veneer, 74, 134, 142, 166
ventilation, 34
veranda, xxiv, 26, 51, 54, 75, 79, 82, 97, 105, 107,
    160, 174
vernacular architecture, 20, 37, 87, 109, 128. *See also*
    traditional
        joints, 67, 91, 116, 122, 126, 137, 150, 157, 158,
            163
        posts, 98, 125, 133, 141, 152, 159, 181
            door, 137, 138, 140, 161
            wall, 49, 116, 120–123, 167
            window, 68, 138, 150
villa, 17, 54, 145, 179, 184, 188 n. 32
    rural, 180
vineyard/viticulture, 19, 21
Vitruvius, 180, 187
volcano/volcanic, 1, 4, 6, 7, 9, 12, 19, 20, 21–23, 38,
    39, 86, 92, 111, 113, 114, 116, 121, 124, 126, 138,
    153, 168, 169, 173, 175–178, 178 n. 3, 183, 186
        deposits, 10, 15, 19, 25, 39, 98
        destruction, 45, 69, 177, 183
        volcanism, 173
        volcanologist, 4, 9

wall
    ashlar, 26, 34, 38, 54, 57, 73, 82, 86, 90, 92, 96,
        157, 159, 160, 162, 164, 168, 169, 174, 180, 181
    bracing, 174
    clay, 57, 153
    double, 29, 71, 74, 75, 83, 85, 95, 103
    hammered, 54, 120
    partition, 51, 61, 66, 78, 86, 88, 89, 93, 95, 104,
        121
    retaining, 29, 33, 34, 36, 38, 75, 79, 90

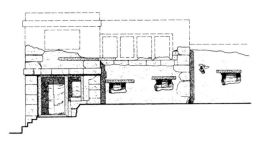

Color Plates

PLATE 1

A. Hagios Nikolaos, in the Akrotiri region. The bright red rock bordered the west side of the prehistoric harbor.

B. Colorful stones from the debris of a prehistoric rubble wall.

C. Ashlar stones outside the excavation: red and black lava and scoriae, dark brown ignimbrite, white tuff (small fragment on the top of the pile), and dark gray volcanic slabs.

PLATE 2

A. The buildings around Triangle Square seen from the west. Computer reconstruction by A. Kassios.

B. The West House and its surroundings seen from the north. Computer reconstruction by A. Kassios.

C. The West House as seen from inside the room above the Gate of house Delta-West. Computer reconstruction by A. Kassios.

PLATE 3

A. The West House, Room 5. Computer reconstruction by C. Palyvou.

B. The West House, Rooms 4 and 4a. Computer reconstruction by A. Kassios.

PLATE 4

A. House Beta-South, Room B1. Computer reconstruction by C. Palyvou.

B. House Delta-East, Room 2. The Spring Fresco.